The COMPLETE IDIOT'S Guide to

Exploring Canada

- ♦ Province-by-province listings of highlights and attractions
- ♦ The hottest must-see places in major cities
- ♦ A complete listing of Web sites featuring Canadian travel info

An Alpha Books/Prentice Hall Canada Copublication

Prentice Hall Canada Inc., Scarborough, Ontario

Joe Chidley

Canadian Cataloguing in Publication Data

Chidley, Joe, 1963– .
    The complete idiot's guide to exploring Canada

ISBN 0-13-080125-9

1. Canada – Guidebooks. I. Title.

FC38.C44 1998   917.104'648   C98-930420-5
F1009.C44 1998

 © 1998 Prentice-Hall Canada Inc., Scarborough, Ontario
A Division of Simon & Schuster/A Viacom Company

Prentice-Hall, Inc., Upper Saddle River, New Jersey
Prentice-Hall International (UK) Limited, London
Prentice-Hall of Australia, Pty. Limited, Sydney
Prentice-Hall Hispanoamericana, S.A., Mexico City
Prentice-Hall of India Private Limited, New Delhi
Prentice-Hall of Japan, Inc., Tokyo
Simon & Schuster Southeast Asia Private Limited, Singapore
Editora Prentice-Hall do Brasil, Ltda., Rio de Janeiro

ISBN 0-13-080125-9

Acquisitions Editor: Robert Harris
Production Editor: Kelly Dickson
Copy Editor: Heather Lange
Assistant Editor: Joan Whitman
Production Coordinator: Katherine Pummell
Cover Design: Kyle Gell
Cover Image: V. Hurst/First Light
Page Layout: Gail Ferreira Ng-A-Kien
Maps: Anthony de Ridder
Illustrations: Craig Francis Design

1 2 3 4 5 RRD 02 01 00 99 98

Printed and bound in the USA.

Visit the Prentice Hall Canada Web site! Send us your comments, browse our catalogues, and
more at **www.phcanada.com**.

Contents

Contents

Introduction

I was just a kid, but I still remember the road trips I used to take with my family back in the '60s. Like many Torontonians, we used to pile in the car on summer weekends and drive north to the cottage. My brother and I would expectantly take dibs on who would see the lake first. Then there was the time we all drove to Montreal for Expo '67—I recall being particularly frightened by some ride that (I think) was called "The Gargantua." We went farther afield a couple years later, driving to Prince Edward Island and spending a week on the North Shore, near a lighthouse and sandstone cliffs and a really good oyster bed. I remember sand down my swim trunks, eating cod we'd caught with baitless hooks, and playing board games in our cabin until way past bedtime.

While writing this book about exploring Canada, I've been trying to think of a trip or a tour that would be *the* quintessentially Canadian experience. I didn't have much luck, except those childhood memories kept coming to mind, perhaps because they provided a glimpse of something special about this country. Which one is the definitive Canadian experience? Well, they all are.

Trying to define the national identity is something of an obsession among Canadians, who are always trying to distinguish themselves from their brasher, more powerful neighbours to the south. But maybe they wouldn't spend so much time worrying about it if they knew their own country better. I've seen quite a bit of Canada since those childhood road trips, but I still haven't seen as much as I feel I should. And I'm not alone. A lot of Canadians will guiltily admit that their own country is usually second or third on the vacation wish list—after, say, Florida in the winter or New York in the summer. A lot of Americans, meanwhile, think that Canada is just an extension of the United States, so why bother visiting?

Since you've bought this book, it's clear that you're not among the Canada-doubters. But just in case you're not sure about the Great White North as a travel destination, here are some good reasons to vacation here.

First, the cities. Canadian cities are among the cleanest and safest in the world. For the tourist, they provide no end of cultural and culinary attractions. Each has its own character and style, making them metropolises well worth exploring.

Second, the outdoors. Canada is a huge country, and much of its area is unpopulated. For the outdoors enthusiast, that means virtually inexhaustible opportunities for fishing, camping and hiking, along with some of the best skiing venues in the world.

Third, the dollar. The Canadian loonie (that's a dollar, for you non-Canucks) is worth only about 70 cents US on world markets. For Canadians, that means that travelling within their own country is a good way to save money on a vacation. For Americans, the low loonie means everything north of the border is relatively cheap.

So let's say you're convinced, and have decided to vacation in Canada. Where do you start? What should you look for? This book is designed to help you answer those questions. It covers the basics of exploring Canada—plus a little bit extra. If you're planning a trip, the book will give you an idea of what you can do and where you should do it, along with a list of parks and other outdoor areas in each region. Since many tourists spend all their time in Canada in its major cities, I've also included neighbourhood guides to the important urban centres, with detailed descriptions of their histories, what you can do there, and how to get around.

The list of activities and attractions is by no means exhaustive, and some reflect personal taste. You won't find restaurant or hotel ratings here: they are widely available (and well done) in other tourist guides, and their quality or reputation can change from year to year. What I've tried to do, based on personal experience and research from a wide range of other sources, is include the ones that are either big draws for visitors or simply worth visiting in their own right. Where available, I've included telephone numbers where you can get more information.

The book is divided into four sections.

Part 1 gives an overview of the country and its history. Here, too, you'll find tips on what you need to do to prepare for your trip, and how you can plan it most effectively.

Part 2 begins our tour of Canada with a look at Eastern Canada—Newfoundland, Prince Edward Island, Nova Scotia and New Brunswick, provinces steeped in British and Acadian traditions. Here you'll find detailed guides to St. John's and Halifax.

Part 3 continues on to Central Canada, stopping by Quebec, centre of Canada's francophone culture, and ending up in Ontario, the country's economic powerhouse. Here you'll find closer looks at Quebec City, Montreal, Toronto and Ottawa.

Part 4 rides on out to Western Canada—Manitoba, Saskatchewan, Alberta and British Columbia—along with neighbourhood guides to Winnipeg, Edmonton, Calgary and Vancouver.

In Part 5, we head to the trackless lands of the North—the Yukon and Northwest Territories.

At the back of the book, you'll find some bits of information that will help you plan your trip and come in handy while you're on the road. The appendices list important telephone numbers, other books and publications, and World Wide Web sites that (if you're hooked up to the information highway) you might want to check out before you go.

Along the way, there are a few highlighted elements designed to enhance your understanding of the places described in the book. Here's how they look:

By the Way

Interesting facts and trivia about a particular place or event.

Local Knowledge

Useful advice for getting around—and getting along.

Out of the Way

Side trips, remote locations or little-known off-roads where you'll be far from the madding crowd (or just off-course!).

Canada by Web

Relevant Web sites where you can get more information about a place or attraction.

I've tried to balance simplicity with detail in the book. If you've never heard of Canada but wonder what it's like, you'll get a taste of it here. If you've been everywhere in the country but Newfoundland, the book will tell you what to expect if you go there. And if you're stuck in Edmonton for a week on business and don't know what the heck to do in your spare time—well, it's a tough task, but the book gives you some pointers.

I hope this book gives you some sense of the diversity and natural wonder that Canada offers. And if it convinces you to get in a car or plane or bus or train and start exploring, then (as we Canucks like to say) *Good on ya!*

Acknowledgments

Writing this book has been fruitful not only because it broadened my understanding of Canada, but also because it allowed me to work with such bright and diligent publishers. To all those who worked behind the scenes at Prentice Hall to get the book done, many thanks. In particular, Robert Harris showed commendable courage in allowing me to write it in the first place, and the close scrutiny and judicious changes from Heather Lange, my editor, have been invaluable. Joan Whitman at Prentice Hall deserves more praise than space allows. Without her encouragement, sound advice and last-minute pep talks, this book would never have been written. And finally, my thanks and my love to Sara, whose advice helped me avoid the potholes, and whose support got me over the many bumps in the road. On the trip of a lifetime, no one could ask for a better travelling companion.

Joe Chidley

February 1998

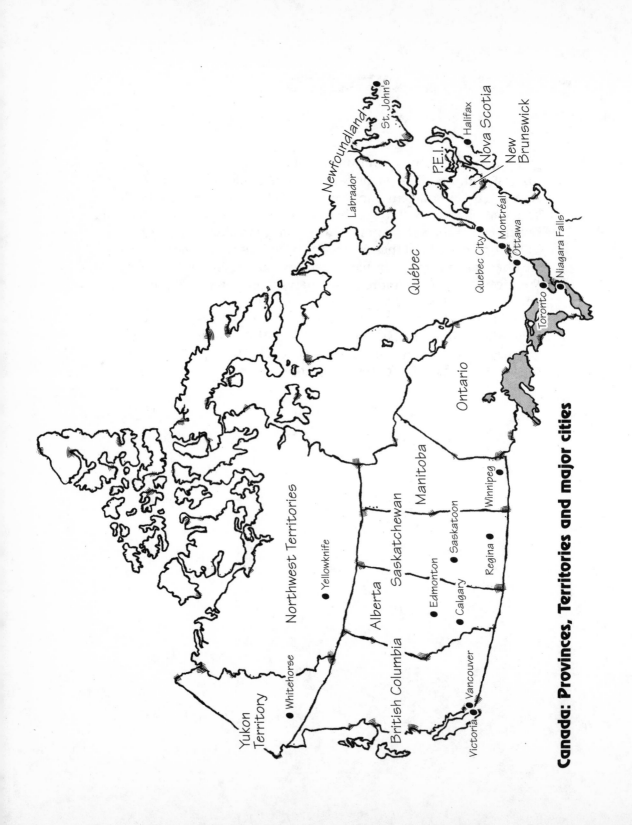

Canada: Provinces, Territories and major cities

St. John's
Halifax
Nova Scotia
New Brunswick
P.E.I.
Newfoundland
Labrador
Montréal
Ottawa
Niagara Falls
Québec
Quebec City
Toronto
Ontario
Northwest Territories
Yellowknife
Manitoba
Saskatchewan
Winnipeg
Saskatoon
Alberta
Edmonton
Regina
Calgary
British Columbia
Yukon Territory
Whitehorse
Vancouver
Victoria

Part 1
Getting Started

Canada is the second biggest country in the world, but don't be intimidated—you're sure to enjoy yourself no matter where you go.

Eastern Canada offers maritime vistas and coastal pleasures. Western Canada boasts mountain ranges and some of the best skiing in the world. Central Canada is chock-full of metropolitan entertainment and historically rich experiences beyond compare. The North holds its own special appeal: rugged mountains, frozen tundra and pristine wilderness areas that are unrivalled by any other place in the world. Given the seemingly endless variety that Canada offers, it's not easy to decide what to take in first. But this section will get you started on the right track by providing all the information you need. In fact, this part of the guide may well be the most important. Here you'll find a general overview of Canada and its history, advice on planning your trip, ideas about what to take with you, and tips on how to use the World Wide Web and other sources of information to get the most out of your travels.

Chapter 1

An Overview of Canada

In This Chapter

➤ Canada's size and population

➤ Languages and ethnicity

➤ The political landscape

If you've ever looked at a map of Canada, you've probably noticed something: it's a pretty darned big place. For both visitors and Canadians themselves, the sheer size of the country can be intimidating. Add to that the diversity of its people—French and English, plus Chinese, Italian, German, Indian, Pakistani and on and on—plus regions that have their own cultures and traditions, and things are getting pretty complicated. So let's break the country down (not up!), piece by piece.

The Tale of the Tape

Every Canadian has a story like this. You phone somebody in the United States, and in the course of the conversation you mention that

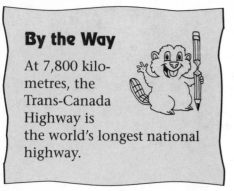

By the Way

At 7,800 kilometres, the Trans-Canada Highway is the world's longest national highway.

you're calling from, say, Toronto. And the voice on the other end says something like: *Jeez, that's in Canada, right? I've got friends in Vancouver, Mr. and Mrs. So-and-So. Do you know them?*

Chances are pretty slim. For those who don't know, Canada is the second largest country in the world in terms of area, after Russia. It takes up almost 10 million square kilometres (or more than 3,850,000 square miles) of the northern half of the North American continent. The Trans-Canada Highway, which runs from St. John's, Newfoundland, to Vancouver, BC, is 7,800 kilometres long.

Let's put that in accessible terms. You're a football fan? Think of 78,000 football fields, placed end to end. If you walked the Trans-Canada from St. John's to Vancouver (if you could, that is, since you have to take a boat over some of it) at a leisurely clip of 5 kilometres an hour, the trip would take you a little over two months—but you would have to walk 24 hours a day, seven days a week.

We, the People

Canadians tend to think that their country is small in terms of population. Part of the perception no doubt comes from living so close to the United States, whose 300 million or so citizens dwarf the 30 million Canadians to the north. And part of it has to do with the fact that Canada's people are spread out over such vast distances.

But it's all relative. In worldwide terms, Canada is really not that small. Population-wise, it is about half the size of France and three-quarters the size of England. It's nearly twice as big as Australia, and the Swedes (even though they're pretty good at hockey) just can't compete in the numbers game: Canada's population is more than three times larger than Sweden's.

From É to Zed

Canada is officially bilingual, which means that all government and judicial services (and, by the way, product labels) have to be available in both English and French. The official bilingualism reflects one aspect of

Local Knowledge

There's this theory about Canadians, that the one thing uniting them is their fascination with the weather. That may be overstating the case, but it's true that Canucks from sea to shining sea seem ready and willing to chat about rain, snow, heat, humidity, cold—if it's weather, they'll talk about it. One reason is obvious: Canadians' livelihood, whether fishermen, farmers or hunters, has historically depended to a large extent on climatic conditions. Another reason is that the Canadian climate really *is* fascinating, ranging from the wet warmth of the BC coast and the fog of Newfoundland to the changeability of southern Ontario and the bitter cold of the Arctic.

Anyway, if you want to initiate a conversation with a Canadian, just start talking about the weather. It's kind of the northern equivalent of "What's a nice girl like you doing in a place like this?"

Canadian history—that white society in the country was "founded" by French and English forces—but also the major linguistic groups. About 60 per cent of Canadians speak English, and about 25 per cent are francophone (French-speaking), mostly in Quebec.

There are many neighbourhoods, however, where you are unlikely to hear either language spoken. Canada has a large immigrant population, historically from Italy, Germany, Poland and other European countries, but lately from Southeast Asia, India and Pakistan. Perhaps more than in any other country, those ethnic groups have retained their culture and their language. That's especially true in the cities, where three-quarters of Canadians live. In Toronto, for instance, about one-third of residents speak a language other than English or French, as do a quarter of Vancouverites and about a sixth of Winnipeggers. So if you're walking around a Canadian city, don't be surprised to see street signs in Chinese or Greek.

The Body Political

Canada, unlike the United States, is a constitutional monarchy, and uses a sort of hybrid of the British and American systems of government, although it closely resembles the former. The head of state is the governor general, an appointed personage who functions as the Crown's representative in Canada and (in theory, at least) can make all the decisions about legislation. In practice, however, the Gee-Gee's job is largely ceremonial, and has been since the 1920s.

The focus of federal politics in Canada is Parliament, which has two elements, an appointed Senate and an elected House of Commons. The more powerful is the House of Commons, whose 300 members are elected in ridings (electoral districts) throughout the country.

The leader of the political party that gets the most seats becomes prime minister, who is the head of government in Canada (as opposed to the head of state). In the Commons, majority rules, and if one party wins more seats than all the others combined, it can do pretty much what it wants. At the moment, most of the MPs (members of Parliament) are affiliated with one of three political parties: the Liberals, who have held power for much of the 1990s, the western-based Reform Party, and the Bloc Québécois—a Quebec-only party that is actively separatist. Two other parties, the Conservatives and the socialist New Democratic Party, were traditionally the second and third most powerful parties in 20th century Canadian politics, but recent elections have left them with few seats.

Local Knowledge

The Senate has limited powers of veto over legislation coming from the House of Commons—it is not allowed, for instance, to kill bills that have to do with the country's finances. There have been repeated calls to reform the Senate in Canada. Many think it is useless and ineffectual, and many find it politically offensive since it is a non-elected body. So far, however, schemes to abolish the Senate or make it elected have gone nowhere—largely because one of its main functions is to reward retired politicians and other friends of the governing party. Anti-Senate feelings are most prominent in the Western provinces.

The Provinces

A similar system works in the 10 provinces. Each has its own legislative assembly, occupied by elected members, and they oversee provincial matters.

The division of powers between federal and provincial governments has a long and tortuous history in Canada, and explaining it would take up volumes. The issue is important in the continuing discussions about Quebec sovereignty, as well as in the other regions. But let's face it: if you think about it too much before you head out to explore Canada, you'll just ruin your trip.

By the Way

If it strikes you as strange that a separatist party is sitting in the federal legislature, then consider this: it's nothing new. In fact, in the first election after Confederation in 1867, nearly all of the MPs elected from the new province of Nova Scotia were separatists who wanted to get out of Canada almost before it started.

The Least You Need to Know

➤ In terms of area, Canada is the second largest country in the world.

➤ Canada's two major languages are French and English.

➤ Canada is a constitutional monarchy with a governor general, Senate and House of Commons.

A Quick History of the Great White North

I know, I know—people always skip over the history sections in travel books.

But there's a reason for going over all this spilt milk yet again: becoming familiar with the history of a place will help you more fully savour your visit. On top of that, Canadian history—with its characters, conflicts and catastrophes—is anything but dull.

Later on, you'll find more details about Canada's rich past. But here are the basics.

In the Beginning...

There was nobody. As near as scientists can figure out, people first came to the North American continent from Asia sometime between 10,000 and 45,000 years ago, when an 88-kilometre land bridge existed between Siberia and Alaska. In other words, they walked.

Over the centuries, the first peoples—we call them First Nations now, or simply natives—ranged throughout North and South America. In Canada, despite the hardships of weather and changing climate patterns, they established a rich network of cultures and languages. Historians estimate that there were more than 50 First Nations groups in Canada before Europeans arrived. On the BC coast, natives lived in relatively permanent settlements, close to their primary source of food, the sea; on the Plains, the tribes were largely nomadic, following the great herds of bison; in the east, especially around the Great Lakes, there were complex and rich agricultural nations.

Although these disparate peoples together did not represent any kind of single "country," they did interact, not only through wars and skirmishes but also along complex trading routes. White historians have only recently begun to appreciate and understand the diversity of native culture in Canada as it existed before the arrival of Europeans.

A New Leif

The first European to set foot in North America (again, as near as anybody can tell) was not Christopher Columbus, but a Viking named Bjarni, who "discovered" Greenland in 986. In the year 1000, fellow Norseman Leif "The Lucky" Erickson sailed from Greenland to the coast of what would later become Canada. He named the island of Newfoundland "*Vinland*," which means Wine-land, because he thought it had an abundance of grapes. Along its coasts, he established settlements and, in very-un-Viking-like fashion, got along pretty well with the native peoples, whom he dubbed "Skraelings."

But the Viking settlements didn't last long. Perhaps relations soured with the indigenous folk, or perhaps the winters were too harsh or food supplies ran out. Whatever happened, the Viking settlements were abandoned by the year 1016. You can still see one of them, however, at the northwest tip of Newfoundland, in the UN World Heritage Site at L'Anse aux Meadows.

The Explorers

From the late 15th century on, the world's three great powers, France, England and Spain, were busy extending their empires into the New World. The Spaniards dominated the South; the French and English stuck largely to the North.

The first Englishman—well, he was Italian really, but he was working for the King of England—to reach North America was Giovanni Caboto, whom the Brits called John Cabot. In 1497, he landed in either Newfoundland or Cape Breton Island (there's still some debate about that), and claimed the land for England. That set up the British presence in the Grand Banks fishery, which proved the economic lifeblood of the Atlantic coast for centuries to come.

In 1534, Jacques Cartier of France sailed to North America and explored the St. Lawrence River, bringing back promises of untold wealth in gold and furs. Cartier returned twice, including a trip in 1535, when he and his men survived a brutal winter at what would later become Quebec City—withstanding incredible hardships and a plague of scurvy.

Cartier's explorations in North America opened up the continent's abundant natural resources—mostly fish and furs—to France. They also had a more enduring legacy: when Cartier asked what the native Iroquois called the land north of the St. Lawrence, they replied *"kanata,"* which means a gathering of houses. The name stuck, and eventually was transliterated into Canada.

It took 70 years and Samuel de Champlain to firmly establish France's presence in North America. Unlike his predecessors, Champlain

By the Way

When Cabot arrived in Newfoundland, he encountered the Beothuk, a native people who (thanks to European-caused plague and conflict) had completely died out by the early 19th century. The Beothuk had a habit of dying their skin with a dye made from hematite, a reddish-brown substance. Some researchers suspect that is how North America's native peoples got their inaccurate but long-standing nickname Red Indians.

was bent on settling Canada. It wasn't easy. In 1604, he set up a town on St. Croix Island on the Bay of Fundy—it barely survived the winter. Champlain and his men moved on, to present-day Nova Scotia, where they settled Port Royal, which was a little more successful, lasting two years. (The French returned a few years later, however.) Finally, he ended up at Stadacona. As it grew, the settlement would become known as Quebec—and the age of New France had begun.

Battle of the Empires

Although they established agricultural settlements, the French in Canada relied largely on the fur trade. To make it work, they needed large and ever-increasing tracts of land, as well as the co-operation of the natives, their main workforce.

Over time, land and the natives proved their biggest problems. France's allegiance with the Hurons ran them into trouble with the Iroquois, culminating in the attacks on and eventual abandonment of the French missionary outpost Sainte-Marie-among-the-Hurons, in modern-day Ontario.

And then there were the British. For one thing, they had established a permanent colony in Newfoundland, and the Treaty of Utrecht gave them control of Nova Scotia in 1713. Their settlements to the south—later the states of the US seaboard—were growing at a frantic rate, and cutting into New France's fur territory. On the other side of the Atlantic, meanwhile, France and England started duking it out back home in 1756, and their conflict—the Seven Years' War—was imported to North America.

It didn't go well for the French. In 1758, Louisbourg, their military fortress on Cape Breton Island, fell to the British. A year later, on the Plains of Abraham outside of Quebec City, British forces led by General James Wolfe confronted the French under the Marquis de Montcalm. Both generals died as a result of their wounds—along with about 1,500 soldiers on both sides—but the British carried the day. And New France was effectively crushed.

The Road to Confederation

Like so much else, events south of the border changed the face of Canada in the late 18th century. The American Revolution, despite its

Local Knowledge

After the fall of New France, the British actually gave a pretty good deal to the losers. Under successive pieces of legislation, the French were allowed to keep their language, their Roman Catholic religion, and their civil legal system. It wasn't just a matter of being nice, however: the new British rulers were acutely aware of the troubles going on in their southern colonies—later the United States—and they did not want similar unrest to start up in their new possession.

Today, criminal courts are the same throughout Canada, and follow the Criminal Code. In civil matters, English Canada follows the traditions of the British common law, but in Quebec civil law still follows the *code civile*, a hold-over from the 18th-century guarantee of the French-speaking area's unique legal system.

usual depiction in Hollywood movies, was not a uniform revolt against an overseas oppressor—many Americans were loyal to the British Crown, and wanted to remain that way even after the Thirteen Colonies had won the Revolutionary War. Faced with mounting perse-cution by the new regime at home, many of the non-revolutionaries—so-called Loyalists—fled the country, and about 100,000 of them settled in Nova Scotia and Quebec.

That was fine for Nova Scotia—it needed people anyway—but in Quebec it created two populations, English and French, that had differ-ent cultures, different economic interests and different religions. Eventually, a political solution was reached, dividing the land on the west end of the St. Lawrence River and that to the east into Upper Canada (later Ontario) and Lower Canada (just Quebec).

In 1812, the Americans came calling. Acting on real or perceived affronts to their nationhood from England, US forces invaded what is now southern Ontario. As wars go, the ensuing War of 1812 (sometimes called "The Second War of Independence" in the States) wasn't all that remarkable. There were victories and losses on both sides, and in the end the border between Canada and the United States remained pretty much unchanged.

But among Canadians, successfully repelling superior American forces was a point of pride, and it helped to define a sense of nationhood among the disparate British colonies north of the United States.

By the 1860s, those colonies had begun to think about getting together. The political division of Upper and Lower Canada wasn't working very well, and many thought that federation would ease and enhance trade. As well, the building of an inter-colonial railroad required a bigger government—and more money—than any of the colonies could provide on their own. And there was still a lingering fear of invasion from the south.

In 1864 in Charlottetown, delegates from Nova Scotia, New Brunswick and Prince Edward Island met with leaders from Upper and Lower Canada, and the idea of confederation was broached. It took three more years—and heightened political tensions with the United States—before the idea became a reality.

On July 1, 1867, the Dominion of Canada came into being under the *British North America Act*. The new country had four provinces: Ontario, Quebec, Nova Scotia and New Brunswick. Manitoba joined up in 1870. A year later, lured by the promise of a transcontinental railroad within 10 years, British Columbia entered Confederation. (The railway ended up being a few years later, but BC stayed part of Canada anyway.) Prince Edward Island, even though it was the place where the ball really started rolling, did not join Canada until 1873.

Thanks to the railway, the West boomed in the late 19th century. In 1905, two new provinces—Saskatchewan and Alberta—were carved out of the vast area that was previously called the Northwest Territories.

Newfoundland, after a long debate and a narrowly decided referendum, joined Canada in 1949. And with that, the country assumed the makeup that it still has today—a dominion of varying interests, different histories, sometimes clashing cultures, and more hockey fans than you can shake a stick at.

The rest, as they say, is history.

But Will It Last?

Canada has been on the brink of disintegration several times in its history—although it has avoided the kind of civil war that the United

States suffered in the 1860s. The most recent, and the most serious, threat to national unity comes from Quebec. French alienation within Canada has a painful history, and attempting to bridge the "two solitudes" between Quebec and the rest of the country has long preoccupied federal and provincial government leaders. Their successive attempts to rewrite the Canadian Constitution to alleviate Quebec's concerns—based on historical grievances, nationalist zeal and fear of losing the province's language and culture—have largely failed.

In 1995, the problem came to a head when Quebec's separatist governing party, the Parti Québécois, staged a referendum in which it asked Quebecers whether they agreed that the province should become a sovereign nation. The result was unnervingly close: the No forces (that is, a vote for Quebec to stay within Canada) narrowly defeated the Yes side, by a margin of 50.6 per cent to 49.4 per cent.

In the aftermath of the referendum, the issue of Quebec separation has largely dimmed in the public mind—both in Quebec and the rest of Canada. Many Canadians, particularly the young, have simply grown tired of the seemingly endless game of referendums, constitutional accords and political brinkmanship.

Although hostilities have ceased for the time being, the Quebec government has vowed to hold another referendum within a few years, and the result of that will be, at the moment, anybody's guess.

Which provides yet another reason to explore Canada soon—while it's still in one piece.

The Least You Need to Know

➤ First Nations peoples arrived in Canada between 10,000 and 45,000 years ago.

➤ Centuries after the Vikings landed in Newfoundland (and then left), John Cabot for England and Jacques Cartier for France explored Canada.

➤ The driving force in the settlement of New France was Samuel de Champlain.

➤ English forces defeated the French on the Plains of Abraham outside Quebec City.

➤ The War of 1812 helped to stir a sense of nationhood among Canadians.

➤ Nova Scotia, New Brunswick, Quebec and Ontario created the Dominion of Canada in 1867; the other provinces followed in later years, and Newfoundland was the last to join, in 1949.

Exploring Canada's Cities

When it comes to Canadian urban centres, it's hard to generalize, because each has its own style. On the other hand, they share certain characteristics. For a lot of reasons, Canada's cities have largely escaped the pattern of urban decay that has been so common in the United States. Downtown areas still tend to be a focus of social and economic activity. Most importantly, people of all races and incomes live downtown; the city cores don't become deserted after 5 p.m. Add to that safety, cleanliness and (usually) friendly people, and it's small wonder that Canada's cities are increasingly becoming tourist destinations in their own right.

Later in the book, the major cities are discussed in detail. But here's a quick look to give you some idea of their diversity.

St. John's

One of the oldest settlements in North America, St. John's embodies the quirkiness and good humour of Newfoundland. And it's said that the city has more pubs per capita than any other town in the world.

Halifax

Rich in Canada's maritime heritage, the capital of Nova Scotia is a modern city with a small-town feel. Thanks to its substantial student population, it also has a very active night life.

Montreal

Long the economic centre of Canada, Montreal, in the southwest corner of Quebec, has ceded that status to Toronto. But it remains a cosmopolitan and urbane city, where French and English—and a few more languages—meet.

Quebec City

The capital of Quebec has some of the country's most historic and well-preserved buildings. Primarily French, Quebec City is probably the most European-feeling place in Canada.

Toronto

The capital of Ontario, Toronto is Canada's largest city. It is one of the most ethnically diverse places in the world, and the capital of culture in English Canada—theatre, film and the fine arts.

Ottawa

The nation's capital, Ottawa is a government town, and it's a great start to exploring Canada's history. It also is home to some of the country's finest museums and art galleries.

Winnipeg

Lying near the geographic centre of North America, Winnipeg is where the East ends and the West begins. It's the capital of Manitoba, and in recent years the city centre has been substantially revitalized and restored.

Edmonton

In the heart of Alberta, Edmonton is the northernmost provincial capital in Canada, which has earned it the nickname "Gateway to the North." Despite being Alberta's largest city, Edmonton still has the feel of a frontier town.

Calgary

Buoyed by oil and natural resources, Calgary is a city eternally on the move—sort of like an Albertan version of Dallas. It's best known as the site of the annual Calgary Stampede.

Vancouver

The Gateway to the Far East, Vancouver is one of the country's fastest-growing cities. And it is certainly among the prettiest, set amid the mountains and splendid vistas of the British Columbia coast.

Where to Stay

All Canadian cities will present you with plenty to choose from when it comes to accommodations. Which you decide upon ultimately depends on your budget. The major hotel chains—Holiday and Comfort Inns, in particular—have at least one establishment, and sometimes more, in most cities. Independent hotels, meanwhile, offer accommodations ranging from the flea-bitten to the ritzy.

The most important thing, besides cost, is location. Basically, you have two options: the airport or downtown. If you're in town just overnight, then sure, stay near the airport. But if you plan to stay a few days and explore the city, stay as close to downtown as possible. That's where the action is, and that's where you will want to be. It might cost you a little extra, but staying downtown will end up sparing you both the expense of transportation and the aggravation of wasted time.

Local Knowledge

If you're visiting an unfamiliar city for a week or two and aren't sure which hotels are good or bad, you might try the "bivouac" approach. Book yourself for a couple nights into a chain hotel, where you already know what sort of accommodation is offered: pretty good, but not spectacular, and probably lacking character. That will be your bivouac. Then, while you're exploring the city, look around for smaller, more elegant or more out-of-the-way hotels. Look around the lobby, even ask to see one of the rooms. Find one you like, then move from the chain into your new digs.

The Better Way—Use It

Most cities of any size in Canada have cheap and efficient public transit systems. In general, they are clean and safe, and not too difficult to follow.

Compared to cars, the buses and trains of public transit systems are better for the environment. In places where traffic jams are a fact of urban life, taking the subway can actually be quicker than driving. And riding a bus or a streetcar is a terrific way to get a feel for the city.

Public transit is a great alternative to expensive taxis and traffic hassles. So use it.

Local Knowledge

The emergency telephone number is the same across Canada and the United States. If you run into trouble and need police or other emergency assistance, dial 911.

Stick 'Em Up, Eh?

Compared with American cities, the crime rate in Canada's urban centres is remarkably low. That's especially true of violent crime, thanks to a lot of factors: a relatively low level of racial tension, social programs, cultural differences and—here's the big one—the fact that the right to bear arms is not written into the Constitution. Although handguns are still too numerous in Canadian cities, they are not common by any means.

Walking is the best way to experience all that Canada's cities have to offer. In most of the places you'll want to go, you should have little fear of being robbed or assaulted. Note: *little* fear is not *no* fear. Crime does exist in Canada, and it makes sense to take the same precautions you would anywhere else.

The first and foremost is know where you're going. If you're not sure about the safety of an area, ask the staff at your hotel or motel.

A money belt is always a good idea, and carrying traveller's cheques instead of cash can prevent your vacation from turning into a nightmare.

Don't take unnecessary risks—walking alone at night, flashing money around, or getting so intoxicated you don't know which way is up. You won't need a black belt in karate to explore the city. But you do need to think.

The Least You Need to Know

➤ Major Canadian cities include Toronto, Montreal, Vancouver and Ottawa, as well as St. John's, Halifax, Quebec City, Winnipeg, Calgary and Edmonton.

Local Knowledge

Toronto police have recently reported a surge in pickpocketing, especially around the city's convention areas and popular tourist attractions. Forewarned is forearmed.

➤ Choosing a hotel will depend on your budget and your expectations, but try to stay as close to downtown as possible.

➤ When you can, use public transit.

➤ Crime rates in most Canadian cities are low, but you should still take precautions.

Chapter 4

Canada's Great Outdoors

In This Chapter

➤ Camping and hiking in Canada

➤ Boating and fishing

➤ Skiing

➤ Wildlife observation

➤ Dealing with bears

Although the country reaches from the lower 48 United States to well above the Arctic Circle, the vast majority of Canadians live along a relatively narrow strip of land running along its southern perimeter. The rest of Canada remains largely hinterland, supporting a rich diversity of plants and animals, and much of the area is freshwater.

There are still places in Canada that have probably never been seen by humans, but many wild areas have been extensively explored and exploited for their natural resources—first for furs, then for minerals and lumber. As in other developed countries, the use (or abuse) of the hinterland is a matter of active social and political debate in

Canada. Still, a good deal of land is protected as part of the national and provincial parks system.

Some of the country's most popular or interesting wilderness areas are described in the following chapters. Here's a quick list of things to do.

Pitching the Ol' Tent

Canada's national parks comprise over 200,000 square kilometres of land and water—about 2 per cent of the country's total area. And there are more than 800 provincial parks. Together, they offer nearly unlimited opportunities for camping, hiking and canoeing.

Some, particularly the provincial parks, cater to the weekend camper or outdoor enthusiast: they tend to be closer to urban centres, and provide more amenities. National parks, on the other hand, tend to be wilder, more remote places, and many of them offer few creature comforts at all. An exception is Banff National Park, the country's oldest and the most popular, which has two full-fledged resort towns, as well as three commercially run skiing areas, within its borders.

Water, Water Everywhere

No one knows the exact number, but it's estimated that Canada has more than two million lakes. Combined, they take up more than 7.5 per cent of the country's total land mass, and if their contents were poured out, they would flood Canada to a depth of more than 6 feet.

For boaters and fishermen, that spells opportunity. For the former, every major urban centre has a favourite weekend getaway spot just a couple hours' drive away. Around Toronto, for instance, there are three

Local Knowledge

If motor boating is your passion, make sure that it's allowed where you're going before you plunk the 30-footer on the trailer. Most parks place restrictions on motorized vessels, as do some residents' associations around lakes and rivers in their areas.

By the Way

A lot of anglers consider the northern pike, which is wildly abundant throughout northern Canada, as a "trash fish"—rarely worth catching, and never worth eating. On the other hand, the pike has its supporters, who argue 1) that their abundance is a good thing, because they're easy to catch; 2) they put up a good fight; 3) they taste really good, once you get used to all those bones; and 4) they are largely immune to the parasites that can render other species unpalatable, especially in late season. So, hey, give the pike a break!

popular areas—Georgian Bay, the Kawarthas and Muskoka—all of which have literally oodles of lakes.

For anglers, there are dozens of gamefish species to pursue. In Central Canada, the most popular are pickerel (or walleye), trout, large and smallmouth bass, perch, northern pike and muskellunge (which are hard to catch—trust me). On the east and west coasts, salmon are the prime catch, although their numbers have been declining in recent years. In the north, the pike is nearly ubiquitous, but there are also world-record whitefish, lake trout, arctic char and grayling in its waters.

Management of sport fishing in Canada is largely left up to the provinces, and each has its own system of seasons, licences and fees, which are strictly enforced. On top of that, parks often have special restrictions and/or fees that apply within their borders. So before you head out to cast your lure, call ahead and make sure you're not breaking the law.

Things Are Going Downhill

Mountains plus snow equal skiing. And Canada has plenty of all three.

When it comes to places to strap on the skis, none is better than British Columbia, whose Rocky Mountain peaks offer some of the best alpine opportunities, not only in North America, but the world. Next most popular is Alberta, especially in the twin national parks of Banff and Jasper, followed by Quebec, which has Mont Ste. Anne and Mont

Local Knowledge

There are two cardinal rules for safe skiing: know the conditions, and know your own abilities. Especially in the Rockies, avalanches are a danger, so be sure to obey warnings and check local weather conditions before heading to the slopes. Just as important, don't take on more than you can handle. Tackling a tough slope or going *off piste* (outside the marked ski runs) when you really don't know what you're doing can get you hurt—or even killed.

Tremblant—real winter hot spots. If you're not too serious or just want to get out for a day, then Ontario, Manitoba and most other provinces also have ski hills. They tend to deliver the same chills, with less thrills.

All the Long-Leggedy Beasties

Getting out into the wilderness is more than just nice views and pristine lakes. It's also an opportunity to see how those other Canadians—the animals—live. In fact, as hunting has fallen out of fashion among city dwellers, an increasing number are making wildlife observation—with a camera, binoculars or just with the naked eye—the major reason for exploring the outdoors.

Canada's development has long depended on its animals—fish, beaver and whales, in particular. Certainly, their numbers have declined as a result, and ever-spreading urbanization is pushing natural ecosystems farther and farther into the frontier. But there are still many areas in Canada where Nature can be observed in the wild.

Some animals can be found practically anywhere in the country. Beaver, muskrat, moose, white-tailed deer and black bear are among them. But some of the more interesting species are found only in certain areas: the muskoxen of the Arctic Lowlands, the mountain goats and marmots of the Rockies, the pronghorn antelopes of the prairie. As well, Canada lies on several important migratory routes for birds, and 425 species are known to breed here. Small wonder bird-watching has become an increasingly popular pastime—or passion—among Canadians.

Whale-watching off the east and west coasts is an increasingly popular activity among tourists, from the beluga of the St. Lawrence and the right and humpback off the east coast, to the killer and grey whales that populate the waters off BC. In many coastal areas on both coasts, charter boats and tours can be arranged where you can see the whales up close.

Please Don't Feed the Man-Eaters

Being safe in the wilderness includes respecting the wildlife. There are relatively few animals in Canada that will or can attack people. The wolf, for instance, which has long been considered a man-eater, in fact almost never takes on a human, unless it has been provoked or is rabid. Moose and muskoxen present a greater threat: they will charge people who get too close, particularly during rutting season.

Every summer, there are a handful of bear attacks in Canada; some have been fatal, although most injuries are minor. Bears will usually put up with the presence of humans—but you need to be careful.

For one thing, remember that bears are not pets and they are not friendly. They will often come to campgrounds and other areas where they can get easy food, or you might see them at town dumps. That's where a lot of bear attacks happen, because the bears have lost their fear of people. (Just because they're near humans does not mean they are tame.) When camping, try to avoid having smelly food around, and make sure you store and dispose of it properly.

Grizzly bears often attack suddenly, charging at their victims out of the brush with little warning. Mostly, they are acting out of surprise. If you must hike through grizzly territory, make as much noise as possible—many people carry a whistle or wear bells.

If you find yourself too close to a bear, the experts recommend backing away slowly, keeping your eyes on the bear. Whatever you do, don't run.

What you do if a bear attacks—if you can do anything at all—depends on what kind of bear you're dealing with. If you're attacked by a black bear, chances are that the injury will be minor and you will be able to back away. If not, and the bear tackles you, some experts recommend giving it a sharp punch on the nose.

Apparently, playing dead doesn't work with black bears. On the other hand, it *just might* work with a grizzly. When you've got 700 pounds of bear trying to kill you, anything's worth a try.

The Least You Need to Know

➤ Canada has over 200,000 square kilometres of national parkland and more than 800 provincial parks.

➤ There are more than two million lakes in Canada.

➤ Popular game fish include salmon, trout, pickerel, bass and pike.

➤ Wildlife observation is an increasingly popular outdoor activity.

➤ Bear attacks are rare, but you need to take precautions.

Chapter 5

Getting It Together

In This Chapter
➤ Planning your trip
➤ Compiling an itinerary
➤ Some tips on packing
➤ Using the World Wide Web for travel

How extensively you plan your trip depends on a lot of factors: where you're going, the length of stay, whether it's a city or an outdoor vacation, and your own personal taste and style. Some people plan their trip months in advance, and down to the smallest detail—right down to where they're going to eat and how much toothpaste they're planning to use. Others prefer to just hop in the car or the plane and go—and damn the details.

There's something to be said for both approaches. But the smartest way is probably to aim for a golden mean, balancing caution with spontaneity. In other words, cover the basics, and then improvise once you get to where you're going.

Here are a few tips to get you started.

We Want Information!

The first step is deciding where you want to go. Simply put, there is no substitute for being informed. Reading this book will get you started, giving you an idea of what each region in Canada has to offer and providing you some basic information about what to do once you decide on a travel destination.

If you plan on an extended vacation or want to explore an area more deeply, however, you should look up other sources of information. Tourism is a big industry in Canada—it employs about 10 per cent of the workforce—and Canadian governments and businesses are eager to let prospective travellers know what's offered. Take advantage of that eagerness when you plan your trip. A good place to start any vacation to unfamiliar territory is to call the tourism department of the province you're planning to visit. (Their telephone numbers are listed in an appendix to this book.) Often overlooked, provincial tourism ministries publish a host of brochures and pamphlets, and they can direct you to tour operators, outdoor outfitters, hotels and restaurants in their areas. Best of all, the advice they give and the material they will send you is free, and it's usually very reliable.

Government information is not exactly objective, however, since it's their business to make you want to visit them. So if a place looks interesting, you should consult secondary sources. This book is one of

Local Knowledge

So you've just arrived in an unfamiliar city, checked into your hotel, and have no idea which way is north, where the main street is, or what the place is like. Here's one approach: take a bus tour of the city. They're cheap, they're readily available at most hotels and they will give you the quick once-over of your new surroundings. Sure, you may feel like a complete idiot staring at the locals from a double-decker bus. But the information the tour guides give you can be helpful (although it's not always reliable), and letting somebody else do the driving at least gives you a chance to scope out the territory and get your bearings.

them, but there are plenty of other regional and city tourist guides that explain the attractions—and the pitfalls—of places throughout Canada in greater detail.

If you're connected to the Internet, the World Wide Web is a great place to get both kinds of travel information. We'll talk more about that later in the chapter.

When it comes to outdoor travel, being informed about your destination is absolutely essential, especially if you're planning to explore the back-country. You will need to find out what equipment is required, what sort of restrictions apply (especially in parks) and what weather conditions you can expect. When you're in the wilderness, your circumstances can change in a matter of minutes, and you need to be prepared for any possibility.

If It's Tuesday, This Must Be Moose Jaw

A lot of people overlook this, but it's a good idea to have at least a rough itinerary before starting a vacation. You can get as detailed as you like—from check-in time at the hotel to where you're going to have dinner every night.

Your itinerary should begin a few days before you leave, listing things you need to take care of: taking the dog to the kennel, arranging for someone to water your plants, finishing up projects or work duties, cancelling newspaper delivery—that sort of thing.

If you're going on a road trip, jot down your destinations, relevant telephone numbers and things you want to see—they'll serve as a useful reminder while you're behind the wheel. Be flexible, however, and don't plan to pack in too many activities or destinations. Travel should be fun and relaxing, not a chore.

It's also a good idea to give your itinerary to someone back home before you leave. Put on it the places you are going to stay (along with telephone numbers) and when you plan on returning. If you don't show up, then your friends at home will know something is wrong. Sharing your itinerary is especially important if you're travelling alone, and many people like to schedule telephone calls to friends or relatives back home to let them know everything is all right.

Again, back-country exploration requires special caution, and an itinerary is usually required by authorities before they will let you into the wilder sections of national and provincial parks. In this case, it's important both that the itinerary is realistic and that you stick to it—you don't want park staff to send out a search-and-rescue team just because you decided to lollygag by a pretty lake for an extra day.

Honey, Where's My Nose-Hair Trimmer?

Okay, packing can be a nightmare. Too many people leave it to the last minute, and then find out they're missing something essential once they're on the road. Another common mistake is over-packing—forcing you to carry around heavy bags filled with stuff you'll never need. To avoid packing hassles, here are a few tips.

First, consider the weather conditions at your destination, and plan on bringing suitable clothing. You won't need to pack a parka in July (for most places in Canada, at least!), but weather throughout the country can change quickly even from day to night. An extra sweater is usually a smart idea.

Second, find out what facilities and amenities are available at your destination. Hotels often provide toiletries, shoe-shining, laundry and other services. Take them into account before you pack 14 shirts for a two-week holiday.

A week or so before you leave, start compiling a list of things you think you'll need to take with you. That way, you'll have a handy checklist once you start to pack, and it will give you a chance to think twice about what you really need. It will also allow you time to go to the store if you're missing anything, so you won't be rushing around at the last minute.

Last but not least, leave yourself plenty of time. You should pack the day before you leave—at the latest. Try to confine yourself, for most

Local Knowledge

If you're going on a road trip, it's a good idea to take a cellular phone. If your car breaks down, if you have an accident or if you need to book a hotel at the last minute, a telephone will come in handy.

trips, to two pieces of luggage: a handbag or rucksack for small items (sunglasses, itinerary, camera, magazines, travel guides) that you will need to use often, and a larger piece for clothing and toiletries.

Surfing to Saskatchewan

Travel and tourism comprise one of the fastest-growing subject areas on the World Wide Web, and if you've got a computer and a modem, you can get plenty of information with just the click of the mouse. Some of it is good, some of it is downright bad. But with a little foreknowledge of what's out there on the electronic highway, surfing the electronic highway can be a useful tool in planning your trip. Best of all, aside from connect-time charges, it's free.

You'll find some of the more useful travel Web sites for Canada scattered throughout this book, as well as in an appendix at the back. In general, they can be broken down into four categories.

Services: By following simple instructions, it is now possible to arrange most aspects of your trip on the World Wide Web. Most major airlines have Web sites where you can not only find flight and fare information, but also buy tickets. As well, many hotels offer reservation

Canada by Web

Learning to use search engines is vital to successfully navigating the World Wide Web. Typically, the engine allows you to type in a key word, and then it searches for Web sites that are related to that word. Often, you'll find the engine returns a mind-boggling number of relevant pages. So use the process of elimination, narrowing your search terms (there's a different way to do this for each search engine) until you find what you're looking for.

For instance, if you're looking for restaurants in downtown Ottawa, first type in the word "Ottawa," then search those results for "restaurant." If you still have too many hits, try refining your search again, including the word "downtown" or even a particular street name. With a bit of practice and patience, you'll be an old hand at Web-surfing in no time.

services on the Web, and if you're planning to go to the theatre or other events at your destination, you can book ahead on-line.

Whether you use these services or not depends ultimately on your faith in the technology. If you're doubtful that you'll ever get the tickets or other things you've bought online, it's not a bad idea to resort to an older form of communication: telephone the airline or agency to confirm your purchase.

Government information: All provincial governments have Web sites devoted to tourism (they're listed at the back). They can provide a good overview of things to see and do across the country, and they're a smart place to start your travel surfing. Remember, though, that it's in the interests of tourism officials to make their provinces seem as attractive as possible, so take some of the more boastful claims with a grain of salt. The government sites usually provide useful links to other, perhaps more objective, travel pages.

Businesses: If you do a basic Web search for, say, "Canada" and "travel," you are bound to get a lot of hits for businesses that make their living off the tourist dollar—hotels, restaurants, resorts, outfitters, and the like. Many of these pages are little more than advertising, and their information may or may not be accurate. They are, after all, trying to put the best face on their businesses. On the other hand, browsing through these pages can provide you with valuable info on what sorts of activities and services are available and how much they cost. As well, the best business Web sites have links to other resources. And the sites of some resort areas, especially ski resorts, provide up-to-date weather and snow conditions.

Independent travel guides: The quality and objectivity of online travel guides can vary widely, but the better ones take advantage of the Web to provide more data than would be possible in any printed book. There are several very good commercial travel guides on the Internet—some are listed in the appendix—and they are best used to get more detail on a particular destination.

Don't overlook individual travel contributions on the Internet. Many people, with no self-interest beyond sharing their experiences, post comments in Usenet newsgroups or chat rooms devoted to travel in Canada. An increasing number use personal home pages as travel-ogues, including not only their impressions but also photographs. You can usually find such pages through a standard Web search, and they can be useful sources of objective information.

Canada by Web

For travellers, one of the more handy uses of the World Wide Web is checking the weather at destinations. There are plenty of weather sites dealing with Canada (see the back of the book), and they'll let you know whether you're going to be wearing shorts or buttoning up your overcoat.

The Least You Need to Know

➤ Find out as much you can about your destination before you leave.

➤ Make an itinerary and leave a copy with friends or relatives, especially if you're travelling alone.

➤ Make a list of things you need to pack, and start packing early.

➤ With patience and practice, the World Wide Web can be a valuable source of travel information.

Part 2
Eastern Canada

Canada's east coast is a unique and breathtaking place with quiet seaside towns and spectacular shoreline, where history is intimately entwined with the sea and its bounty. Atlantic Canada includes Newfoundland, the last province to join Canada but the first to be settled by Europeans; Nova Scotia, home of the Bluenose and the bustling city of Halifax; Prince Edward Island, the birthplace of Confederation and the setting for the Anne of Green Gables novels; and New Brunswick, where you can witness the world's highest tides and check out the oddity of Magnetic Hill, one of the Maritimes' strangest attractions. If you go, you'll find that Down East in Canada—with its colourful people and rich traditions—is a place quite unlike any other.

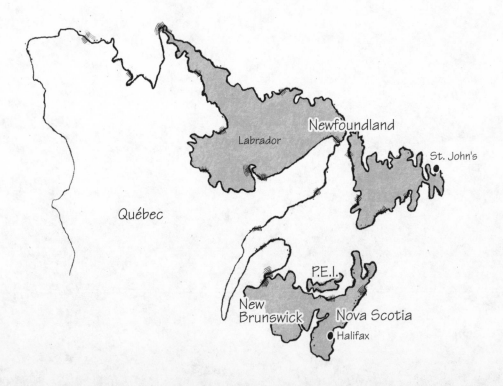

Newfoundland

Chapter 6

In This Chapter

➤ Exploring St. John's, Newfoundland's premier city

➤ Out and about in Newfoundland

Welcome to Newfoundland

Canada's newest province, Newfoundland, which joined Confederation officially in 1949, is also one of the least visited by other Canadians. One reason is its relative remoteness: the main island, plum in the Atlantic Ocean, is of course impossible to reach by land, and the province's mainland area, Labrador, is cold and forbidding for much of the year. A benefit of Newfoundland's seclusion, however, is that its unique culture and deep history remain an integral part of life there.

With the decline of the province's staple fisheries industry in the 1990s, Newfoundland's government and businesspeople turned increased attention to developing tourism—a trend that culminated in 1997 with the massive 500th anniversary celebrations in honour of the discovery of Newfoundland by Giovanni Caboto, better known by his English name, John Cabot. The tourism industry in Newfoundland may

By the Way

Before you go, try to get the pro-nunciation of "Newfoundland" straight. Some Canadians pronounce it "*newf*-in-lund," stressing the first syllable, and some weigh in with "new-*fownd*-lund," with the stress on the second syllable. Both are wrong (at least to a Newfoundlander's ears). The correct pronunciation is "new-fun-*land*," placing stress on the last syllable and hitting it hard. It's easier for the natives to say—but do your best!

still be in its infancy—an advantage to many visitors, since it means many areas still have a fresh, non-touristy feel about them. But increasingly, travellers from around the world are discovering the Atlantic province's wonders—from friendly St. John's to the natural beauty of the island's parks and the forbidding coastal areas of Labrador.

Newfoundland is a big province, stretching for 1,800 kilometres from its northernmost tip, Cape Chidley in Labrador, to the south coast. Most visitors will restrict their tour of the province to the main island. But once you're there, be prepared to stay for a while.

St. John's

The largest city in Newfoundland, St. John's is also one of the oldest settlements in North America. It is also the most visited place on the main island, and not only because it is home to the main airport for international and domestic flights. As the centre of province's cultural, political and religious life, St. John's has a style all its own, part urban sophistication and part Down East charm. Rich in history and culture, the city is also renowned for its friendliness—and it probably has more pubs per capita than any other place in the country. One thing is for sure: few who have visited St. John's have anything bad to say about it.

St. John's Past and Present

Thanks to its natural harbour, located on the east side of the Avalon Peninsula and protected by high hills on either side, St. John's got an early start. Local legend has it that John Cabot arrived in its sheltered bay on the night of June 24, 1497—St. Jean Baptiste Day—and therefore named it St. John's. While the truth of that story remains in question, it's pretty certain that European ships plying the nearby Grand Banks for fish frequently stopped in the St. John's harbour from the early 1500s, and by 1583, when the British officially declared Newfoundland a colony, a permanent settlement had sprung up on the channel's north side.

For the next two centuries, fish—particularly the then-abundant cod—drove the local economy, and St. John's grew into the administrative and economic capital of Newfoundland. The city's real heyday (it became the seat of the colony's legislative assembly in 1832) was the latter half of the 19th century, when St. John's pre-eminence as a port fuelled the growth of manufacturing and commercial industries. Its population, meanwhile, had steadily grown throughout the 1800s, thanks largely to the immigration of Irish Catholics, who contributed a Celtic flair to its otherwise largely Anglo-Saxon inhabitants.

But if St. John's lived by fish, so too did its prosperity wax and wane with the fortunes of the East Coast fishery, leading

By the Way

It's hard to keep track of all the things that set Newfoundland apart, but here's another one: it is the only Canadian province with its own breed of dog. The good-natured and massive Newfoundland dog was probably developed by islanders way back in the 17th century, and they can weigh up to 150 pounds. Besides their size, though, they are also excellent swimmers—a factor that has helped them remain popular with Newfoundlanders (the people), since the dogs have often saved lives.

it through times of boom and deep bust—particularly after the First World War and during the Great Depression. After Newfoundland joined Confederation in 1949, the public sector played an increasingly important role in the local economy of its capital, which created new problems.

After 1949, the St. John's fishery experienced a sharp decline, from which it never recovered, thanks largely to shifting distribution practices of major fish producers. People from the fisheries-dependent outports, encouraged by the government of Joey Smallwood, flooded into the provincial capital to take advantage of new civil service jobs, doubling the population in 25 years. The result—since there were only so many jobs to go around—was chronic unemployment and St. John's becoming one of the poorest Canadian cities.

Local Knowledge

When planning a trip to Newfoundland, take the weather into consideration. Although St. John's lies further south than Vancouver, it is not as warm, thanks to ocean currents that are downright chilly. Although winters can be relatively mild, many of the city's attractions may well be closed during the colder months. The same goes in spades for the rest of Newfoundland, especially in the north, where winters can be harsh and summers never get very far above cool. The best time to go is between June and September—October is pushing it.

St. John's has rebounded well from those dark times, thanks in part to the continuing importance of the provincial government and to the health of its port, a major centre for servicing fishing vessels from around the world, at least until the cod fishery was closed in the early 1990s. Even then, the city did not suffer as much as many other places in Newfoundland, since its business and retail industries are largely self-sustaining. Today, it is home to about 175,000 people—by far the biggest city in Newfoundland.

It used to be that the highest buildings in St. John's were its Catholic and Protestant churches—but not anymore. The city's characteristic streets of eclectic clapboard rowhouses are now overshadowed by office towers and large hotels. In recent years, fuelled by the presence of Memorial University, on the city's northern edge, museums, art galleries and theatre companies have flourished in St. John's—yet another reason to pay it a visit.

How to Get There

By air: The easiest way to get to Newfoundland's capital from the mainland is by air. St. John's international airport serves flights from across Canada and international flights, and is located just a short drive from the city centre. Other, smaller airports are also dotted around the island, particularly Deer Lake and Gander, but they typically serve only regional airline flights. **By water:** The Marine Atlantic company runs regularly scheduled car ferry services to Newfoundland from North Sydney, NS. The shortest ferry trip is to

Local Knowledge

While in Newfoundland, you are bound to hear a few unfamiliar phrases—part of the island's dialect that has both preserved and mutated the English of Newfoundland's early inhabitants. If you want to bone up, dictionaries of Newfoundland English are available, or you can check out the highly entertaining Newfoundland Expressions Web site at http://www.dis.on.ca/newfexpr.html. Here are a few of the more common or colourful phrases:

b'ye: boy, fellow
dory: a small fishing boat
slew around: turn around
Lard tunderin' Jesus: a general expletive
Whattya at?: What are you doing, or what's your problem?
I'll be dere da rackley/dere by da by: I'll be there soon
Grivelled up like a kipper: Uh, no one's really sure what this means.

Port aux Basques, on the "nose" of southeastern Newfoundland. The Port aux Basques ferry runs year-round, but from there to St. John's is a very long drive—at least 12 hours. The other ferry arrives at Argentia in Placentia Bay, just 100 kilometres southeast of St. John's, but it operates only from June to September and takes a whopping 14 hours. In other words, unless you have time to burn, plan on flying into St. John's. **By car:** The main highway into St. John's from the west is Highway 1, part of the Trans-Canada system, which turns into Kenmount Road within the city limits.

Getting Around

It is possible to explore the bulk of attractions in St. John's proper by foot in a day or two. But many of the interesting sites are scattered farther afield, and the easiest way to get to them is by automobile. Chances are that visitors will want to expand their exploration of Newfoundland beyond the Avalon Peninsula, and while there are bus tours available, the easiest method is simply to rent a car if you didn't take the ferry over. The province's highway system is very well maintained, and traffic into and out of St. John's is rarely heavy.

By the Way

If you plan on driving around St. John's, then first purchase a good road map. Part of the charm of the city is its winding, seemingly nonsensically placed streets—the product of a quirk in history. Large tracts of St. John's were destroyed by several fires in the 19th century; the most devastating one was set by one Tommy Fitzpatrick in 1892, when a spark from his pipe started a blaze that destroyed half the town. In the wake of fire, roads had to be re-planned and rebuilt. The trouble was, municipal officials didn't have enough money to buy the land they needed to build straight roads.

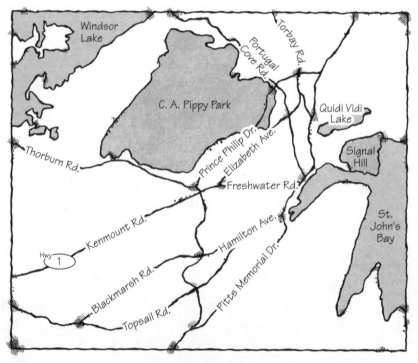

St. John's area

A Guide to St. John's and Area

One of the things visitors notice immediately about old St. John's is the strange-looking mix of architectural styles among its homes and commercial streets. The look is uniquely St. John's, and it's the result of a series of devastating fires and patchwork rebuilding during the 19th and early 20th centuries. The odd cityscape sets the tone for a tour of St. John's—a city that is all its own.

Downtown

Most visitors start a tour of St. John's in the place where it all began: on the waterfront. Walking along Harbour Drive, you'll get a sense of the international importance of the St. John's Harbour, where ships from all over the world are tied up at any given time of the year. **Water Street**, which runs along the west side of the harbour, is one of the main commercial strips in the old downtown, and there is a collection of pubs, restaurants and novelty stores. Among the quirkiest sights on the street is the **James O'Mara Pharmacy Museum Apothecary Hall**, a heritage drug store restored to circa 1895, with displays of old medicines, bottles and mortar-and-pestles. Call (709) 753-5877.

Another major commercial section is **George Street**, which intersects with Water Street at the gorgeously named Yellowbelly Corner. George used to be a laneway for fish pedlars, but now it is a centre of St. John's cultural and night life, and locals boast that it has more pubs per square foot than any other place in North America. If you want to get a taste of St. John's social life—and pick up Newfoundlanders' unique dialect and turns-of-phrase—then by all means stop in for a pint and a meal. On George, too, is the **Prince Edward Plaza**, a concert and performance venue during the summer months. Once pretty seedy, George Street is now benefiting from the city's heritage revitalization program.

Another important street is Duckworth, running roughly parallel to Water Street, where you'll find an array of restaurants and craft shops. Here, too, is the **Newfoundland Museum**, with permanent galleries on the province's rich history and on the cultures and traditions of its indigenous peoples. Phone (709) 729-2329 for information.

In the heart of downtown are some of St. John's greatest treasures: its churches. Worth looking for is the Anglican **Cathedral of St. John the Baptist**, on Church Hill Road, a fine example of neo-Gothic architecture. Call (709) 726-5677. Don't confuse it with a nearly equally impressive church, the Roman Catholic **Basilica of St. John the Baptist**, also in downtown, on Military Road. According to popular folklore, Queen Victoria personally donated the land for the church back in 1838, as long as it was named for St. John the Baptist. (Like anyone in St. John's needed to be asked!) The stones used in the basilica are from all over Newfoundland, including Signal Hill, and some come all the way from Ireland. Inside are rare sculptures and religious symbols, including the "Dead Christ," a somewhat chilling sculpture that lies at the foot of the basilica's altar. Call (709) 754-2170.

Nearby is the **Commissariat House**, on Kings Bridge Road, a precious Georgian home where interpreters in period costume will show visitors through the former home of the British garrison's assistant commissary general. Farther up Military Road, check out two remnants of Newfoundland's colonial past. The aptly named **Colonial Building**, a stately manor built of Irish limestone, was the seat of the Newfoundland government from 1860 to 1960, and is now home to the provincial archives (a good place to trace your ancestors if your family is from the Rock). Nearby is an oddity that stands out even in this town of oddities: **Government House**, one of the few buildings in North America that actually has a moat. According to local legend, its designer feared that lizards and snakes would invade the spacious home—apparently unaware that there are no reptiles in Newfoundland. Today, the building is the private residence of the province's lieutenant-governor.

Canada by Web

For general information on Newfoundland tourism, check out the following sites:

http://www.gov.nf.ca/tourism *(the provincial government Web site)*

http://www.nfld.com

http://www.wordplay.com/tourism *(a privately operated site)*

For more specific information and links about St. John's, try the municipal site at:

http://www.city.st-johns.nf.ca

Signal Hill and Quidi Vidi

You can walk to Signal Hill, northeast of the city core, if you feel up to it: it's only about a mile along a well-maintained pathway, but it is rather steep. Alternatively, you can drive, taking Signal Hill Road out of downtown. Once there, you will find the **Signal Hill National Historic Park**, once the old fortifications at the narrows to St. John's Harbour, now reduced to a wooden palisade marking the walls. The vantage point of Signal Hill—500 feet above the harbour below—gives an excellent view of the city, and it's a good place to watch icebergs float by during the spring. The site long had military significance: St. John's changed hands many times in the 17th and 18th centuries, and the final battle for the city occurred on Signal Hill in 1762.

By the Way

Although it is now a tourist attraction, Signal Hill used to have a more frightening effect on visitors to St. John's. In the 1700s, the local constabulary would hang thieves and other ne'er-do-wells, dip their bodies in tar and then hang them from a yardarm on Signal Hill—a warning to pirates and rowdy sailors to behave themselves while visiting the city. Today, the site of the gruesome displays is a mere knob of rock near the Signal Hill Park interpretation centre.

At the summit of the hill is **Cabot Tower**, built in 1897 to celebrate both the 400th anniversary of Cabot's landing and the Diamond Jubilee of Queen Victoria. Near the tower in 1901, Gugliemo Marconi received the first wireless transatlantic message—the single letter S—in morse code from Cornwall, England. Today, park staff at an interpretation centre guide visitors through the area's history, and there are well-marked trails to explore the harbour and the park surrounding the tower.

From Signal Hill, you can easily walk or drive to **Quidi Vidi Village**, a picturesque fishing community that is within the St. John's city limits. (It's pronounced "kiddee-viddee," by the way.) Overlooking the village is the Quidi Vidi Battery, an old French fortification later restored by the British. Open from June to September, the battery features guided tours. Call (709) 729-2460.

In the village too is **Mallard Cottage,** a quaint little structure revered as the first cottage in North America, and now a provincial and national heritage site. Call (709) 576-2266. West of the Village is **Quidi Vidi Lake**, a picturesque body of water and a nice place for a stroll. Every August, the lake is the site of the **Royal St. John's Regatta**, touted as the oldest sporting event in North America. Rowing races between fishermen took place on the lake since the 1700s, and the regatta has been an organized competition since the early 19th century.

Other St. John's Excursions

If you're in the mood for a longer walk, the **Rennies River Trail** runs for 3 miles to a freshwater resource centre, which features the only **Fluvarium** in North America. Maintained by the Quidi Vidi Rennies River Development Foundation, a local organization dedicated to preserving the St. John's area's freshwater ecosystems, the Fluvarium, on the shores of Long Pond, is a sprawling building that contains nine underwater viewing windows into a stream. Visitors can witness trout and other freshwater creatures in their natural environment, including their spawning rituals every fall. Featuring a host of other environmental exhibits, the Fluvarium lays claim to being one of Newfoundland's most popular tourist attractions. Call (709) 754-3474.

The Fluvarium is in **C. A. Pippy Park**, a vast green belt that skirts the northwest part of St. John's. At 1,342 hectares, the park has picnic areas and a full-service campground/trailer park, as well as a golf course, and during the winter it is a favoured site for cross-country skiing. Fishing is allowed in the park's several ponds, and Pippy is home to a wide range of animal species—you might even see a moose.

On the park's southern edge are the grounds of **Memorial University**, the province's largest post-secondary institution. Worth checking out, on the west side, is the Memorial University Botanical Gardens, a 110-acre natural area on the shores of Oxen Pond. The gardens attempt to re-create indigenous Newfoundland ecosystems, with peat beds, rock gardens and native plant collections, and a system of trails lends itself to bird-watching and walking. Guided tours are also available. Call (709) 737-8590.

West of downtown is another large park, **Bowring Park**, located on Waterford Bridge Road. Landscaped in the Victorian style, Bowring—with its stone bridges and green glades—is in part a tribute to the area's British ancestry: there is even a replica of the famous Peter Pan statue that stands in London's Kensington Gardens. Other statuary includes *The Fighting Newfoundlander*, a sculpture by Basil Gotto in honour of the province's military contributions to the British Commonwealth. The park also features picnic sites, a swimming pool and a playground—all in all, a pleasant place to while away a few hours.

Just a few minutes' drive out of St. John's on Route 11 is **Cape Spear**. If you don't count Greenland, it is the most easterly point in North America, and it regularly draws early birds who come to catch a glimpse of the sun rising over the vast Atlantic Ocean. For centuries, Cape Spear has been a beacon to ocean-going vessels, and today the lighthouse still stands (although it is now fully automated). A Second World War military installation—emplaced to counter the threat of German U-boats—is also at the Cape Spear site, which is surround by a national park lending itself to whale- and iceberg-watching in the spring.

Out and About in Newfoundland

One of Newfoundland's attractions is the way that its tiny outport communities blend in with the natural surroundings. For tourists who are not into camping, hiking or other extreme activities, getting out of St. John's and into Newfoundland's more remote areas is well worth the trouble. And for those who want to experience the great outdoors to the fullest, the province has plenty to offer.

Off the Beaten Path

To get an idea of the natural splendour surrounding St. John's, drive down to Bay Bulls (a half-hour drive south of the city) and arrange a boat tour. Several companies offer them, and most will take visitors out into the ocean and past the **Witless Bay Ecological Reserve**, home to puffins, murres and other seabirds. In the early summer months (before August), humpback and minke whales often venture inshore in search of capelin, and the best way to see them is from a boat.

Labrador

Québec

L'Anse aux Meadows

Gros Morne
National Park

Terra Nova National Park

Gulf of St. Lawrence

Island of
Newfoundland

Bonvista

Port aux Basques

St. John's

St. Pierre and Miquelon

Newfoundland: Outdoor attractions

The Avalon and Bonavista Peninsulas

The Avalon Peninsula south of St. John's is largely a wilderness, and yet it is dotted with small communities of Irish ancestry that define the southern Newfoundland landscape and have a rich history all their own. Two seaside towns are the sites of recent archeological digs. The first (driving from St. John's) is **Ferryland**, an old village where sat (briefly) the British Colony of Avalon; there is an archeological exhibit and laboratory here. Call (709) 432-3200.

To the west, in the delightfully named town of **Cupids**, archeologists have begun exploring the site of a colony established by the British in 1610. Although significant, there is not much to see at the site, although some pieces from the dig are on exhibit at the community museum. If you're driving the Avalon Peninsula, keep your eyes open wide farther south along Route 10, between Chance Cove and Portugal Cove South. You will probably see hundreds of caribou gathered on the

Off the Beaten Path

If you go to Newfoundland in search of postcard-perfect villages, then **Grand Bank** comes highly recommended. About four hours south of Highway 1 near the tip of the island's Burin Peninsula, the town was at the centre of the Atlantic fishery for centuries—historians estimate that it was used as a base for French fishing vessels as far back as 1650. Its importance as a fishing centre led to prosperity, and the town is filled with unique Victorian buildings that stand out from other Newfoundland architectural traditions.

barrens. The best time to see them is spring, when adults are accompanied by new calves.

On the Bonavista Peninsula, a two-hour drive northwest of St. John's on Highway 1, is **Terra Nova National Park**, a 400-square-kilometre reserve of rugged coastline, muddy bogs—and some terrific golfing. Terra Nova is easily accessible—Highway 1 runs right through it—and there are two large campgrounds with more than 500 sites. The park is a popular spot for salmon fishing, although you'll need to buy a special permit to ply the waters of the Northwest River.

In the summer, park staff conduct guided walks and interpretive exhibits explaining the area's hard-bitten flora—stunted black spruce and balsam, mostly—and boat tours to take in some whale- and bird-watching are also available.

For duffers, the Twin Rivers Golf Course is one of the most scenic courses in the country, and the clubhouse has dining facilities. Call (709) 533-2801 for park information.

History buffs will want to pay a visit to **Cape Bonavista**, about 100 kilometres away on the eastern tip of the peninsula (take route 230—a beautiful drive). It is here that explorer John Cabot was reputed to have first landed in the New World in 1497. Cape Bonavista is mostly a barren stretch of rock, but a few tourist facilities have popped up thanks to its historical interest. The lighthouse on the cape is one of the oldest in Newfoundland (built in 1843) and, recently restored to its 1870 appearance, is now a museum.

By the Way

Whether or not John Cabot actually landed at Cape Bonavista is still a point of contention among historians. Some think that rather than Newfoundland, the Anglo-Italian explorer in fact landed first on Cape Breton Island, in modern-day Nova Scotia. In any event, for his discovery Cabot received a whopping £10 from King Henry VII after the adventurer returned to England in 1497. After receiving royal assent for a second expedition, Cabot sailed from England to Greenland, and then perhaps as far as Chesapeake Bay off what is now Massachusetts. But history may never know how far he got: although records are sketchy, Cabot (probably) perished at sea on his way back to Europe. If the Atlantic was unkind to Cabot, then so was history: it is now generally accepted that the Norsemen were the first Europeans to venture onto Canadian soil, beating Cabot by nearly 500 years.

The Great Northern Peninsula

Rising sharply north, the Great Northern Peninsula on a map looks like the province's western crest. Up close, however, it is a rugged country of steep fjords and sand dunes, carved out of the Canadian Shield by centuries of glacial activity. It was here that the Norsemen first settled at the dawn of the second millennium, and in subsequent centuries the area's west coast became the focus of Newfoundland's lobster industry. A good place to start a tour is at **Corner Brook**, the second-largest city in the province; for anglers, Corner Brook's nearby Humber River offers some of Newfoundland's best opportunities for salmon fishing. Travelling north along Highway 1 and then taking Route 430—known as the Viking Trail—at Deer Lake, visitors will come across once-isolated communities like Rocky Harbour, Trout River and Port au Choix.

At the southern end of the peninsula is **Gros Morne National Park**, among the most picturesque of all Canada's parks and a UN-designated World Heritage Site because of its geological uniqueness. If you're travelling the west coast of Newfoundland, it's a must-see, and plan to spend three days or more exploring its wonders.

The geography of Gros Morne varies wildly, from the seashore dotted with fishing villages to the coastal plain of fjords and forests, and finally to the alpine plateau of the Long Range Mountains. You can see some of the area's scenery by car, but the real treasures of Gros Morne are best experienced on foot. By the sea, there are trails that wind by sheltered coves, waterfalls and gigantic caves carved out of the shoreline, as well as a historic lighthouse at Lobster Cove Head.

On the coastal plain, those in the know recommend the Western Brook Pond hike, which starts near the north end of the park. After trekking through boreal forest, visitors can take a boat ride on the so-called pond—actually, a deep, land-locked fjord resplendent with waterfalls and sharp cliffs. Real adventurers, on the other hand, will get a thrill out of scaling Gros Morne Mountain, rising 2,600 feet in the park's interior and providing hikers a spectacular view of the coastline—after a three- or four-hour climb, that is. The park offers almost 300 campsites to visitors, and staff maintain cross-country ski trails in the winter. Gros Morne is also a popular salmon and trout fishing spot for anglers. For information, call (709) 458-2066.

Off the Beaten Path

One of the many oddities of Newfoundland is that it is so close to France—really. The islands of **St. Pierre and Miquelon** are the only remaining French lands in North America, and they lie just 20 kilometres south of Newfoundland's Burin Peninsula.

For much of their history, the islands passed back and forth between England and France, finally being ceded to the latter in 1814. Most of the islands' more than 6,000 inhabitants live on the smaller St. Pierre, and they have maintained a little pocket of French culture and language for almost two centuries—thanks in part, it should be added, to heavy funding from the government of France, which is intent on maintaining a fishing outpost in the Gulf of St. Lawrence.

Two ferry services run between St. Pierre and Fortune, in Newfoundland, and visitors to the island can take advantage of its tranquil setting and fine French cuisine. For information, call the St. Pierre tourist board, at 1-800-565-5118.

On the far northern tip of the peninsula, about 230 kilometres above Gros Morne, is another World Heritage Site—so designated by the United Nations not just because of its scenery, but also for its historic significance. **L'Anse aux Meadows** is a small inshore fishing community, but it is now internationally recognized as the place where Europeans first put down stakes on North American soil. Discovered in 1960 by Norwegian explorer/archeologists Helge and Anne Stine Ingstad, L'Anse aux Meadows harbours one of the most significant archeological sites in the world. There are three building complexes, made up of a long sod house and surrounding workhouses. Archeologists have discovered Norse artifacts—like pins and darning needles—suggesting that the Vikings, believed to have been led by Leif (the Lucky) Eriksson, lived on this spot for a significant period of time, probably between 990 and 1050 AD. Parks Canada has a very good visitor's centre at the site, and there are even a few inns and restaurants in the area to make a visit to this remote location more enjoyable. For L'Anse aux Meadows information, call (709) 623-2608.

The Least You Need to Know

➤ St. John's is the largest city in Newfoundland, and one of the oldest European settlements in North America.

➤ L'Anse aux Meadows, where Vikings settled, and Cape Bonavista, where explorer John Cabot may have landed, are two of the province's most popular historic sites.

➤ Major outdoor areas include Terra Nova and Gros Morne national parks.

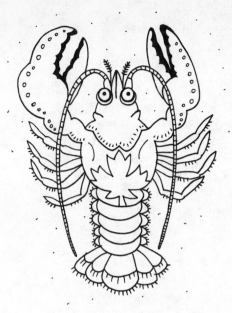

Chapter 7

Prince Edward Island

In This Chapter

➤ Exploring Charlottetown, cradle of Confederation

➤ Out and about in PEI

Welcome to Prince Edward Island

As soon as you arrive, you know that Prince Edward Island is something completely different. Perhaps it's the characteristic red soil—the product of iron oxides left behind by receding glaciers more than 10,000 years ago. Or perhaps it's the unique culture and history of the island, eked out of the land and out of the plentiful sea that surrounds it. For years, the only way to the island was by air or by ferry, and that isolation has allowed much of PEI's rural way of life to remain intact.

Islanders have long cherished their insularity from the rest of Canada, and with a few exceptions, the land and the people are much the same as they were decades ago. The recent construction of a fixed link from the mainland—Confederation Bridge—was perceived as a threat to the island way of life by many residents, who feared an onslaught of outsiders would transform PEI's seaside communities and

61

rolling farmland into theme parks and tourist traps. So far, that hasn't happened.

PEI is—by far—Canada's smallest province, both in terms of land mass and in terms of population: with only 130,000 or so residents, it is more than 20 times less populous than Metropolitan Toronto. It is also Canada's most rural province, with only about 40 per cent of its population living in urban areas. For visitors, however, the island boasts a wealth of down home attractions. For many, the main one is the industry that has grown up around Lucy Maud Montgomery's *Anne of Green Gables*, the beloved novel written and set in PEI. For other visitors, PEI is an island of tranquillity, whose gorgeous beaches, stunning sandstone cliffs and quaint fishing villages make it one of the country's most popular tourist destinations. You won't find bustling city life or many happening nightclubs on Prince Edward Island—but that, after all, is part of its charm.

Getting There

By air: Charlottetown, the capital of PEI and its largest city, is served by both major Canadian airlines and takes flights from all over North America, usually after connecting at Halifax, NS—about 25 minutes away by air. The Charlottetown airport is only 5 kilometres north of town. **By rail:** There is no passenger rail service to the island, but VIA Rail does run from other Canadian destinations to Moncton, NB. From the Moncton bus station, you can catch an SMT bus (1-800-561-5151), which takes passengers to any of Borden-Carleton, Summerside, Kensington or Charlottetown. **By car:** Until 1997, automobiles got to the island via ferry from the New Brunswick mainland. But since the

Canada by Web

The government of PEI maintains an informative and well-designed visitor's guide on the Web, detailing all the major places of interest, at:

http://www.gov.pe.ca/vg

A virtual tour of the island is available at:
http://www.peisland.com

opening of Confederation Bridge, auto-mobile travel to PEI is easy. The 13-kilo-metres-long bridge runs from Cape Tormentine in New Brunswick to Borden-Carleton, on the island side of the Northumberland Strait. **By sea:** Although the Confederation Bridge re-placed the major passenger ferry route from the mainland, two services are still available. One ferry runs from Caribou, NS, to Wood Islands, on PEI's southeast-ern tip, a journey of about 75 minutes. Call Northumberland Ferries, 1-800-565-0201. Another longer route runs from Quebec's Îles-de-la-Madeleine to Souris, on the northeastern tip of the island. The trip takes about five hours. Call CTMA at (902) 687-2181 for information.

Getting Around

The opening of Confederation Bridge made travelling by car perhaps the most convenient way of getting to the island. Similarly, the best way to explore PEI once you're there is by private car. An al-ternative to driving is cycling—increasingly popular in the warmer months of the year. The island is only 224 kilometres from end to end, and it has a good main road system (although the back roads, which you *will* want to explore, can get a little rugged). A healthy, experienced cyclist can see the better part of the island in three or four days.

But PEI is, first and foremost, a place to get away and relax, and to enjoy the beauty of the sea and the landscape. So even if you have never been there, plan to take your time—a week is the ideal minimum—and although an island tour will in all probability begin in Charlottetown, it should not be restricted to the province's major city. Comfortable accom-modations can be had at all of the larger (and many of the smaller) towns throughout the island. Better yet, cabins and cottages—many on the sea-side—are available for rent by the day, week or even month throughout the warm season. Staying longer does not mean that you have to pack

By the Way

Confederation Bridge is a mar-vel of modern engineering. Spanning the Northumber-land Strait between New Brunswick and the southern shore of the island, the bridge cost a whopping $1 billion, but was constructed in a mere 44 months, from October 1993 to June 1997. At 13 kilometres, it is one of the longest bridges in the world—and the longest to traverse waters that freeze up in winter, as the Northumberland Strait cer-tainly does, with pack ice sometimes forming "cliffs" that are 10 metres high.

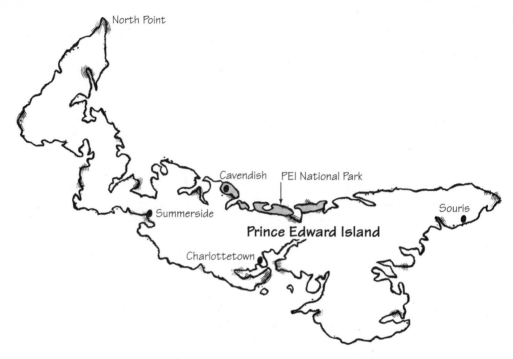

North Point

Cavendish   PEI National Park

Summerside

Prince Edward Island

Souris

Charlottetown

P.E.I.: Major towns and outdoor areas

hoards of food and clothing, since we're not talking remote wilderness here. No matter where you are in PEI, you're never very far from a town or village—yes, the place is that small.

Charlottetown

Charlottetown, the province's capital, is the island's *only* incorporated city, established in 1855, but although (thanks to amalgamation with surrounding communities in 1995) its official population tops 30,000, the central city is home to only about 15,000. In other words, you won't find skyscrapers or many traffic jams here. For a provincial capital, Charlottetown is a pretty small place, and most of what visitors will want to see can be easily covered in a day or less.

The city sits on a natural harbour near the centre of the province, and settlement dates back to French colonial days. After the British took over in the mid-18th century, Charlottetown became the capital of the

Local Knowledge

You may come across ads or books that claim PEI is a great place to go all year-round, with its relatively mild winters and moderate to hot summers. In my experience, that's only half right. The last time I visited the island, the beaches and waters on the north shore were clogged with ice, few if any of the historic sites were open, and—worst of all!—lobster season hadn't started yet. This was the final week of April. Only once I was there did I find out that lobster season doesn't begin till the first week of May—a fact that was even harder to swallow than having to wear a parka around all the time. Here's the point: there *are* things to do in the cooler months, but first-timers should play it safe and not plan on visiting the island before late spring or early summer.

new colony of Prince Edward Island. From then on, it served as an administrative and commercial centre for the island's agricultural economy. But Charlottetown is best known for its role in the creation of Canada, serving as the site for the first discussions of union—a role that earned both Charlottetown and PEI as a whole the nickname "Cradle of Confederation."

So when visiting Charlottetown, it's a good idea to begin where Canada began: in **Province House**, on downtown Richmond Street. In this stately sandstone building, representatives from the three Maritime colonies (Nova Scotia, New Brunswick and PEI) met with political leaders from the province of Canada from September 1 to September 9, 1864—the first conference in a process that would culminate, three years later, in Confederation.

Today, Province House is the only site of a Confederation meeting that is still standing. Although it remains home to the provincial legislature, many of the building's rooms have been lovingly restored to mid-19th-century appearance, and for anyone interested in Canadian history a visit to the Confederation Chamber is a must. Open year-round, admission to the building is free (although donations are gratefully accepted). For information, call Province House at (902) 566-7626, or the PEI Capital Commission, at (902) 629-1864.

By the Way

Although PEI is known as the cradle of Confederation, it actually got a late start as part of Canada. When other British North American colonies got together in 1867, the island held out—few of the famously insular PEI'ers were interested in joining. Six years later, however, the island, suffering under massive debt thanks to an expensive railway-building project, reconsidered its stand on Confederation, and became the seventh Canadian province.

Just west of Province House is the **Confederation Centre of the Arts**, the focal point for much of Charlottetown's cultural activity. Built in 1964 in honour of the 200th anniversary of the Charlottetown Conference, the sprawling complex houses a 1,100-seat theatre, a public library, a restaurant and an art gallery/museum. The latter is the largest of its kind in Atlantic Canada, with more than 15,000 contemporary and historical works of art, including a fine collection of works by Robert Harris (1849–1919), one of the country's foremost portrait artists. The theatre, meanwhile, mounts productions throughout the year, but is best known for the musical adaptation of *Anne of Green Gables* that it has staged for more than 30 years—one of the country's longest-running and most popular plays. In July and August, Confederation Centre also serves as the hub of activities for the **Charlottetown Festival**, an annual celebration of the island's heritage through plays, concerts, tours and other special events. For information and ticket reservations, call 1-800-565-0278.

History buffs will also want to check out **Beaconsfield House**, a splendid Victorian mansion northwest of Province House on Kent Street featuring a huge double drawing room, a nursery, a galley and a belvedere—an observation room from which you can see much of the city. Tours are available year-round, and the house is also the site of regular lectures, musical performances and plays. Call (902) 368-6603.

Farther afield (and less visited) is **Ardgowan National Historic Site**, on the corner of Mount Edward Road and Palmers Lane. The summer home of William Henry Pope—politician, lawyer and one of PEI's strongest supporters of Confederation—Ardgowan has been substantially restored, and its Victorian garden (maintained by Parks Canada, which has an office on the site) is a Charlottetown landmark. Call (902) 566-7050 for information.

Most of the shops, restaurants or nightspots in Charlottetown can

Local Knowledge

William Henry Pope, who lived at Ardgowan, was not the most universally liked man in Charlottetown—his very profitable real estate deals before becoming a member of the PEI legislature earned him the enmity of many locals. Still, the Pope name is intrinsically linked with the development of Canada. Not only was W.H. Pope a Father of Confederation who argued tirelessly for union with the rest of British North America, but his son, Joseph, went on to become an influential federal civil servant under Canada's first prime minister, Sir John A. Macdonald. In 1921, the younger Pope came up with the motto for Canada's new coat of arms, derived from a biblical psalm: *A Mari Usque Ad Mare*—from sea to sea.

be found on or along Queen Street, which runs roughly north from the harbour. But be sure to check as well **Great George Street**, running north-south between Richmond and Water streets. Designated a national historic site, Great George Street was the path the Fathers of Confederation took on their way to the Charlottetown Conference, and it is lined with architecturally and historically significant buildings. (Look especially at St. Dunstan's Basilica, south of Sydney Street, one of the largest churches in the country.) At the base of Great George is **Confederation Landing Park**, marking the area where the founding fathers landed in 1864. Nowadays, it's a great place to get a view of Charlottetown Harbour—and nearby is the Peake's Wharf complex, home to restaurants and small artisan shops.

Out and About in PEI

You can divide your tour into three parts, central, eastern and western PEI. The benefit of having your own transportation is that three scenic highways—all well marked and fairly easy to follow—pass through the most interesting spots on the island, and each can be easily travelled in a day or less by car. Blue Heron Drive winds through central PEI for a little under 200 kilometres, while the Kings Byway and Lady Slipper Drive traverse the east and the west respectively.

Central PEI: The Land of Green Gables

The best way to see this part of the island is along the so-called Blue Heron Drive, which heads north out of Charlottetown on Route 15, then turns west on the North Shore and circles back around to the South Shore in a roughly circular route of 190 kilometres.

Much of the drive along the North Shore—just 20 minutes or so out of Charlottetown—is taken up by **Prince Edward Island National Park**, a wildlife and camping area spanning 40 kilometres of spectacular coastline from the towns of Dalvay in the east to Cavendish in the west. The main attractions here are the high, rolling dunes, which create a unique ecosystem of birds, plants and marine life. The dunes are punctuated, in some areas, by dramatic red sandstone cliffs looming out of the water and providing wonderful views of the ocean and beaches below. In the southern parts of the park, forested areas criss-crossed by trails are perfect (and not too arduous) places for hiking and cycling—the latter made easier by special bicycle lanes on the Gulf Shore Parkway, which runs through the park.

As one of the more popular tourist and weekend getaway areas on the island, the park also offers interpretive beach walks and guided bird-watching tours. There are more than 500 campsites spread out across four campgrounds, which are booked on a first-come, first-serve basis and can get very busy in the summer—the park is a haven for beach-combers and swimmers, who take advantage of some of the warmest

Local Knowledge

While driving around PEI, keep an eye out for signs (usually on telephone poles or in front of churches and community centres) advertising a unique island experience: the lobster supper. Put on by church groups and community associations, the suppers start in May and run throughout the summer. The menu is always the same: salads, steamed mussels, fresh rolls, home-made pies and fresh PEI lobster. It's delicious and cheap—typically under $15. And it's a great way to meet the locals.

ocean waters north of Bermuda. If you can't get in, the area has plenty of private campsites, and there are many hotels and motels in the towns in and around the park. For information, call (902) 672-6350.

On the west end of the park is the second most popular tourist destination on the island: **Cavendish**, whose environs were both the setting for the *Anne of Green Gables* novels and the place where their author, Lucy Maud Montgomery, lived for much of her life. There are only about 150 permanent residents in this small seaside community, but the enduring popularity of the books draws more than 200,000 visitors every year, including a healthy contingent of tourists from Japan, where Anne has become all the rage.

The major attraction is **Green Gables**, a green and white farmhouse that actually belonged to Montgomery's cousins. Still, it served as the main setting for the Anne books, and fans will get a kick out of walking through the Haunted Wood, or along Lover's Lane and the Balsam Hollow Trail—all on the grounds. Regularly scheduled tours of the house and grounds are available for a small admission fee (about $3), but Green Gables is open only from May to November. Call the PEI National Park for information.

Also in Cavendish is another Anne-related attraction, the **Site of Lucy Maud Montgomery's Cavendish Home**, where the author lived with her paternal grandparents, the Macneils, and where she wrote *Anne of Green Gables*. Maintained by Montgomery's descendants, the home itself has been reduced to the foundation and the white picket fence, but there are a museum and a bookstore for those interested in all things Anne. The site is open from June to November. Call (902) 963-2231.

Cavendish is home to an amusement park and sideshow area, with a Ripley's Believe It or Not Museum and even a re-creation (sort of) of an Egyptian pharaoh's tomb. It's one of the few overtly touristy areas on the whole island, and although kids will probably like it, others may find it detracts from Cavendish's innate charm and history. In August, the town plays host to a three-day Lucy Maud Montgomery Festival featuring period games, barn dances and even a fish-eating contest. If you are not at all interested in Anne of Green Gables, a visit to Cavendish is still worthwhile: the beach on the north end of the area offers some of the best swimming in PEI, and it's a good place to arrange a sea-kayaking tour or charter a fishing boat.

Off the Beaten Path

On the southern stretch of Blue Heron Drive, the South Shore is a land of rolling hills and red sandstone cliffs. Although there are plenty of small communities here that seem frozen in time, be sure to check out **Victoria-by-the-Sea**. It has a gorgeous natural harbour, and there are plenty of shopping opportunities in the craft and antique stores that line its quiet streets. Only a few minutes out of Charlottetown, Victoria-by-the-Sea is also home to the **Victoria Playhouse**, which in the summer runs highly regarded theatrical productions. For ticket information, call (902) 658-2025.

Eastern PEI

To explore the beautiful coastline and charming villages in the eastern part of the island, take the Kings Byway, which runs out of Charlottetown east on Route 1 and winds along the shore for nearly 400 kilometres.

The southeast corner of the island has long been overlooked by tourists, but that is quickly changing, as visitors are discovering the joys of exploring PEI's agricultural heritage. Nowhere is that more in evidence than **Orwell Corner Historic Village**, a faithfully re-created 19th-century farming community with an old school, farmhouse, church, general store and blacksmith shop. In the summer and autumn, the sound of fiddles is in the air as the village hosts ceilidhs—Celtic musical concerts—every Wednesday night, and on Sundays the locals mount a musical production of Lucy Maud Montgomery's *The Blue Castle*. Call (902) 651-2013.

Passing through such pleasant seaside communities as Eldon, Belfast, Little Sands and Murray River, the Kings Byway arrives at **Montague**—also called Montague the Beautiful—perched on the southern extension of St. Mary's Bay on the island's east coast. It is home to a marine museum and a pretty marina, and has inns, motels and plenty of shopping opportunities for those looking to purchase the unique crafts that flourish in southeastern PEI. From the marina, you can also book tours that will take you past a substantial harbour seal colony in the

Local Knowledge

A ceilidh (pronounced kay-lee) is about as Celtic as you can get—a sometimes raucous, but always fun, celebration of fiddling and step-dancing that harkens back to the island's Irish and Scottish roots. As in the rest of Atlantic Canada, Celtic music is experiencing a revival in PEI, and ceilidhs are mounted during summer evenings in communities all across the island. Besides Orwell, check out Rustico, Woodleigh and Rainbow Valley if you're in the mood for a foot-stomping good time.

area. Nearby is the county seat, **Georgetown**, home to the charming McDonald Memorial Gardens and, like many island communities, a local theatre company, the King's Playhouse, which mounts children's and classic stage productions during the summer months.

The largest community in the northeast is **Souris**, a town of about 1,300 people that was first settled by the French. Still an active port—it is the terminus of the ferry from Îles-de-la-Madeleine—it sustains the island's only offshore fishery, but tourists will also enjoy its thriving lobster industry and its wonderful (and not too busy) beach on Northumberland Strait. Just south of Souris, Rollo Bay plays host to an annual Fiddle Festival, attracting Celtic musicians and step-dancers from all over Atlantic Canada in July.

Off the Beaten Path

Knocking around the seaside communities of PEI, you may well come across a rather strange sight: draft horses walking in the surf, dragging behind them what looks to be a huge rake and pulling up salty, smelly masses of gelatinous gunk. What they are doing is harvesting Irish moss, the country's most valuable commercial seaweed, which in its refined form is used in beers, wines and coffees, as well as for a gelling agent in a host of convenience foods—despite the smell.

By the Way

Skinner's Pond, in the northwest of the island, is known by legions of Canadians as the home of the province's most famous export: Stompin' Tom Connors. Although he was born in Newfoundland and now lives in Ontario, the legendary folk singer spent his youth in PEI—a land he paid tribute to in one of his most popular songs, *Bud the Spud*, a toe-tapping anthem to the island's potato industry.

Western PEI

Lady Slipper Drive—named after the province's official flower, a delicate orchid—begins at Summerside, the island's second-largest community, and winds northwest to the tip of PEI and then around to the south-western shore.

Summerside, 70 kilometres west of Charlottetown, was long the centre of the island's prosperous ship-building and fox-farming industries. Both, unfortunately, have fallen into steep decline, but Summerside is still redolent with the area's history. The waterfront (where there are also a couple good hotels) is where most of the activity happens. The boardwalk, known as Spinnaker's Landing, is lined with inexpensive restaurants and shops, and during the summer it is a popular spot for a stroll. Here, too, is the **Eptek National Exhibition Centre**, which explores the history of PEI and features fine art exhibitions from across Canada. Call (902) 888-8375.

During the summer, the city plays host to two of the island's most popular festivals. If you're a music fan, don't miss the Highland Gathering in June—a bagpiping, dancing and fiddling extravaganza featuring many performers from the College of Piping and Celtic Performing Arts of Canada, based in Summerside. And in the third week of July is the Summerside Lobster Carnival, with livestock exhibitions, even more fiddling and plenty of servings of the tasty crustacean that gives the festival its name.

The island is still home to a small but sturdy French population largely scattered throughout the west. In Miscouche, stop by the **Acadian Museum**, which introduces visitors to the history of the French presence in PEI and houses an extensive genealogical listing of Acadian names. Call (902) 436-6237 for information. In nearby Mont-Carmel, Le Village is an authentic Acadian village (and a craft shop), which also offers regional cuisine and a popular French-language supper theatre, La Cuisine à Mémé.

Off the Beaten Path

PEI is the potato capital of Canada, the largest producer of eating potatoes in the country and a shipper of seed potatoes to more than 20 countries. There are over 100,000 acres of potato farmland in the province, and half of it is on its western arm. If you've got the time and the inclination, head east off Lady Slipper Drive's western length and go to the town of O'Leary, where you can visit the **Prince Edward Island Potato Museum**—the only museum in Canada dedicated to the noble spud. Call (902) 859-2039 for information.

Lady Slipper Drive meanders northwest through charming fishing villages and some stunning ocean views—with the added benefit of being one of the least-visited areas on the island. At the northwestern tip is **North Cape**, dotted with huge wind turbines that are part of the Atlantic Wind Test Site, a significant research facility trying to develop economically feasible wind-generated power. The cape is also home to a large seal colony just offshore, and there is an **Interpretive Centre and Aquarium** with exhibits on the area's history and on marine life. Call (902) 882-2991. Nearby, on the western side of the island, make sure you take a look at **Elephant Rock**, a weird rock formation carved by wind and water resembling a huge pachyderm lumbering off shore. (It is reachable by foot during low tide.)

Confederation Trail: Another Way to See PEI

While the three major tourist roadways—Kings Byway, Blue Heron Drive and Lady Slipper Drive—are a good way to see the province by automobile, Confederation Trail promises to provide hikers and cyclists with a convenient, alternative route for exploring PEI's wonders. Still not completed, the trail will eventually run all the way from Elmira, on the eastern tip, to Tignish, on the northwest arm of the island, a total of 350 kilometres. The plan is for the trail to run along the old PEI railway line which traverses the heart of PEI through inland places and sites that are often overlooked by shoreline-fascinated travellers.

The longest section runs between Kensington, just north of Summerside, and Tignish, near North Cape. On the way, it passes through Summerside, the town of Wellington, and the heart of PEI's Acadian community. The next longest section runs in the northeast, from Elmira to Mount Stewart, a distance of 75 kilometres, and winds around Souris and St. Peters Bay.

By the mid-1990s, about two-thirds (or 225 kilometres) of the Confederation Trail was open to hikers and cyclists in the summer, and snowmobilers in the winter. The finished parts of the trail are an outdoor enthusiast's dream: 10 feet wide, paved in stone dust, and slicing through some of the island's most interesting rural and urban areas. The existing trails are well marked, with rest areas and shelters along the way. For information, call the PEI government tourism service at 1-800-463-4PEI.

The Least You Need to Know

➤ Prince Edward Island is Canada's smallest province.

➤ The major attractions in Charlottetown, PEI's largest city, are Province House and the Confederation Centre of the Arts, along with Great George Street and the waterfront.

➤ Outside Charlottetown, the must-see attractions are Cavendish (home to *Anne of Green Gables* author Lucy Maud Montgomery), PEI National Park and North Cape.

Nova Scotia

Chapter 8

In This Chapter

➤ Exploring Halifax, Nova Scotia's capital

➤ Out and about in Nova Scotia

Welcome to Nova Scotia

Nova Scotia is not, by any stretch of the imagination, a big province. Jutting out into the North Atlantic, most of it is a long, narrow spit of land which at its widest is only about 130 kilometres across. And yet, within that relatively small area, historical and cultural variety flourishes.

Halifax, Nova Scotia's capital and the largest city in Atlantic Canada, offers all the excitement and night life of any comparable urban area, while the south shore, with its deep maritime roots, harkens back to a time when fishermen made their living from surf and sail. The north shore, meanwhile, is rich in French-Canadian heritage, the centre of Acadian culture for a hundred years. And Cape Breton Island is a land apart, both Acadian and Celtic, with some of the most breathtaking natural scenery in the world.

Canada by Web

The Nova Scotia government maintains a good general tourism site, as well as a virtual tour of Halifax and the province's other major tourist areas:
http://explore.gov.ns.ca

For a detailed guide to Halifax's attractions, check out:
http://ttg.sba.dal.ca/nstour/halifax/hfxwalk.htm

Halifax

Sitting on one of the largest natural harbours in the world, Halifax, the capital of Nova Scotia, is the largest and most cosmopolitan city on the east coast. On one hand, it is steeped in British military tradition, still evident in its importance as a naval base and in its best-known land-mark, the Citadel. On the other hand, it is a modern and bustling city, the seat of financial and administrative power in Nova Scotia and home to four universities—a mix of money and youth that gives the city its characteristic energy by day and by night. A town where past and present get along well, Halifax seems to have accomplished that rarest of urban feats: it's a nice place to live—and to visit.

Halifax Past and Present

Although its huge harbour, on Nova Scotia's south shore, had been used intermittently by Micmac natives and later by French soldiers, Halifax's modern history began with the British military. In the middle of the 18th century, the British had two military concerns that made establish-ing a presence in southern Nova Scotia seem like a good idea: the large French Catholic community in nearby Acadia, and the French fort of Louisbourg on Cape Breton Island.

In 1749, 2,500 settlers arrived in Halifax (then called Chebucto) from England, and went about establishing under the leadership of Colonel Edward Cornwallis the first government-sponsored and -planned community in North America, heavily fortified by a stockade. (You can see evidence of the military planning that went into Halifax's creation in the grid road pattern that survives today in the older parts of the city.) Getting people to stay in Halifax was something of an uphill battle. Out of the 2,500 settlers shipped over from Britain in 1749, about 1,000 left for America and better economic prospects. At one point, the government imported hundreds of Protestants from Germany to keep the population up. Were it not for the arrival of a merchant class in the 1750s from New England—where goes government spending, business follows—Halifax may never have gotten off the ground at all.

After the passing of the French threat just a decade later, Halifax remained an important military base for the British. During yet another war with France from 1793 to 1815, the city established itself as a port, and extended its influence west across the Atlantic and south to the Caribbean. In the years that followed—the great Age of Sail—Halifax boomed as a centre for international shipping and trade, not to mention privateering, and many of its merchants acquired vast wealth.

With the advent of steamships and the railroads, the Age of Sail

By the Way

Privateering—the practice whereby governments hire private companies to attack the enemy—was big business in Halifax's early days. Among the most famous privateers was Enos Collins, an accomplished sailor who owned and operated the *Liverpool Packet*, a ship that was estimated to have captured $1 million worth of treasures during the War of 1812. A shrewd businessman and war profiteer, Collins parlayed his winnings into a vast fortune, and by the 1830s he was widely known as the richest man in the Maritimes, so wealthy, in fact, that in 1825 he set up his own private financial institution, the Halifax Banking Co. As a historical side note, one of his partners in the venture was Samuel Cunard, founder of the Cunard sailing and steamship company, whose most famous (later) vessels were the *Mauritania*, the *Lusitania* and the *Queen Elizabeth 2*. Collins's warehouse and the site of his bank still stand, in the Historic Properties area of the Halifax waterfront.

ended and Halifax's economic importance to the British colonies waned in the middle of the 19th century. Still, it had established itself as a naval base, and served as the administrative and political centre of what later became Atlantic Canada. The two world wars of the 20th century enhanced Halifax's status and its economy, and its importance to the international shipping trade remains to this day.

Today, as the province's capital, Halifax remains the hub of economic and political activity in Nova Scotia. Many of its historic sites and buildings still exist, although they now compete for attention downtown with soaring (and visually uninteresting) office towers that bear witness to the city's prominence as a financial centre. It is also the

Local Knowledge

Halifax's greatest setback this century was the explosion of 1917, when two military vessels collided in the harbour and touched off a blast that destroyed the north end of the city. The blast severely damaged the city and its institutions, and it took years—as well as millions of dollars in charitable donations from around the world—for Halifax to rebuild and recover.

The Halifax Explosion began in the early morning of December 6, 1917, when the Belgian vessel *Imo* rammed into the *Mont Blanc*, a French ship carrying munitions, in the narrows of the city's harbour. The collision created sparks that eventually reached more than 2,500 tons of explosives the *Mont Blanc* was carrying in its hold. At 9:06 a.m., the harbour literally blew up. The blast reached a mile into the air, and could be heard as far away as Prince Edward Island. Between 1,500 and 2,000 people—many of them standing on the shores of the harbour to watch the aftermath of the ships' collision—were killed instantly, and another 9,000 were injured. The explosion levelled 300 acres on the north end of Halifax, obliterating 1,600 buildings, and then it touched off a fire that raged throughout the city for days. The event, which inspired author Hugh MacLennan's 1941 book *Barometer Rising*, held the dubious distinction of being the worst man-made explosion in history—until the dropping of a nuclear bomb on Hiroshima in 1945.

east coast's largest educational centre, home to St. Mary's, Dalhousie and Mount Saint Vincent universities, as well as the Technical University of Nova Scotia and the world renowned Bedford Institute of Oceanography.

Although Halifax proper has a population of a little over 100,000, its 1996 amalgamation with the surrounding municipalities of Dartmouth and Bedford created a metropolitan region with more than 300,000 residents—easily making it the largest city in Atlantic Canada. Despite its size, Halifax has managed to retain much of its small-town appeal, thanks largely to the preservation and, in some cases, restoration of many of the historic sites in the downtown area. Halifax is urban without being hectic or bewildering—an inviting place for party creatures, sightseers and history buffs alike.

Getting There

By air: Halifax International Airport is 40 kilometres northeast of the downtown, and serves both major Canadian airlines, which run regular flights from Toronto, Montreal, St. John's and several cities in the United States. For airport information, call (902) 873-1223. Taxi trips from the airport are quite expensive ($40 or more), so consider catching one of the several shuttle buses that go to downtown hotels like the Delta Barrington for about half the price. **By rail:** VIA Rail runs six trains a week from Montreal to Terminal Station in Halifax, about 15 minutes by foot from downtown. **By car:** There are three major road routes into the Halifax/Dartmouth area. Highway 102 is the primary route from the Trans-Canada Highway (in Nova Scotia, Highway 104), exiting south at Bible Hill just west of Amherst. From the northwest, Highway 101 leads into Halifax from Wolfville and the north side of Nova Scotia's western peninsula, while Highway 103 runs along the peninsula's south coast, from Yarmouth through Lunenburg, and then into Halifax.

Getting Around

The best way to see the rest of Nova Scotia is by car, but driving around Halifax can be a confusing experience for first-time visitors, thanks to its odd layout in the outlying areas and a couple turnarounds that are downright perplexing. Once you're in downtown Halifax, however, you can easily see the major attractions simply by walking around. It's made easier if you stay downtown, although the several hotels near the harbour tend to be upscale and (for the area) relatively expensive. If you are relegated to the cheaper accommodation of the suburbs and don't have your own automobile, the municipal bus service is inexpensive (less than $2) and easy to use. Late at night, however, you will probably end up taking a taxi back to your hotel, since buses are hard to find in the evenings.

A Guide to Halifax and Area

Visitors can easily take in most of Halifax's major attractions, which are centred in the downtown and harbourfront areas, in a single day, then expanding their tour to see the rest of Nova Scotia by car. If you go, however, consider staying in Halifax longer. Elsewhere in the Maritimes, you will likely spend much of your time travelling through small, remote communities that certainly have charm aplenty. By contrast,

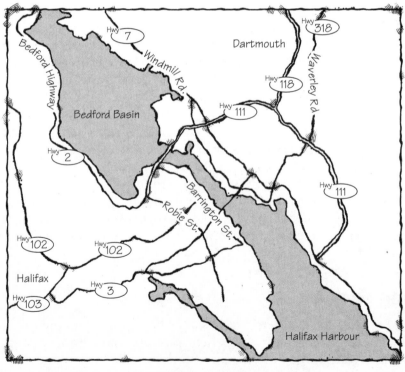

Halifax area

Halifax, with its happening bars, good restaurants and active nightlife, offers a cosmopolitan change from all that peace and tranquillity, along with the comforts that only a big city can provide—a good place to recharge your urban jets for a couple of days.

Downtown

This is where it all happens in Halifax, the centre of social and economic activity in the city just as it has been for centuries. Here, in an area roughly bound by Cogswell Street in the north, Spring Garden Road in the south, and Barrington and Summer streets in the east and west, you will find restaurants, cafés and shops catering to all tastes, from the chic to the bohemian, as well as the major sites of historical interest that Halifax has to offer.

A tour of the downtown should begin at the **Halifax Citadel National Historic Site**, a star-shaped fortress looming above the city at the top of George Street. (The path up to it from downtown runs near the Georgian Clock Tower, one of the city's best-known landmarks.) Walking around the grounds of the Citadel, you can get an idea of why Halifax was never attacked by the French or Americans: its fortifications are truly imposing. Inside the Citadel's Cavalier Building, there is a small army museum tracing the history of the fort and of Canada's military past, and in front of the building soldiers run through their drills every day. Guided tours of the site are available year-round, but many visitors come to the Citadel simply for the view it affords of Halifax and its harbour. Ticket prices and hours of operation vary. Call (902) 426-5080 for information.

Down George Street is the **Grand Parade**, the original square around which the rest of the planned settlement was built in the 1750s. Officers posted at the Citadel used to frequent the parade in their off-duty hours, making it the hub of high society throughout the 18th and 19th centuries. Nearby is **Province House**, an imposing example of Georgian architecture. Built in 1819, the sandstone edifice is the oldest legislative building in Canada, and it is still home to the Nova Scotia legislature. Free tours of Province House are available; call (902) 424-4661. On the corner of Prince and Argyle streets is the oldest building in Halifax, **St. Paul's Church**, built in 1750 to serve the spiritual needs of the Protestant settlers imported by the British government; it is the oldest Anglican church in Canada. Call (902) 429-2240.

Local Knowledge

St. Paul's Church has plenty to distinguish it. It was the first British cathedral built overseas, and its simple architecture gives a sense both of the aspirations of the early settlers and the austerity that they must have endured. If you visit the church, be sure to take a glance at an oddity of local history: a piece of metal embedded in the interior wall on the north side of the building—put there by the Halifax Explosion of 1917.

Near Province House on Hollis Street, be sure to visit the **Art Gallery of Nova Scotia**, housed in an old Victorian building that used to be Halifax's courthouse. Today, it is home to an extensive collection of over 4,000 works. The gallery is best known for its holdings of maritime and folk art, although it also has an impressive, although small, exhibit of paintings by Group of Seven artists. Admission is $2.50; call (902) 424-7542. Culture vultures will also want to pay a visit to the **Neptune Theatre** on Argyle Street, the oldest repertory playhouse in Canada, which stages both contemporary and classical dramas year-round. Call (902) 429-7300 for tickets and information.

You will find plenty of restaurants, pubs and shops scattered throughout downtown Halifax—and some of the better ones tucked away on small side streets and laneways. But if you're looking for something to eat or items to buy, the surest bets are on and around Barrington Street, the main north-south thoroughfare, and on Spring Garden Road, in the south end of the downtown area.

South on Barrington is an area frequented by Halifax's large student population, and its shops and cafés tend to cater to bohemian tastes. The businesses get more upscale (and more expensive) on Spring Garden past the public library, a favoured hang-out for students to lunch, lounge and chat in. There are also plenty of night spots on and around Spring Garden, and some pretty good jazz and dance clubs which typically stay open past 2 a.m.—on weekends, they can get pretty raucous.

Off the Beaten Path

If you're looking for a place to get away from it all in Halifax, take a stroll through the **Halifax Public Gardens**, north of Spring Garden Road east of Summer Street. Opened in 1875, the 17-acre park is among the oldest Victorian gardens in North America. Surrounded by a wrought iron fence, the gardens' beautifully maintained flower beds are punctuated by duck ponds, fountains and winding pathways. If you're there on a Sunday, be sure to stop by the glorious 19th-century gazebo for a concert. To the north is the **Nova Scotia Museum of Natural History**, with exhibits exploring the flora and fauna of the province. Call (902) 424-7353.

The Harbour

Long the economic lifeblood of Halifax, the harbour area today has largely been transformed from a rough-and-tumble port of call to a tourist-oriented waterfront of shops, restaurants and other attractions. A good example is the former warehouse district now called the **Historic Properties**, on the north end of Lower Water Street near the foot of Duke Street. The wharves and old maritime warehouses—like that of 19th-century privateer and merchant Enos Collins—have been extensively refurbished into upscale clothing stores, boutiques, pubs and offices. The aptly named Privateer's Warehouse, located in the properties, is a huge entertainment complex of restaurants and bars, popular both with locals and with tourists.

If you're lucky, the schooner *Bluenose II*—a replica of the famous *Bluenose*—will be docked nearby. Although its permanent home is in Lunenburg, east of Halifax, *Bluenose II* is available for tours and cruises when it is in town. A sail around the harbour costs $20 for adults. Call 1-800-763-1963 for schedule information.

South of the Historic Properties along the harbour's pleasant boardwalk is the **Maritime Museum of the Atlantic**, a restored warehouse that offers exhibits of maritime artifacts, as well as a fascinating historical look at the Halifax Explosion and a few relics from the *Titanic*.

(Much of the wreckage—and the bodies—from the famous 1912 disaster washed ashore at Halifax.) A World War II corvette, *HMCS Sackville*, is docked outside the museum during the summer months, and serves as a naval memorial, and behind the museum the *CSS Acadia*, Canada's first hydrographic vessel, is on display. Call (902) 424-7491 for information.

Dartmouth

Dartmouth is usually overlooked by visitors to Halifax, but if you're in the area for a few days and are in the mood for an excursion, Nova Scotia's second city (population 68,000), with its many lakes, parks and a picturesque boardwalk, may be worth a day-long trip. Although you can easily get there from Halifax by car, along either the Angus L. Macdonald or A. Murray Mackay bridges, the most evocative way is from the Dartmouth Ferry Terminal in the Historic Properties area of the Halifax waterfront. During rush hours, the ferry ride is jammed with commuters, but it provides a great view of both Halifax and Dartmouth and a one-way trip is cheap—only about $1.10. Call (902) 421-6600 for schedule and ticket information.

Dartmouth is largely a suburban residential area, but its roots go all the way back to 1750, and it was long a centre for a Quaker-run whaling industry. If you're interested, check out the **Historic Quaker Whalers' House** on Ochterloney Street, the oldest home in Dartmouth, which offers a taste of the city's ocean-going history. Of similarly specialized interest is the **Black Cultural Centre for Nova Scotia**, on Cherrybrook Road. Dedicated to the preservation of black culture in the province—which in the 18th and 19th centuries had the largest ethnic African population in Canada—the centre has a library, auditorium and exhibits on African-Canadian history. Call (902) 434-6223.

Off the Beaten Path

If you're in the mood for a pastoral retreat, **McNab's Island**, at the mouth of Halifax harbour, will fit the bill. To get there, for $8 you can take the 20-minute ferry ride from Cable Wharf on the Halifax waterfront. Five kilometres long, the island formed part of the area's substantial military fortifications, but today more than half of McNab's is made up of parkland with hiking trails and secluded picnic spots—a good place to get away from it all.

Halifax Festivals and Events

Halifax's best-known festivals celebrate something that all Easterners love: music, in all its forms. From May to early June, the city plays host to the **Scotia Festival of Music**, which features classical performers from around the world who give concerts at venues throughout Halifax. Call (902) 429-9469. In July is the **du Maurier Atlantic Jazz Festival**, (902) 492-2225, and the **Nova Scotia International Tattoo**, which coincides with the city's Canada Day celebrations and honours the Celtic roots of the area.

Halifax is home to an increasingly important film and television production industry, and in September the focus is on the **Atlantic Film Festival**, an exhibition of movies and television productions that is steadily gaining a reputation on the Canadian film-fest circuit (call (902) 422-3456). Also in September, the **Atlantic Fringe Festival** caters to lovers of the trendy performing arts, with dozens of alternative dramatic productions staged throughout the city.

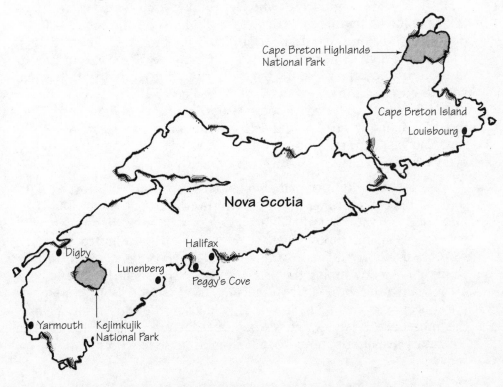

Nova Scotia: Major towns and outdoor attractions

Out and About in Nova Scotia

Although it is the second smallest province in Canada after Prince Edward Island, Nova Scotia offers plenty to see and do beyond the borders of Halifax. The best way to explore the seaside villages, wilderness areas and historic towns is by car, following any of the dozen or so scenic highways that meander through the province's most popular sites. For first-time visitors, however, three areas are required travelling: the Lighthouse Route stretching along the south shore from Halifax to Yarmouth; the Evangeline Trail from Yarmouth along the north shore; and finally, Cape Breton Island in the eastern end of the province, circled by the stunningly beautiful Cabot Trail. Although not separated by great distances, the three areas are remarkably different, each rooted in Nova Scotia's nautical, Acadian or Celtic histories.

The Lighthouse Route

From the Greater Halifax area, the Lighthouse Route—marked with distinctive blue-and-white signs depicting a lighthouse and waves—starts on Route 3 just on the outskirts of the metropolitan area. From there, it wanders through some of the most picturesque seaside communities in the country. You can drive the length of the route easily in a day, and if you need to make time, get off Route 3 and on to Highway 103, the most direct path to the Lighthouse Route's terminus at Yarmouth. On the other hand, the best way to explore the south shore is to take it slow and easy. Surprises and beautiful views seemingly await around every corner.

Everybody will find their own favourite spot along the route, but some of the communities on the south shore are not to be missed. The first obligatory stop out of Halifax is **Peggy's Cove**, a charming harbour that is synonymous (thanks to its popularity as a postcard photo) with Nova Scotia. The main landmark here is the lighthouse, towering above a rock outcropping that is a great place to watch huge waves crash against the shore. Less spectacular, but every bit as interesting, are the collection of fishing boats and fish sheds in the community below the lighthouse. Peggy's Cove is a popular tourist spot—and nearby is an obligatory restaurant and tacky gift shop, festooned with lighthouse souvenirs.

About 90 kilometres west of Peggy's Cove, turn off Route 3 and visit **Lunenburg**, one of the south shore's most beautiful towns.

Local Knowledge

While at Peggy's Cove, you will see signs warning visitors not to stray too close to the water's edge and to be careful while exploring the rocks by the lighthouse. The warnings are to be taken seriously. The rocks in the cove have been worn smooth by water and wind, and even on sunny days they can be very slippery. The action of the spectacular waves, meanwhile, is highly unpredictable, and they can wash over dry areas of the rocks without warning. Stories of careless visitors being swept out to sea are by no means uncommon in Peggy's Cove.

Settled largely by German immigrants in 1753 with the encouragement of the British government, the Old Town of Lunenburg has been extra-ordinarily well maintained, and the United Nations declared it a World Heritage Site in 1995. Among its 250-year-old buildings are some good restaurants and inns, as well as plenty of shopping opportunities. Central to the 19th-century cod fishery, Lunenburg is also the home base of the *Bluenose II*, a replica of the famous schooner that was the fastest sailing ship of its day. Worth a look is the **Fisheries Museum of the Atlantic**, which has exhibits on the history of commercial fishing in the area, as well as a theatre, restaurant and gift shop. Call (902) 634-4794.

Nature lovers will want to make a stop, at the midway point of the Lighthouse Route, in **Kejimkujik National Park**, known to locals as the Kedge. At nearly 400 square kilometres, the park takes up a good chunk of the western peninsula's interior, and a 22-square-kilometre seaside adjunct was recently added near the Lighthouse Route at the town of Liverpool. At the centre of the park is Kejimkujik Lake, and although much of the area was heavily deforested after European settlement, it has largely recovered into a pristine wilderness populated by deer, beaver and muskrat.

There are over 140 kilometres of hiking trails with primitive camp-sites, and for the experienced canoeist the Kedge's many lakes and rivers are joined by 23 portages. For less adventurous visitors, the park also has a visitor information centre, more than 300 well-maintained camp-sites with running water and toilets, and pre-set tours conducted by

By the Way

The *Bluenose* was launched at Lunenburg in 1921—and sailed on into Canadian history. Fast and sleek, the schooner captured the prestigious International Fisherman's Trophy races three years in a row, in 1921, 1922 and 1923. It was also a famous fishing boat, and held the record for the largest cod catch ever brought into Lunenburg's harbour. Wrecked off Haiti in 1946, the *Bluenose's* memory lives on, both in *Bluenose II* (docked at Lunenburg) and on the Canadian dime, where its profile has been etched since 1937.

park staff. The seaside adjunct to Kedge, meanwhile, is a great place for bird-watching, although it is intermittently closed to tourists in the spring and summer to allow its rare species to nest in peace. For park information, call (902) 682-2772.

The Evangeline Trail

Winding along the north shore of the Nova Scotia peninsula, the Evangeline Trail begins at Yarmouth, then follows Route 1 through the heartland of French Acadian life in the province. On the western coast of the Bay of Fundy, many of the communities from Yarmouth to Digby are still French-speaking, and don't be surprised if you see the tricolour Acadian flag flying on many of the homes and businesses.

As it has been for two centuries, **Yarmouth** is still a major port for ship building and trade, and it's the departure point for ferry services running to and from Maine. It's a natural place to stop for the night while exploring southern Nova Scotia, and while you're there you might want to take in an idiosyncratic attraction, the **Firefighters Museum**, dedicated to the history of firefighting in the province (call (902) 742-5525). The short drive to the Yarmouth Light, a lighthouse originally built in 1840, is one of the most scenic in the area.

Further along Route 1, stop for lunch in **Digby**, a modest little town perched on the Bay of Fundy. Digby is renowned worldwide for its scallops—which during the scallop season you can buy and have cooked up

By the Way

The Evangeline Trail skirts the Annapolis Valley, once the centre of francophobe culture in Nova Scotia. In the mid-18th century, however, Acadian territory was controlled by the British, and during the Seven Years' War with France, the British demanded an unconditional oath of allegiance from the area's Acadians. They declined, and in 1755 Britain began a seven-year project of deporting Acadians to England and to other British colonies, or forcibly repatriating to France. In all, about three-quarters of the Acadian population of 13,000 was deported. The event—which caused untold hardships for a community that had been in Nova Scotia for 150 years—inspired Henry Wadsworth Longfellow's famous poem *Evangeline*, from which the Evangeline Trail takes its name.

Off the Beaten Path

If you've got time, take a drive out of Digby on Route 217 along the Digby Neck, a narrow spit of land that juts out into the Bay of Fundy, and take the two ferries that arrive in **Brier Island**. There are two lighthouses on the small island, as well as hiking trails along which you can explore the bay's unique ecosystem. It is also a great place to watch whales; the area is frequented by finback and minke, as well as the occasional humpback. Whale-watching tours can be arranged in the town of Tiverton on Long Island, the first ferry stop, during the summer months.

right on the town wharf. If you're more adventurous, try the local variation of smoked herring, called (appropriately enough) Digby chicks.

Two other stops along the Evangeline Trail are of major historical interest. The first is **Annapolis Royal**, halfway along the north shore about 30 kilometres from Digby. Graced with large mansions and more than 150 heritage buildings, this small, picture-perfect town has shops,

Canada by Web

The Evangeline Trail Association's Web site details attractions and points of interest along the route:
http://www.valleyweb.com/evangelinetrail

antique stores and galleries. It is also home to a pleasant historic gardens, and to the **Fort Anne National Historic Site**, a military outpost established by the French in 1643, and later fortified by the British. It's free to roam around the fort's grounds, but a small admission fee is charged for the site's museum, which is in the old officers' quarters. Call (902) 532-2397 for information.

Just a few kilometres farther on Route 1 is **Port Royal**, the earliest European settlement in North America north of Florida. Founded by Sieur de Monts in 1605, the town is now a national historic site, and its buildings have been restored based on sketches of the original settlement made by Samuel de Champlain. Open mid-May to October; call (902) 532-2898.

Cape Breton Island

Cape Breton is virtually a country unto itself, holding fast to its Celtic and Acadian roots, and home to one of the most distinctive cultures in Canada. It is—still—a land of fiddle music and step-dancing, but also is stunningly beautiful in its natural attractions: rolling seaside hills, gorgeous harbours and pristine wilderness. A drive around the Cabot Trail, which circles the Cape Breton Highlands, is simply one of the most spectacular drives in the world. Plan to spend at least three days driving around and exploring Cape Breton—it's a great place to simply soak up the atmosphere.

There are a few places you will not want to miss. A good place to start is in **Baddeck**, a town of about 1,000 people on the shores of Bras d'Or Lake in the Cape Breton interior, at the intersection of Highway 105 and Route 205. Billed as one of the finest resort communities in Eastern North America, it is also the most overtly tourist-oriented spot in Cape Breton. Part of the attraction is the lake itself—a huge inland sea that comprises almost 1,200 square kilometres of clear, sparkling

Local Knowledge

Simply put, the best time to tour Cape Breton is in the summer and early fall. If you go in the spring, chances are that many of the attractions—not to mention the restaurants and inns—will be closed up, and they certainly will be during the winter. Better to wait until at least June, and don't delay a visit beyond early October.

water. It's a favoured spot for yachting and fishing, and is also one of the most productive breeding sites in the world for the American bald eagle—keep an eye out for them. In Baddeck, a major tourist draw is the **Alexander Graham Bell National Historic Site**, where the inventor summered during the last 37 years of his life. Featuring a huge exhibit of Bell's inventions and his research into deafness, the site also has interactive learning lessons geared towards children. Call (902) 295-2069.

North of Baddeck, the Cabot Trail (Route 205) winds along the rugged shoreline of Cape Breton. On its northern loop—a winding, rolling stretch of road—it cuts through **Cape Breton Highlands National Park**, one of the country's most interesting wilderness areas. From rocky coasts to sandy beaches and pleasant wooded trails, the park offers a wide variety of outdoor experiences, thanks to its location between the Atlantic Ocean on the east and the Gulf of St. Lawrence to the west. The Cabot Trail through the park is lined with roadside exhibits and lookouts, but you can also stay a while in Cape Breton Highlands. There are many walking trails and nearly 500 campsites in the park, about evenly divided between its Atlantic and St. Lawrence coasts, and Cape Breton Highlands is a good spot for salmon and sea trout fishing. For information, call (902) 285-2270.

On the Gulf shore south of the park, stop in at **Chéticamp**, an old Acadian village famous for its hooked rugs (many of which are on display at the **Dr. Elizabeth LeFort Gallery and Museum**). It is also perhaps the most popular whale-watching spot on the island, and charter boat tours can be arranged at the government wharf in town.

Far on the other side of the island, on Cape Breton's eastern tip half an hour north of Sydney, is **Louisbourg**, the historic French

Off the Beaten Path

On your way to Cape Breton Highlands, pay a visit to **Mabou**, an overwhelmingly Scottish town on Route 19 west of Baddeck. There are plenty of reminders here of this part of Cape Breton's Gaelic roots, including a shrine to early pioneers and a historical museum called An Drochaid (The Bridge). On Canada Day, the locals hold a Scottish picnic, and during the summer months it's a good spot to join in on a traditional ceilidh (fiddling and step-dancing concert). Adding to the Scottish air: the only distiller of single malt whisky in North America, the **Glenora Inn and Distillery**, which offers tours of the facility, a gift shop and a very good restaurant, as well as accommodation. Call (902) 258-2662.

stronghold that was completely destroyed by British forces in 1758. Today, beyond being a thriving fishing community, it is home to the largest national historic site in Canada, the Fortress of Louisbourg, which is a partial re-creation of the old town. It's a lively tourist spot, with costumed staff leading visitors through the history of the French presence in Cape Breton, and offers period cuisine and handicrafts, as well as exhibitions of 18th-century military drills. Open from June to September; call 1-800-565-9464.

The Least You Need to Know

➤ Halifax is Nova Scotia's largest city, and its major attractions are the Citadel and the waterfront.

➤ The Lighthouse Route explores Nova Scotia's south shore, passing through Peggy's Cove, Lunenburg and Kejimkujik National Park.

➤ Nova Scotia's north shore features many Acadian villages, and Annapolis Royal and Port Royal are its most popular attractions.

➤ A tour of Cape Breton Island should include Baddeck, Cape Breton Highlands National Park and Louisbourg.

New Brunswick

Welcome to New Brunswick

Compared with the rural charm of PEI, the thriving seaside life of Nova Scotia or the idiosyncrasies of Newfoundland, New Brunswick has often *seemed* like the poor cousin of the Atlantic provinces when it comes to tourism. Many visitors' only experience of the province is driving through it—on the way to the more popular destinations to the east. Part of the reason is that New Brunswick is so large, and most of its land—85 per cent—is taken up with seemingly endless tracts of forest, a higher percentage than any other province. In recent years, however, the provincial government and New Brunswick businesses have been carefully promoting the region as a tourist destination.

An officially bilingual province, New Brunswick boasts a vibrant mix of French and English cultures. The northeastern reaches are home to some of the best sport fishing in the world, and its shore on the Gulf of St. Lawrence has spectacular beaches. The major cities of Fredericton, Saint John and Moncton are increasingly sophisticated spots, rediscovering their own history and putting it on display, and the south shore along the Bay of Fundy boasts the natural wonder of the world's highest tides and seaside communities that seem untouched by time. In short, for those visitors willing to take a closer look, New Brunswick has plenty to offer.

Getting There

By air: Both major domestic airlines (or their regional services) have regularly scheduled flights to Saint John, Fredericton and Moncton, New Brunswick's three largest cities, from Montreal and Boston; Canadian Airlines flies also from Ottawa, while Air Canada has flights from Toronto to all three cities. **By rail:** You can take the VIA Rail train to Moncton, the Gateway to Acadia, from Montreal or Halifax, but it runs only six times a week. **By car:** The Trans-Canada Highway (Route 2) enters New Brunswick from Quebec near Edmundston, and exits just past Moncton and into Nova Scotia. **By water:** If you're coming into New Brunswick from Nova Scotia and early mornings don't bother you, you can take a ferry from Digby, NS, to Saint John. Call Marine Atlantic for more information; 1-800-565-9470.

Getting Around

You can arrange bus tours in any of New Brunswick's major cities, but a tour of the province is best conducted through self-guided exploration. In other words, by car. The Trans-Canada Highway skirts most of the prime

Canada by Web

An informative virtual tour of New Brunswick, listing its main attractions and dividing the province into scenic drives, can be found at:
http://www.cybersmith.net/nbtour

For descriptions of New Brunswick's provincial parks, see:
http://www.gov.nb.ca/dnre/parks

destinations, including Fredericton, Saint John and Moncton, and there are also excellent roads leading through Acadian country in the north and its many attractions. Routes 1 and 114, meanwhile, are the major roads for exploring the south (Bay of Fundy) shore of the province.

New Brunswick is deceptively large, and much of the province is sparsely populated, so plan on driving good distances between sites of interest. In fact, it would take you well over a week to properly see the whole province, so consider breaking up your tour into two- or three-day excursions. One of those should be Saint John and the Bay of Fundy shoreline in the south; the other should be Acadian country and the St. Lawrence shore in the north.

Fredericton

The capital of New Brunswick, Fredericton is one of the province's prettiest cities, with quiet, tree-lined streets and historic buildings that

New Brunswick: Cities and outdoor attractions

Out of the Way

New Brunswick's highway system is well maintained and extensive, but you still may be tempted to get off the main road and do a bit of side exploring. If you know where you're going—and you're sure there's a town at the end of the side road—that's fine. But in many areas, the muddy byways of New Brunswick put the acid test to that adage, "Every road leads somewhere." This advice comes from personal experience, and the memory of how one detour along the "scenic route" between Saint John and Moncton led to a very dirty car, a missed dinner reservation—and one seriously upset travelling companion.

evoke the city's Loyalist past. In the late 1600s, the site of the city, set beside the sparkling waters of the Saint John River, was briefly the capital of French Acadia. In 1783, however, it was a haven for thousands of Americans still loyal to the British crown who were fleeing the revolution, and Frederick's Town (named after the son of King George III) quickly became the Loyalists' capital and an oasis of genteel society.

Today, the economy of Fredericton, once a lumbering and cotton centre, relies for the most part on a nearby military base and on the provincial government. In recent years, thanks to aggressive government courting of high-tech companies, the city of 46,000 has also become a hub (along with Moncton) of New Brunswick's burgeoning information-technology industry. But despite such modern aspirations, the past seems very much alive in Fredericton, and many of the city's old Loyalist buildings are still standing. You can see many of them along **Waterloo Row** on the banks of the Saint John River, an area of residential buildings where you can see many fine (and well maintained) examples of Georgian and Victorian architecture.

Fredericton's other major attractions bear witness to its cultural and political importance. Art lovers will get a kick out of the **Beaverbrook Art Gallery**, established by the Canadian-born British lord and newspaper magnate. The gallery, on Fredericton's main thoroughfare of Queen Street, has a wonderful collection of nearly 2,000 artworks by Canadian and international artists, including paintings by

Out of the Way

Twenty minutes west of Fredericton on the Trans-Canada Highway, **Kings Landing Historical Settlement** is an open-air museum re-creating New Brunswick life in the 19th century. The settlement features 10 homes, a working saw mill, a school, a store, a small theatre and a cooper's shop, among other period buildings that evoke the area's Loyalist roots. Set amid some of the prettiest rural landscapes in New Brunswick, Kings Landing is open from June to October, but hosts special events throughout the year. Call (506) 363-5090 for information.

Salvador Dali and Cornelius Krieghoff. Call (506) 458-8545. Across the street is the only professional theatre company in the province, **Theatre New Brunswick**, whose Callithumpian players offer tours of the city during the summer. Call (506) 458-8344.

Also on Queen Street is the **Military Compound**, a restored former base for Canadian and British forces which during the summer is used for colourful changing-of-the-guard ceremonies and musical concerts. In the compound, as well, are the **York Sunbury Museum**, tracing native, French and Loyalist settlement in the area (call 455-6041), and the **New Brunswick Sports Hall of Fame**, which has a large collection of sport memorabilia; call (506) 453-3747. Be sure also to take in the gorgeous **City Hall**, built in 1876 and home to a tapestry collection that portrays the history of Fredericton. Free guided tours are available; call (506) 452-9508.

Saint John

The largest city in New Brunswick, with a population of 125,000, Saint John is also the oldest incorporated city in Canada, dating back to 1785. Nestled on a natural harbour where the mouth of the Saint John River meets the Bay of Fundy, the city had its heyday during the 19th century, when it established itself as the centre of economic activity in the Atlantic region thanks to its thriving ship-building and lumbering industries. The development of railways and steamships in the late 1800s,

Local Knowledge

Saint John was discovered by Europeans (actually, it was Samuel de Champlain) on St. Jean Baptiste Day, June 24, 1604—the same day on which John Cabot is believed to have arrived in St. John's, Newfoundland, 107 years earlier. As a result, the two cities have similar names, and many people confuse them. So remember, St. John's (with the possessive) is in Newfoundland; Saint John (no possessive) is in New Brunswick. Do try and get it straight: when visitors mix the two, it drives New Brunswickers and Newfoundlanders to distraction.

however, was a blow from which the local economy never fully recovered, and Saint John eventually lost pride of place to Halifax.

Once, Saint John endured a rather unflattering reputation as a working-class, dirty city of little interest to visitors, thanks largely to its smelly pulp and paper mills and to the general dilapidation of its historic areas. In recent years, however, the municipal government and Saint John's citizenry have undertaken a major civic beautification project.

Much of the city's Georgian and Victorian architecture has benefited from recent restorations. Downtown, in the area known as **Market Square**, a historic section of waterfront along King Street has been substantially restored, and now features malls, a trade and convention centre and a hotel. In the Market Square area is the **New Brunswick Museum**, featuring a full-size model of a right whale and an interactive gallery—good fun for kids and adults alike. Call (506) 643-2300. Also worth checking is the **Old Courthouse** at the intersection of King and Sydney streets. Built in 1829, it is still in use today.

A big tourist draw in Saint John is the world-famous **Reversing Falls**, just a kilometre away from the city centre along Main Street. An intriguing side effect of the Bay of Fundy's phenomenally high tides—at more than 40 feet, the highest in the world—the Reversing Falls look like just a regular rapids during low tide. During high tide, however, ocean water rushing in looks like it is trying to push the river back onto itself, and the flow of the river seems to reverse. Call ahead, at (506) 658-2937, to ensure that you see the falls at their most spectacular.

Canada by Web

New Brunswick's three major cities have their own Web sites, listing the prime attractions.
Fredericton—**http://www.city.fredericton.nb.ca**
Saint John—**http://www.city.saint-john.nb.ca**
Moncton—**http://www.greater.moncton.nb.ca**

Moncton

Known as the Gateway to Acadia, Moncton reflects the bilingual character of New Brunswick, a city where you are as likely to hear French as English. Ironically, the area was first settled by Germans, who called it The Bend, since it sits on an elbow of the Petitcodiac River. For decades, the major industry in town was ship building, but that has since been replaced by the railway, and Moncton is sometimes called the Hub of the Maritimes because the rail lines to the rest of Atlantic Canada pass through it. Today, Moncton is also a hub of French culture in New Brunswick, and the Université de Moncton is a completely French-language university. About a third of the city's 60,000 residents are francophones. Thanks to its student population and the mix of culture, downtown Moncton has an agile nightlife and bar scene, and is a good place to enjoy traditional French cuisine.

For visitors, however, the main attractions of Moncton are its unique natural wonders. It used to be more spectacular than it is now, but check out the **Tidal Bore**—a wall of water up to 3 feet high that surges up the Petitcodiac, driven by the high tides of the Bay of Fundy. Best times for viewing are posted in nearby Bore Park, and the bore tends to be higher in the spring.

More popular is **Magnetic Hill**, just off the Trans-Canada Highway. For $2, you drive to the foot of the hill and, at a clearly marked point, stop, put the automobile in neutral—and then start rolling uphill. Magnetic Hill is one of the most frequently visited natural attractions in Canada, and a large entertainment and tourist complex has been built up around it. **Magnetic Hill Theme Park** comprises a re-created Maritime fishing village with shoppes (yes, with the "e") and restaurants, a water theme park, a scenic 2-kilometre train

Local Knowledge

Acadian culture is unique, and has its own literary, cinematic and theatrical traditions. If the culture interests you (and you can speak French), two of the region's best-known theatres are worth a look. **La Coopérative de Théâtre L'Escaouette** in Moncton specializes in the often-eclectic works of playwright Herménégilde Chiasson. Call (506) 855-0001. In the town of Caraquet, meanwhile, the **Théâtre Populaire D'Acadie** is known for its productions of plays by Jules Boudreau and other Acadian playwrights. Call (506) 727-0920.

ride and a zoo with more than 80 animal species. Call (506) 384-0303 for zoo information; 1-800-331-9283 for water theme park info. Adults may want to try out Magnetic Hill and then move on—but kids will probably want to stay longer.

Out and About in New Brunswick

Beyond the cities, most places of interest in New Brunswick can be found along its two coastlines. In the northern part of the province, the Gulf of St. Lawrence shoreline is home to thriving Acadian communities, swimmable beaches and some world-renowned fishing rivers. On the southern shore, the dramatic tides of the Bay of Fundy have created some of the most picturesque scenery in the country, while west of Saint John are quaint seaside villages that are great for leisurely exploring.

The St. Lawrence Shore

A hundred kilometres north of Moncton off Route 11 is **Kouchibouguac National Park**, a popular camping spot and a great place to go for a dip in the relatively warm waters off New Brunswick's eastern shore. The main attraction here are the beaches, backed by rolling dunes of white sand and ringed by lagoons and salt marshes. The two most popular are Kellys Beach, which has supervised swimming between June and September, and Callander's Beach, which has large picnic areas. To see the rest of the park, one of the best ways is by bicycle, and Kouchibouguac is laced with an extensive network of cycling trails. The park has more than 350 campsites, many with electrical hookups, but if you're going during the summer call ahead and make sure a spot is available—Kouchibouguac can get very busy in July and August. Phone (506) 876-2443.

North along Route 11, you'll pass through a string of Acadian fishing villages and then come upon **Miramichi City**—a pocket of English, Scottish and Irish settlement in the heart of contemporary Acadia. The region is known for two things—lumber and salmon—and the latter has made the Miramichi River among the most famous sport-fishing rivers in the world. (In recent years, however, Atlantic salmon stocks in the river and elsewhere in New Brunswick have sharply declined, thanks to overfishing, pollution and unknown causes.) Fittingly, the town is home to an interesting little museum dedicated to the

By the Way

Beyond Miramichi, another salmon fishing mecca is Campbellton, on the north shore of New Brunswick by the Restigouche River on the Baie des Chaleurs. So important are salmon to the town's livelihood that its mascot is Restigouche Sam—a 28-foot-long steel model of the gamefish on the Campbellton waterfront. The town bills itself as the home of the World's Largest Salmon. For tourist information on Campbellton, call (506) 789-2700.

In fact—perhaps as a sign of an increasing penchant for tourist dollars—New Brunswickers seem to have a thing for "World's Largest Whatever" claims. In Hartland, north of Fredericton off the Trans-Canada Highway, is a bridge built in 1921 that, at 1,282 feet, is billed as the world's longest covered bridge. Another "big" attraction can be found in Nackawic, a town in the heart of northern New Brunswick's timber region (where, by the way, the legend of Paul Bunyan got its start). Here, looming 60 feet into the air and weighing approximately 55 tons, is the unrivalled spectacle that is the World's Largest Axe.

salmon, and another museum traces the roots of the lumber trade along the Miramichi.

You will get a better sense of the region's Acadian heritage in **Caraquet**, along Route 11 on the Baie des Chaleurs. Home to the professional French drama centre Théâtre Populaire d'Acadie, Caraquet plays host every August to an Acadian festival, and also boasts some of the finest beaches in New Brunswick. Nearby is the **Acadian Historical Village**, a living history site that re-creates Acadian life in the wake of the French Loyalists' expulsion from Nova Scotia in the 1700s (an event called *La Deportation*). Open from June to October, the historical village is made up of more than 40 original Acadian buildings, including a grist mill, a tavern and a pioneer chapel, and there are demonstrations of such pioneer skills as soap-making and haying. Call (506) 726-2600.

The South Shore

Lining the Bay of Fundy to the east and west of Saint John, the south shore of New Brunswick is characterized by quaint seaside villages and dramatic scenery. An absolute must-see in any tour of Atlantic Canada is **Fundy National Park**, about 130 kilometres east of Saint John on Highway 114 off the Trans-Canada Highway. The many outlooks along the road or on any of the park's trails give a wonderful view of the events below. The Bay of Fundy has the highest tides in the world, twice a day rising to heights sometimes in excess of 45 feet. All that tidal action has had a dramatic effect on the shoreline, creating steep sandstone cliffs that fall off into the waters below.

From the town of Alma, on the park's eastern boundary, you can walk out for a kilometre during low tide and explore the Fundy ecosystem. (But beware: the tide comes back in quickly, so don't tarry too long.) Fundy National Park is also home to deer and myriad bird species—including peregrine falcon—and it is a popular camping spot, with more than 600 well-furbished sites. There is also a very pretty nine-hole golf course in the park. Call (506) 887-6000 for information.

If you want to see even more of the Bay of Fundy's quirks, check out **The Rocks Provincial Park**, east of the national park at the mouth of the Petitcodiac River. The main attractions here are the

Out of the Way

If you have time for an extended side trip, take a detour and go to **Campobello Island**, the best known of the many islands that dot New Brunswick's south shore. Long a resort community catering to America's rich and famous, Campobello was the summer home of the Roosevelt family, and Franklin Delano Roosevelt's 34-room "cottage" is now part of a nature preserve jointly maintained by the United States and Canada. Visits to the cottage and the grounds are free. Call (506) 752-2922. There are a few hotels on the island, but if you're camping you can stay at **Herring Cove Provincial Park,** which has a pleasant beach (although the water is cold!) and many campsites, including 40 with electrical hookups. Call (506) 752-7010.

"flowerpots," huge and oddly shaped masses of rock that have been carved by the tidal surge. The Rocks has walking trails, a restaurant on-site and an interpretive centre open to visitors during the summer. Call (506) 734-3429.

The jewel of the south shore is **St. Andrews-by-the-Sea**, about 150 kilometres west of Saint John on Route 1. One gets the sense in this pretty little village that not much has changed since Loyalists settled in the area two centuries ago. Many of the buildings in town are well over a hundred years old, and a handful date from the 1700s. Along Water Street by the harbour, shops and restaurants cater to the resort crowd, and tours of the historic old courthouse are available during the summer. Here, too, is the **Algonquin**, a famous and old resort hotel with lazy verandahs, plenty of greenery and a very good restaurant.

The Least You Need to Know

➤ A complete tour of New Brunswick will take more than a week.

➤ The major cities are Saint John, Moncton and Fredericton, the provincial capital.

➤ The prime attractions on the St. Lawrence shore are Caraquet and Kouchibouguac National Park.

➤ On the south shore, be sure to visit Fundy National Park and St. Andrews-by-the-Sea.

Part 3
Central Canada

Central Canada is the place where Canada's two major traditions, French and English, meet and compete. Quebec is home to the world's largest francophone community outside France, and to cultured Montreal and the historic charm of Quebec City. Ontario, meanwhile, is the most powerful of the English-speaking provinces, containing the country's biggest city, Toronto, and the national capital, Ottawa. Bursting with French, English and a few other languages, the cosmopolitan cities of Central Canada are tourist attractions in themselves. This part of the guide provides detailed neighbourhood guides to Montreal, Quebec City, Toronto and Ottawa, along with street maps so you don't get lost.

For travellers, Central Canada offers something for everyone—not just the city-oriented attractions of great restaurants, bustling streets, and

world-renowned theatre. Don't overlook the host of natural wonders offered by the region, where you can take in a Broadway-style play in Toronto one night and then canoe in the Northern Ontario wilderness the next day.

Quebec

Welcome to Quebec

So much media attention has been paid to the national unity debate and the widely publicized separatist aspirations of many Quebecers, it might be easy to forget that Quebec is a wonderful place to visit, offering travellers a wealth of attractions both urban and wild. Chief among them is Quebec's unique French culture, rich in history and still alive in the language, pastimes and cuisine, as well as in the institutions that seek to preserve the centre of *francophonie* in North America. Home to two of the world's great cities, Montreal and Quebec City, the province also offers hikers, skiers and fishermen nothing less than an oasis of outdoor opportunities. If you want to know Canada, its past and its present, then you must explore *la belle province*.

Montreal

Despite its recent troubles, Montreal remains an effervescent and culturally alive town with a deep history, a multitude of diversions and attractions and a vital mix of French, English and a host of other ethnic elements thrown in. As the second-largest French-speaking city in the world (after Paris), for Anglophone travellers it is at once different enough to be interesting, and familiar enough to not be intimidating. For tourists, Montreal remains one of the world's great cities—and a welcoming gateway to Quebec's unique culture and history.

Montreal Past and Present

The history of Montreal dates back more than 350 years, when in 1642 Frenchman Paul Chomedey de Maisonneuve started building a mission-ary colony on what became known as Île de Montréal, an island situ-ated at the confluence of the St. Lawrence and Ottawa rivers. The first stab at settlement of the area was troubled from the start, thanks mostly to a constant state of war with the Iroquois, the area's indigenous peo-ples (and the ones Maisonneuve was trying to convert to Christianity!). But after the French government signed a peace treaty with the natives at the beginning of the 18th century, Montreal started to become a nat-ural centre for trade—the fur trade, in particular. As the coureurs de bois and the voyageurs explored the rest of North America from the Great Lakes to the Rocky Mountains, the small settlement on Mount Royal—a 200-metre-high peak that dominates the Île de Montréal—became an important part of the French colonies, even though Quebec City,

Canada by Web

Interesting and informative Web sites on travelling to and exploring Montreal can be found at:
http://www.tourism-montreal.org (which includes a good guide to Montreal's neighbourhoods)
http://www.pagemontreal.qc.ca (another excellent neighbourhood guide)
http://www.ville.montreal.qc.ca

further down the St. Lawrence to the east, remained its political centre.

Real growth in Montreal did not begin, however, until well after the British conquest of the city in 1760. In the late 18th century and early 19th, immigrants from Great Britain—especially Scottish merchants—came to Montreal to seek their fortunes in a new land. In the process, they transformed the smallish settlement (only about 5,000 inhabitants at the turn of the century) into a bustling metropolis of nearly 45,000 by the 1850.

The import and export trade fuelled the city's economy, taking advantage of its geographical position as a gateway to the Atlantic for ships and their cargo coming from the Great Lakes to the west. In coming years, Montreal became Canada's premiere transportation hub with the building of the transnational railway system, and with the industrial revolution the city boomed. At the turn of the century (and for much of the 20th century), it established itself as Canada's most important metropolis. Immigrants from all over the world—Italians, Jews, Poles, Ukrainians, Balts—came to settle there, pushing the population to nearly half a million by the First World War, and Montreal became the cosmopolitan city that it largely remains today.

By the Way

Among the missionaries who followed de Maisonneuve to Montreal was Marguerite Bourgeoys. She was the colony's first teacher, instructing both French and native children, and she established an arts school, a girls' boarding school and a school only for natives. The non-cloistered order she founded before her death in 1700, the Sisters of the Congregation of Notre-Dame, numbers in the thousands today, and is active around the world. In some ways, she is Montreal's most famous citizen: Bourgeoys became a saint in the Roman Catholic church in 1982.

The second period of boom in Montreal occurred in the 1950s and 1960s, when its borders expanded to encompass the burgeoning suburbs that spread out across the surrounding countryside. (In that way, Montreal is not that different from any other large North American city.) The downtown area, too, was largely restored, as office towers were constructed—and much of old Montreal's history was demolished. With its hosting of the World Exposition in 1967—better known as Expo 67—Montreal's international reputation became firmly established, and it remains today.

By the Way

The rivalry between Montreal and Toronto is part of the cultural and social fabric of Eastern Canada, grounded partly in economics, history and long-standing English-French tensions—not to mention hockey, a sport in which the Montreal Canadiens and the Toronto Maple Leafs, the Habs and the Buds, were long the NHL's two most powerful teams. These days, Torontonians can still get into a good argument with Montrealers over which is the more multicultural or entertaining or lively city, and over which town has the better cuisine. Lately, the animosity has dimmed somewhat, as many Montrealers have grudgingly come to admit that Toronto is not some sort of hell on earth—and vice versa. But if you're a Torontonian visiting Montreal, do your hosts one small favour: don't diss the Habs.

Expo 67 brought more than 50 million visitors to the city—and truly put Montreal on the map. Two years later, with the acquisition of the Expos, Montreal was the only Canadian city with a major league baseball team (a distinction it held until the Blue Jays came to Toronto in 1977). Expo 67 was followed, in turn, by the summer Olympics of 1976. Directed by the leadership of then-Mayor Jean Drapeau, both Expo and the Olympics were huge construction and civil beautification projects, and they left a lasting and visible legacy on the city's landscape.

Toronto, meanwhile, had been slowly asserting itself as the political and cultural centre of Canada. In the late 1970s and right up to the present, however, Montreal has undoubtedly suffered from continuing fears among many of its business leaders—and many of its non-francophone residents—over the province's political future. After the election of a separatist provincial government in 1976, many companies who had long made Montreal their headquarters moved to Toronto. As jobs and businesses fled to English-speaking Canada, so did many citizens. And by the end of the 1970s, Montreal was relegated to second-city status next to its historic rival in Ontario. (There are those who would argue—sending shudders up the spines of Montrealers—that Toronto even has better restaurants!)

Despite a mini-boom in the 1980s, Montreal has never fully recovered, in terms of economy or population. But it remains today a major industrial, commercial and financial centre, with a city population of over one million, and hundreds of thousands more in the over 100 different municipalities that make up the urban area. Like Toronto, much of what Montreal offers to tourists is centred in and around the downtown area, and among its galleries, historic sites, museums and happening nightspots—not as active as they once were, but still a big part of the city's attraction—there is plenty there for any traveller to do and see.

Getting There

By air: Two airports serve the Montreal area. The largest is Mirabel, 55 kilometres north of downtown, a sprawling and distant complex that has had a fair share of economic troubles in recent years. Thankfully, almost all domestic flights to Montreal arrive at Dorval International Airport, the more accessible of the two airports, situated just 22 kilometres northwest of the city, or about a 20-minute trip by car. Together, the two facilities are served by all major domestic and international

Local Knowledge

It's a question that many first-time travellers to Montreal have on their minds: given separatist sentiments in Quebec, will I still be made to feel welcome? The answer is—by and large—yes. The fact is, even among themselves, few Quebecers—or, in particular, Montrealers—care to talk about politics, and their views will not be forced on unsuspecting travellers. A couple of tips, though. If you do not speak French, don't "give it a try" just because you're in Quebec. Most of the people you'll run into in Montreal will be fluently bilingual, and those who aren't will still probably speak English better than you speak French. As a general rule, don't talk about Quebec politics with Quebecers unless your opinion is requested. The fact is, many in the province are as bored with the ongoing national unity debate as people in the rest of the country. And besides, arguing politics with your hosts is just bad manners.

airlines. For Dorval information, call Montreal International Airport (Dorval), at (514) 633-3105. **By rail:** VIA Rail, the national passenger train service, runs regular trains into and out of the city. The main stop in Montreal is Central Station, located beneath the Queen Elizabeth Hotel on de la Gauchetière Street, and is connected to the public transit system. **By car:** From Toronto, the major route into the city from the west is Highway 401. Highway 417, entering from the northwest, is the major direct route from Ottawa, and from Quebec City Highways 20 and 40 (the extensions of the Trans-Canada Highway in Quebec) are the main access routes to the city. **By water**: Montreal remains one of the world's most active seaports, with more than 30,000 passengers arriving there annually. The Iberville Passenger Terminal in the Old Port of Montreal (recently restored) is a main destination for cruise ships on the St. Lawrence River and East Coast.

Getting Around

Montrealers will dispute this, but many visitors to the city find it a confusing and even dangerous place to drive—not that there are many more traffic accidents there than any other place, but residents seem to follow rules of the road that are both unique and mysterious to outsiders. And really, there is little need to drive around the city once you're there, thanks largely to its extensive and well-maintained public transit system. The Métro, as the subway system is called, has four lines running throughout Montreal, with stops at or near all of the major tourist attractions. And like Toronto, Montreal is largely a city of neighbourhoods—get to any one of them by public transit, and you can walk to just about anywhere you want to go. Another reason to use public

Local Knowledge

If you decide to drive to Montreal, don't fall prey to the most common traffic violation tourists to Quebec make: turning right on a red light. Sure, it's legal just about everywhere else in Canada, but not in La Belle Province. If you get nailed by a traffic cop for the slip-up, go ahead and tell them you're from out of town. It won't do you any good, but it might make you feel better.

Local Knowledge

Montreal is the largest French-speaking city outside France, so it's not surprising that many of the street signs and other directions you'll see around town will be in, well, French. Most restaurants, hotels, museums and other tourist areas are staffed by bilingual Quebecers, so there's no need to take a crash French course before you leave. On the other hand, a basic knowledge of what the signs mean will be indispensable in your tour of the city. Here are a few of the most common French signs in Quebec—and what they mean in English:

arrêt: stop
centre-ville: downtown
droite: right
gauche: left
stationnement interdit: no parking
sortie: exit
escalier (or escalier roulant): escalator
ascenseur: elevator
salle de bain: washroom
Métro: subway
billets: tickets

transit: it's cheap, at less than $2 a ride. And maps of the system are readily available at any Métro station. For information, call STCUM, the Montreal area transit authority, at (514) 288-6287.

A Guide to Montreal's Neighbourhoods

Perhaps more than any other Canadian city, Montreal is known for its neighbourhoods. Their rich variety is in part due to immigration and settlement patterns, as first European, then ethnic groups from all over the world, have travelled to Montreal and made it their home. In part, too, many of the neighbourhoods are formerly independent municipalities, swallowed up by the larger metropolis as it boomed in the first half of the century. Each has its own unique flair, and each neighbourhood, in its way, is a vital part of the Montreal experience.

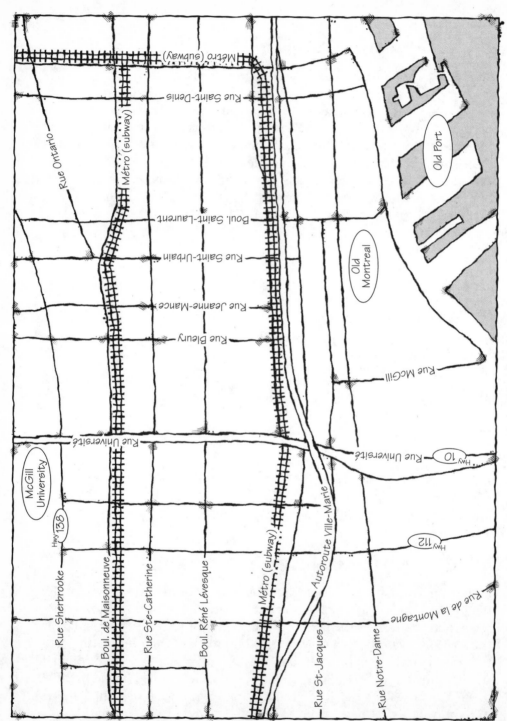

Downtown Montreal, with Métro lines

Old Montreal

For visitors, a tour of Montreal should begin where the city began—in the old port area, which has been substantially restored in recent years and has since become one of Montreal's major tourist attractions. Located at the foot of St. Laurent Boulevard, and running along the shore of the St. Lawrence River roughly between Berri and McGill streets, Old Montreal (take the Métro to any of Champs de mars, Place d'Armes or Square Victoria stations) covers only a few city blocks, so the area is easily accessible by foot. More a preservation area than a real neighbourhood, some of the area's major tourist draws sometimes seem Disneyland-style artificial—a vision of earlier times that is just a little *too* perfectly rendered. And during peak season from May to October, its many attractions can get pretty crowded, so what you planned to be a couple hours in Old Montreal could quickly turn into a day-long affair.

At the heart of the neighbourhood is **Place Jacques-Cartier**, which runs between Notre-Dame and De la Commune streets, and once was the private gardens of the Marquis de Vaudreuil. Its history as a marketplace dates back to 1804, and it is dominated by an 1809 monument to Lord Nelson, the British naval war hero who defeated Napoleon at Waterloo. These days, **Place Jacques-Cartier** is a bustling flower market and hang-out for artists vending their wares. It's also a good meeting place for visitors trying to keep track of their directions among the winding, narrow streets of *Vieux Montréal*, and its many restaurants make it a popular dining spot (for tourists, at least).

Just to the north, at 280 Notre-Dame Street East, is the **Chateau Ramezay**, one of the few early buildings in the old part of town that still survives. Built in 1705 for the then-governor of Montreal, it is a quaint little "castle" that evokes the city's French colonial past. It also houses a small museum of Quebec and Montreal history. Call (514) 861-3708.

Not to be missed in Old Montreal is **Notre-Dame Basilica**, a huge Roman Catholic Church built in 1829 that remains one of the most impressive on the continent. Located on Notre-Dame Street west (at the Place-d'armes subway stop), the church features a neo-Gothic architectural style that is nothing less than awe-inspiring, and one of the largest organs in the world. For information on hours, call (514) 842-2925. To the right of the basilica's front is a lesser-known but important building, the **St. Sulpice Seminary**, built in 1685 and the

Local Knowledge

Because it cuts through so much of Montreal, locals call St. Laurent Boulevard simply "the Main." It used to be that St. Laurent was a kind of border, dividing the English in the west from the French who lived on the east side. But that is hardly the case any more, as the lines distinguishing one community from the other have become increasingly blurred over the past couple decades. For visitors, St. Laurent is a good street from which to get their bearings in Montreal's core, and walking along it will take you through many of the city's most interesting neighbourhoods.

oldest surviving structure in Montreal. It is, unfortunately, closed to the public.

Old Montreal harbours a number of more modern attractions. One of the most renowned is the **Pointe-à-Callière Museum of Archeology and History**, on the south end of Old Montreal at 350 Place Royale. The museum is built around an archeological dig of early Montreal, and the "multimedia" show put on over the remains (including an old cemetery) is both spooky and uplifting. There are also exhibits on everything from bread-making to native Canadian history, and in the summer the museum has begun conducting tours of an archeological dig site. Call (514) 872-9150 for information. If you really get into Montreal's past, then you'll probably want to check out the **Centre d'Histoire de Montréal**, at 335 Place d'Youville, with exhibits on the early and modern history of the city.

Running along the shores of the St. Laurent River, the biggest tourist attraction in the area is the **Old Port of Montreal**. Once the bustling heart of industry in the city, the Old Port is now practically empty of commercial ship traffic. And yet in recent years it has been reborn as a charming promenade for visitors and for locals. Two kilometres long, the boardwalk is a great place for a summertime stroll, and there are plenty of diversions. An **IMAX theatre**, with its trademark huge screen and roaring sound system, is on King-Edward Pier at the corner of de la Commune and Saint-Laurent. Call (514) 496-IMAX for show times.

For the kids, nearby is the **SOS Labyrinthe**, a twisting maze built in an old hangar on King-Edward Pier, designed to look like a cargo ship full of traps and obstacles. Beyond the permanent attractions, the Old Port also stages shows and street performances, as well as guided excursions and cruises around the port area. For information on Old Port events, call toll-free 1-800-971-PORT.

Downtown

The main strip through the heart of Montreal is Ste. Catherine Street, the rough equivalent of Toronto's Yonge Street. There are myriad stores on Ste. Catherine between Bleury and Bishop streets, as well as cheap nickel-and-dime shops, porno galleries, video arcades and fast-food restaurants, not to mention panhandlers and street vendors. Since it's the street that everybody takes to walk through downtown, you'll probably end up on Ste. Catherine at some point on your visit—but you may not wish to stay long. On the street, however, is the **Place des Arts**, Montreal's main live-performance venue, with three theatres and available tours. Call (514) 842-2112.

By the Way

Montrealers take their hockey very, very seriously. If you need evidence, consider what happened in 1955, when then-president of the NHL Clarence Campbell suspended the Canadiens' great star, Maurice "Rocket" Richard, for the rest of the season after the Hall-of-Famer-to-be took a cheap shot at a Boston Bruin. On St. Patrick's Day, outraged Montreal fans attacked Campbell at a Canadiens game, and then spilled out onto the streets and conducted one of the worst riots in Canadian history.

Most of the good shopping downtown can't be found on streets at all, but underground, in the extensive system of interconnected office buildings that take up much of city core. From McGill Métro station, you can easily walk underground from Centre Eaton to the shopping-and-office complexes of Place Ville-Marie and Place Bonaventure, as well as the Bell Amphitheatre's indoor skating rink and the (more professional) Molson Centre, where hockey's Montreal Canadiens took up residence in 1996 after the legendary Forum was put out to pasture.

Above ground, be sure to pass by Sherbrooke Street, in the area known as the Golden Square Mile between Côtes-des-Neiges street on the west and du Parc Avenue to the east. It is still an exclusive little

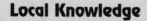

Local Knowledge

The heart of nightlife in downtown Montreal can be found on three streets: Crescent, Bishop and de la Montagne, near Ogilvy department store. (Get off the Métro at either Peel or Lucien-L'Allier stations.) It's an area of trendy stores, upscale eateries and swish bars and nightclubs, catering mostly to those with money and people into the meet-market scene.

community, but at the turn of the century it was home to most of Canada's rich and famous Anglos—a famous estimate is that 70 per cent of Canada's wealth used to reside among the Golden Square Mile's big houses and tree-lined streets. Nearby is the **Musée des Beaux-Arts de Montréal** (near the Peel Métro station), Canada's oldest museum and one of the best fine-arts museums in the country. Founded back in 1860, the Musée is the main venue for visiting exhibitions, as well as offering excellent permanent collections in its two pavilions. Call (514) 285-1600 for information.

The best view of downtown Montreal can be had from Mont Royal Park, a large green space that takes up much of the summit of Mount Royal. Designed by Frederic Law Olmstead—the same man responsible for Central Park in New York—the park is a popular spot for hiking and mountain biking in the summer, and in the winter it plays host to skating at the top of the mountain. An observatory on its east end gives a breathtaking view of east Montreal, while from the Chalet Mont-Royal—a large old flagstone building accessible by trails—you can see a gorgeous vista of downtown.

The Latin Quarter

For most of Montreal's boom period, the Latin Quarter, on the north side of downtown between St. Laurent and St. Denis streets, was the place to be in Canada's first city, thanks largely to the fact that it was home to a very active (and infamous) red-light district. Today, the notorious red-light area has shrunk to a few peep shows and strip clubs—and trendy cafés, restaurants and bars have sprung up to fill the void.

Local Knowledge

Though many of its members have left the city in recent years, a large and vital Jewish community has left an indelible imprint on the economic and cultural life of Montreal. For visitors, one of the most inviting side effects of that community is also one of Montreal's great delights: delis. Two of the most famous are Schwarz's, on 3895 St. Laurent Boulevard, and Wilensky's Light Lunch, at 34 Fairmount Street West—an eatery immortalized by Montreal author Mordecai Richler in *The Apprenticeship of Duddy Kravitz*.

Grungy and hip, the area gets its energy from a large student population, courtesy of the Université de Québec à Montréal (UQAM) nearby. There are only a few real tourist attractions here—the **Just for Laughs Museum** (at 2111 St. Laurent), the first museum in the world to be dedicated to the art of comedy, is one of them. But there are many fine restaurants (some of them increasingly touristy) and plenty of places to simply sit, hang out, and soak up the atmosphere.

Plateau Mont Royal

Simply called "the Plateau" by Montrealers, Plateau Mont Royal lies above the Latin Quarter near Mont Royal Park. It is largely a residential neighbourhood, comprising two- or three-storey apartment buildings and walk-ups that lend the area a bohemian flair. A former working-class area, the Plateau has become an increasingly trendy place to live since the 1960s, as much for its indigenous charm as for the famous people who lived there—among them, poet-songwriter Leonard Cohen and playwright Michel Tremblay. Today, there are some very good restaurants and cafés on the Plateau, as well as pricey food stores catering to the urban-professional crowd that lives there. Most of the upscale stores are along St. Denis Street and Mont Royal Avenue. People on the Plateau don't drive much—it's one of the most densely populated neighbourhoods in the city, and the streets and houses are packed tightly together—so it's a good idea to walk, or to do like the locals and bicycle.

Off the Beaten Path

In the northwest part of the Plateau, the Mile-End district is not as trendy but more ethnically diverse than the rest of the area, and is home to large Jewish, Portuguese and Greek communities (along with some great Greek restaurants). Mile-End is also famous for its bagels, available in bakeries throughout the neighbourhood, which Montrealers like to boast are the best in Canada. They just might be right.

Other Montreal Attractions

Two major fun spots for Montrealers and visitors alike are the former sites of the Olympics and Expo 67. Since 1976, the **Olympic Park** area, in the east end of Montreal (get off at Viau Métro station), has been transformed into a significant amusement and environmental theme park.

Dominating the landscape is Olympic Stadium, with its characteristic tall, sloping tower. The tower was originally designed to hold up a removable canopy for the Big O, as Olympic Stadium is called, but the thing never worked; instead, the stadium was covered with a permanent roof. Guided tours of the stadium, which is home to baseball's Montreal Expos, are available—call (514) 252-8687 for information.

Nearby is the **Biodome de Montréal**, which served as the velodrome (bicycle racing stadium) in the Montreal Olympics. Now, it is an environmental exhibition venue (and one of Montreal's most popular tourist attractions), re-creating to stunning effect four North American ecosystems that visitors can walk through. Call (514) 868-3000 for information. Cross over Sherbrooke Street and you'll find the **Montreal Botanical Garden**, which features 10 exhibition greenhouses and over 30 outdoor areas for visitors to explore (including a rather macabre poisonous-plant garden). And check out the adjacent **Insectarium**, which is bound to provide icky thrills to young and old.

While the Olympic site has largely been transformed into an educational complex, the site of Expo 67 has turned itself over to pure entertainment. Located on two islands in the St. Lawrence River, the site now boasts a huge amusement park, **La Ronde** (take the Métro to Île Ste-Hélène station), which has one of the world's longest roller coasters and is a big draw for Montrealers throughout the warm months—children will probably want to spend a whole day here.

On the other island, Île de Notre-Dame, is an amusement park reserved for adults: **Casino de Montréal**. The Montreal Casino, compared with other Canadian gaming houses, is definitely upscale. It has three very good restaurants on the premises, and the view it provides of Montreal (across the river) is almost worth the trip even if you don't like to gamble. You have to be over 18 to get into the casino. If you go, however, leave your jeans, shorts or sneakers at the hotel. Some of the most sartorially renowned celebrities in Canada—no names, please—have been turned away at the door for not adhering to the casino's strict dress code. For information, call 1-800-665-2274.

Festivals and Events in Montreal

Montrealers love a good party. And throughout the year, they play host to world-class festivals that regularly draw hordes of tourists from around the globe. The most important, for many, is the **Montreal International Jazz Festival**, which runs for 11 days in late June and early July. Typically, the festival—one of the largest in its kind in the world—attracts thousands of the best jazz musicians who perform over 400 concerts; recent performers have included such greats as B.B. King, Etta James and Pat Metheny. Best of all, the majority of the concerts, staged in four downtown blocks that are closed to traffic through the festival, are completely free of charge.

Also in July, Montreal hosts the international **Juste pour Rire/Just for Laughs** festival, a bilingual celebration of the world's finest comedians, who perform at venues throughout the city (and produce fodder for countless TV comedy specials for years afterward). Finally, one of the most overlooked—at least by the rest of the country—Montreal events is the annual **World Film Festival**, held every August just before Toronto's (better-known) International Film Festival. The Montreal festival does not tend to attract the big Hollywood stars that Toronto's does, but many in the know would argue that its offering of films is far superior.

By the Way

By all accounts, explorer Jacques Cartier had a tough time of it at Quebec—and not only because of the difficult winters. In 1541, Cartier returned to France with what he thought was a treasure trove of diamonds mined from the newly discovered frontier. In fact, the would-be precious gems were worthless nuggets of quartz. The myth about Canadian diamonds, however, lives on in the name of the Quebec City promontory: Cap Diamant, or Diamond Cape in English.

Quebec City

Walking through old Quebec, you can almost feel the history in its stone walls and narrow streets. It is the political centre of the province, but Quebec City—perhaps even more than Montreal—also embodies the rich and lasting culture of *la belle province*. The only walled city left in North America, it is at once charming and sophisticated, accessible and slightly intimidating—if only for its age. A little slice of the Old World in North America, no journey to the province would be complete without a visit to Quebec City.

Quebec City Past and Present

The old town of Quebec City sits among some of the most interesting and visually stunning geography in Eastern Canada. Located on the north shore of the St. Lawrence River, where it meets the St. Charles, this is where the mighty St. Lawrence narrows to less than 1 kilometre. (The name Quebec probably comes from an Algonquian word meaning "narrowing of the river.") North of the river's edge, a sheer promontory of rock—now called Cap Diamant—rises dramatically for hundreds of feet above sea level.

Before the arrival of the Europeans, the area was long inhabited by native Canadians. Jacques Cartier was the first Frenchman to arrive, in 1535. He and his party wintered in the region, but did not put down roots. It wasn't until 1608, with the arrival of Samuel de Champlain, that a permanent settlement was established at Quebec.

Champlain's original settlement was beneath the Quebec cliffs, on a narrow strip of land north of the port. Champlain, however, worried about the indefensibility of the lower town, gradually began to move administrative and military operations to the top of the promontory; the inhabitants and Catholic religious institutions followed, although the Lower Town remained the residential and commercial hub of the city.

In the following decades, Quebec became the political centre of French North America, important both as an entry point to the Canadian interior from the Atlantic Ocean, and as a strategic installation on the St. Lawrence River. Small wonder, then, that throughout its history Quebec City has been repeatedly attacked and defended: in fact, the first British takeover of the town was in 1629, when David Kirke (later governor of Newfoundland) captured Quebec in one of his many adventures. (Under a French-British treaty, Kirke had to turn it back over to France just a few years later.)

The conquest that everyone remembers, however, took place in 1759, when British General James Wolfe and his army scaled the cliffs of Quebec and met the French forces, under General Louis Montcalm, on the nearby Plains of Abraham. The battle of the Plains of Abraham has become a paradigm of French-English animosity, and its two generals—both of whom died as a result of wounds sustained in the skirmish—have passed on into heroic immortality. In fact, this epic struggle of two superpowers, as both France and England were at the time, lasted only about 20 minutes. Wolfe's forces won, and Quebec passed into British hands, as did the rest of French North America within only a couple years.

Under British rule, Quebec City's strategic importance continued—American forces repeatedly (and unsuccessfully) tried to capture it in the late 18th century—and the British built the walls for which Quebec remains famous. The city also remained the region's political and administrative centre. In the pre-Confederation period, it (along with Toronto) shared in playing host to Canada's legislative assembly. Following Confederation, it became the capital of the province of Quebec.

Economically, Quebec's importance as a seaport and trade city gradually declined over the 19th century, losing place to Montreal. Despite repeated efforts in the 20th century to bring major industry to Quebec, its primary economic mover remains the provincial government, which employs a plurality of the metropolitan area's inhabitants. Typical suburban sprawl characterizes much of the rest of Quebec City outside the walls: most of what you will want to see and do can be found in the historic areas of Lower Town and Upper Town.

The second most important industry is tourism—not surprisingly, given Quebec City's intrinsic scenic and historical value. Many of the 17th- and 18th-century buildings have been preserved throughout the old city. In 1985, the United Nations declared old Quebec a world heritage site, and it joined the ranks of such other great international cities as Rome and Cairo.

For a time in the 1800s, British immigrants outnumbered French in Quebec. But today—after many anglophones moved elsewhere in the latter part of the 19th century—the city is almost uniformly French: about 97 per cent of the 650,000 residents in the metropolitan area are francophone. For tourists, this is not such a big problem as it might seem. Tourism is big business in Quebec City, and staff at most of the places that visitors will go are friendly and fluently bilingual. In fact, the Frenchness of Quebec City is one of its most appealing traits. By preserving not only the architecture but also the spirit of its past, Quebec City remains the capital—both literally and figuratively—of French culture in Canada.

Getting There

By air: About 20 kilometres from downtown, Jean Lesage International Airport is the main air terminal serving the Quebec City area. If you're flying from other Canadian cities on a major airline, chances are you will have to stop over in Montreal or Ottawa and transfer to a regional airline before landing at Jean Lesage. **By rail:** One of the most interesting ways to get to Quebec, VIA Rail has regularly scheduled trains from Montreal running every day of the week. The main station is the Gare du Palais, right in the old city, so train travel is a good way to dive right into the Quebec City experience. **By car:** The two major routes from Montreal (about a three-hour drive to the west) are Highway 20 and Highway 40. Highway 20 runs along the south shore of the St.

Canada by Web

Several good sites give interesting and useful information on visiting Quebec City:
http://www.otc.cuq.qc.ca/eng (*Quebec City's Tourism and Convention Bureau site*)
http://old-quebec.com

Also, check out the government of Quebec's official tourist site on the city, at:
http://www.tourisme.gouv.qc.ca/anglais/tourisme_a/villes _a/quebecv_a.html

Lawrence, while 40 traverses the north shore. If you're driving from Montreal, why not take one route to Quebec and the other route back?

Getting Around

If you drive into Quebec City, park your car as soon as you get to your hotel—and plan on leaving it there. When choosing a place to stay, pick a

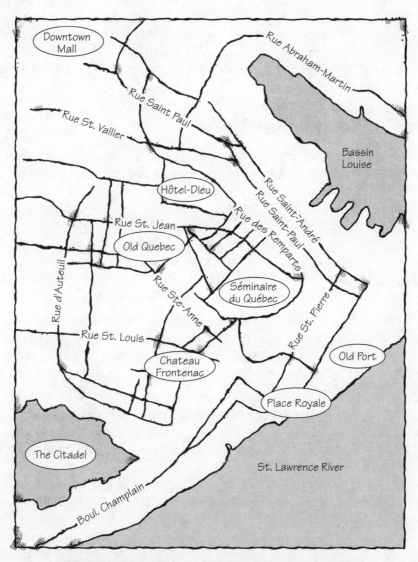

Old Quebec City with major landmarks

hotel as close to the old city as possible; there is plenty of accommodation within and around the city's walls. Beyond side trips to outlying areas, you won't need a car once you are there—most sites of interest are in the old city, and all of them are easily accessible on foot.

A Guide to Quebec City's Neighbourhoods

As it has for centuries, Quebec City can be conveniently divided into three parts: Upper Town, Lower Town, and Outside the Walls. You can easily walk the most popular areas in a day or two, but chances are you will want to linger amid the beautiful architecture and pleasant atmosphere. With the exception of the Plains of Abraham and a few other points of interest, you can safely plan on skipping the rest.

Upper Town (Haute-Ville)

The part of the old city perched high above the river, Upper Town is where visitors will find most of the sites of historic interest, as well as some of the best shopping and eating Quebec City has to offer. It is a wonderful place to (figuratively, at least) get lost, wandering narrow cobblestoned streets and soaking up the atmosphere in its numerous cafés, shops and restaurants. The main commercial strip in Upper Town is Rue St. Jean, whose clothing stores and eateries tend to cater to the tourist crowd, but which typically are less expensive than the other shops and restaurants dotted throughout this part of the city.

In and around Rue du Trésor, further to the east, there is a congeries of artists peddling their creations on the street, as well as a number of souvenir and trinket shops. The art tends to be overpriced for its value (as are the souvenirs), but the area lends Upper Town a certain bohemian, festive air.

A tour of Upper Town should begin and end at the **Place d'Armes**, a square near the cliff at St. Louis and Fort streets, which features a fountain dedicated to Franciscan monks who came to Quebec City in the early 17th century. Government buildings, including the old courthouse, surround the square, as does the structure that dominates old Quebec's landscape: the **Chateau Frontenac**. A sprawling castle perched atop the promontory, the chateau is on the site of the Chateau St. Louis, which since Champlain's day was the administrative and military headquarters of Quebec City. The current structure, built in the late

19th century, is a renowned Canadian Pacific Hotel—if you've got the money and can book well in advance, do by all means stay there for at least a night—and although it is more modern than many of the buildings in the Upper Town, it fits in seamlessly, if imposingly, with its surroundings.

If you're in the mood for a bit of a hike, walk along the Terrasse de Dufferin near the chateau, a wide boardwalk that runs along the top of the cliff and gives a spectacular view of the Lower Town and the St. Lawrence River. Further up the hill, it becomes the **Promenade des Gouverneurs**, leading to Cap Diamant and the Citadel.

Beyond its pleasant parks and squares, the list of historically significant sites in Upper Town goes on and on. North of Place d'Armes is the **Seminaire du Québec** (Quebec Seminary), the first Catholic university in North America, which visitors can tour during the summer. Call (418) 694-1020. Nearby is the **Notre-Dame-de-Quebec Basilica**, which has been destroyed by war or fire, and subsequently rebuilt, three times since the mid-17th century. According to legend, Samuel de Champlain is buried under or near the basilica (but he hasn't been found yet).

Among the many museums in the area is the **Musée de l'Amérique Francaise**, on University Street, which traces the history

Local Knowledge

A visit to Quebec City is not merely a trip through history, but also a gastronomic adventure. Some of the most consistently excellent restaurants in Canada can be found in and around the old city, as well as some of the priciest. Every visitor will find his or her favourite, to which they will return every time they go to Quebec. For me, it's **Casse-Crêpe Breton**, on the Rue St. Jean commercial strip in Upper Town. It's not fancy, but it won't break the bank either—brunch or lunch costs in the neighbourhood of five bucks. Sitting there looking out at the street life at lunchtime, munching on a delicious, made-to-order crêpe while chugging back a bowl of café au lait—well, that to me *is* Quebec City.

of French culture and settlement in North America. Call (418) 692-2843. And if you can find it, check out the **Ursuline Convent**, located on tiny Donnacona Street near Rue St-Louis. A small museum in the convent traces the history of the Ursuline nuns, who came to Quebec in 1639, and on the grounds is a small chapel, built in the mid-18th century, where General Montcalm, hero of the Plains of Abraham, is buried. Call (418) 694-0694.

Lower Town (Basse-Ville)

In some ways, the Lower Town of Quebec is merely a continuation of its neighbour on the cliff. But for some reason—perhaps the change in altitude—it seems more relaxed and in many ways more interesting than the picture-perfect austerity that is Upper Town. Lower Town is the oldest part of Quebec City, where Champlain and his followers first settled, but thanks to the recent restoration of the area, it seems almost new.

More than 20 sets of stairs, as well as a tram car, lead into Lower Town from the upper district of Old Quebec. But one of the most popular entry points is Escaliers Frontenac, leading down from Place d'Armes. From the stairs, just head south and stroll along Rue de Petit-Champlain, which meanders through an old riverside village that now features pleasant cafés and novelty shops with the works of local artisans. Immediately to the east of the stairs, towards the St. Lawrence, you will find the Notre-Dame-des-Victoires church, the oldest church (built in 1688) in Quebec City. Nearby is **Place Royale**, a bustling square that used to be home to the city's wealthy traders, as well as an important ship-building and import/export centre.

To the north, by all means visit the **Museum of Civilization**, a huge, modern limestone-and-glass building that houses an eclectic mix of interactive and interesting exhibits. With plenty for kids to do, the museum features exhibits on international and local culture (in its Objects of Civilization section), as well as a collection of Chinese artifacts gathered by Jesuit priests. Call (418) 643-2158. Nearby is the Old Port of Quebec,

Off the Beaten Path

General Montcalm, the French leader on the Plains of Abraham, is everywhere in the old city. If you're into hero worship, check out his old house, on the north side of the Lower Town on rue des Ramparts, just inside the city walls.

no longer a major seaport, but home to an exhibition centre and a farmer's market.

Beyond the Walls

Most of Quebec City outside the old part of town will prove of little interest to tourists. The exception, however, is the area immediately outside the walls. The main thoroughfare here is the Grande Allée (which turns into Rue St-Louis in old Quebec), a strip of nightclubs and restaurants that also is home to some of the city's finest hotels. Here you will find Quebec's **Parliament Buildings**, a gracious complex of white neo-Renaissance architecture that houses the provincial legislative assembly. Further up the street, away from Upper Town, hang a left and you will come to **Battlefields Park,** a huge greenbelt area that is of significant historical interest. Within its borders is Joan of Arc Park, where *O Canada* was played for the first time back in 1880. Nearby, close to the Grande Allée, is yet another monument to Montcalm; at its south end is a monument to his opponent, General Wolfe. And in the centre of the park are the **Plains of Abraham**, site of the famous battle between English and French forces in 1759. Today, the Plains are home to an interpretive centre from which guided tours are available. Call (418) 648-4071 for information.

At the south end of Battlefields Park is the **Musée de Québec**, one of the province's premier fine-arts museums, which specializes in works by Quebec-based artists. Visitors can also tour an abandoned 19th-century prison on the site. Call (418) 643-2150. At the other end of the park looms the **Citadel**, still an active military installation, which was completed by the British in 1832 as the main base of defence against attack. Weather permitting, you can see the changing of the guard on its grounds, and the Citadel also is home to a small museum dedicated to its regiment, the Royal 22nd, commonly known as the fabled "Van Doos." Call (418) 648-2815 for information.

If you have access to a car while in Quebec City, a few attractions within a couple hours' drive may strike your fancy. On Route 360 just a few kilometres east of the city is **Parc de la Chute Montmorency**, which provides a great lookout point over the St. Lawrence River and Quebec City. It is also home to the Montmorency Falls, which at 83 metres are half-again the height of Niagara Falls. In the winter, the spray from the falls freezes and forms a hill perfect for sliding and ice

By the Way

Back in the early part of the 20th century, La Malbaie (home of the Casino de Charlevoix) used to be called Murray Bay—indicative of the large American and anglo-Canadian influence in the town. In fact, for years the community was known as the summer White House—president-to-be William Howard Taft built a summer residence there in the 1890s, and wealthy merchants and various politicos from the United States and Canada followed suit. Today, local businesses have transformed many of those old summer homes into quaint inns and bed-and-breakfasts for a burgeoning tourist crowd.

climbing. Farther east on 360 is **Ste-Anne-de-Beaupré Basilica**, a shrine to the saint whom Breton sailors credited with saving their ships from wreck back in the 17th century. More than 1.5 million pilgrims from all over the world visit the basilica every year, many of them in hopes of being cured of various physical ailments.

As another side trip, spend a day driving around **Île d'Orléans**, in the middle of the St. Lawrence River east of Quebec City. Rural and charming, the island is an oasis of old orchards and farmhouses, and its centuries-old villages—St. Jean, Ste. Pétronille, St. Francois and St. Pierre—are rife with pastoral splendour.

For a little more excitement farther afield, the resort town of La Malbaie, about 150 kilometres northeast of Quebec City, boasts the **Casino de Charlevoix**, a European-style gambling establishment on the north shore of the St. Lawrence River. Call 1-800-965-5355 for information.

Festivals and Events in Quebec City

Quebec City's standing as the political centre of the province, along with its fame as a tourist attraction, has made it a hot spot for seasonal festivals. The best known is the **Winter Carnival**, held over 11 days in February, when the old city is transformed into a winter wonderland. Street performances, ice sculptures, skating and parades characterize this celebration of the cold season—and since the carnival's inception in the mid-1950s, its mascot Le Bon'homme has become synonymous with the city itself.

In the summer, Quebec City plays host to an **International Jazz Festival** every June, which can't compete with Montreal's July event in size or quality, but which is still very good. And to take advantage of the tourist season, Quebec City stages an annual **Summer Festival**. With its nightly musical performances at venues in and around the historic part of the city, the Summer Festival guarantees that the old town is hopping on just about every summer evening.

Quebec's Outdoors

Quebec is a huge province, covering a sixth of the total land mass of Canada. And yet a mere quarter of that great bulk of land is inhabited: the rest is made up of largely untouched wilderness. For outdoorsmen,

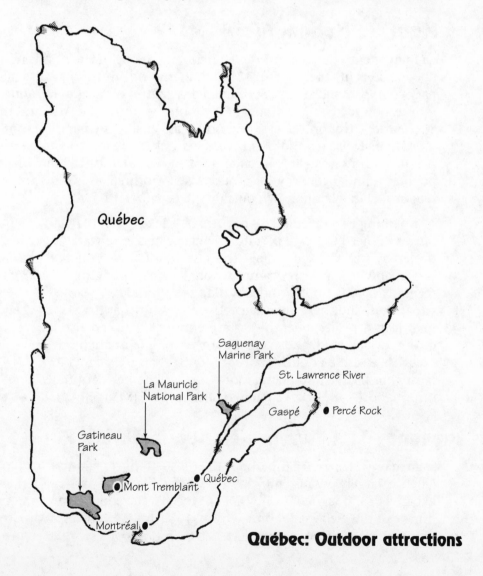

Québec

Saguenay
Marine Park

St. Lawrence River

La Mauricie
National Park

Gaspé   ● Percé Rock

Gatineau
Park

●Mont Tremblant   ● Québec

Montréal ●

Québec: Outdoor attractions

it is a paradise—and Quebec has more than 35 parks and wildlife reserves within its borders. In the summer, while most tourists concentrate on Montreal and Quebec City, the province also offers a wealth of different natural experiences, thanks to its varied geography and ecosystems (underwater included!). In winter, the weather gets bitterly cold, but that doesn't stop native Quebecers from enjoying the outdoors, especially thanks to the fine skiing dotted throughout the province. The better news is, the most popular and interesting outdoor areas are within a couple of hours' drive of either Montreal or Quebec City.

La Mauricie National Park

La Mauricie, in the heart of the Laurentians, is one of the best-kept outdoors secrets in Quebec. Only 200 kilometres northeast of Montreal, the park comprises more than 500 square kilometres of mountains and forests, bounded by the Matawin River on the north and west and the St. Maurice River on the east and northeast. Inside the park, there are more than 150 lakes and ponds, and cascading streams too numerous to count. With its accessible birch and spruce woodlands, La Mauricie is a popular summer getaway for thousands of Montrealers every year, but remains relatively unknown outside the province.

Fishing is allowed on 39 of the park's lakes from May to September, but you'll need to buy a permit. The many bodies of water are connected by well-marked portage trails, so La Mauricie is a good place to canoe, and back-country campsites are located throughout. Park staff regularly conduct both guided walking tours and canoe tours of the park's sites, and there are interpretive slide shows at the visitor's centre in St-Jean-des-Piles, near the eastern entrance. You can also see much of the park by road, and there are three well-maintained campsites. Mauricie is also a popular spot for Montreal-area residents to cross-country ski, and boasts more than 80 kilometres of trails. For information, call Parks Canada in Shawinigan: (819) 536-2638.

Saguenay-St. Lawrence National Marine Park

Saguenay-St. Lawrence is perhaps the most strangely laid-out park in Quebec, largely because most of it is underwater. The park is a T-shaped expanse of the Saguenay and St. Lawrence rivers, about 200 kilometres northeast of Quebec City on Highway 138 (this is Highway 40 between Montreal and Quebec City). Here, the twin flows of the St. Lawrence and the Saguenay, along with Atlantic tides from the Gulf of St. Lawrence, have conspired to create one of the most southerly fjords in the world, with sheer peaks lining the glistening waters of the river below.

More important, the mixing of all that water has led to great depths: the Saguenay fjord is more than 800 feet deep in some places. The result is a startling array of marine life, from fish and sea birds to the real reason most visitors go there: whales. The two main species of whale to observe are minke and beluga, ghostly white denizens of Eastern Canada's waters.

From land, the main lookout points are at Pointe-Noire lighthouse station, just across the Saguenay from the town of Tadoussac, and Cape-de-Bon-Désire, a 20-minute drive north of the river's mouth. If you want to get closer, more than 20 boat tour companies operate out of Tadoussac and surrounding communities—it can get pretty busy on the waters of the fjord in the summer. For information on the marine park, call (418) 235-4703.

There are no campsites in the marine park—not surprisingly, since its borders only go to the high-water mark. But there are a couple of private campgrounds nearby. As well, the park is largely surrounded by **Saguenay Provincial Park**, which has wilderness campsites and a well-maintained system of hiking trails winding throughout the fjord and its environs. Several towns are located within the park, so visitors should take some time to explore the unique culture and history of the Saguenay, a community unto itself within Quebec. For park information, call (418) 544-7388.

The Gatineau Hills

Located near the city of Hull, a tour of the Gatineau Hills can easily be

Canada by Web

For more information on Quebec's provincial parks, see:
http://www.mef.gouv.qc.ca/en/parc_que

wrapped into an Ottawa excursion. The rolling hills of the Gatineau are among the world's oldest, and the many (often English-speaking) communities that dot the area enhance their woodsy splendour—making it a prime getaway and resort destination for Ottawans. In Hull, two main urban attractions are the Canadian Museum of Civilization (see Ontario, Chapter 11) and the Hull Casino, yet another Quebec gambling house, located on a dramatic spit of land in an old quarry.

The Gatineau area proper starts in the town of Chelsea, a few minutes north of the capital, which also serves as the gateway to **Gatineau Park**. During the summer, you can drive through the park and stop at its many scenic views, giving dramatic vistas onto the Ottawa Valley. Check out, as well, Pink Lake, an ancient glacial lake harbouring a unique ecosystem, and the Mackenzie King Estate, a 230-hectare complex where Canada's long-serving prime minister made his eclectic home. There are several houses here, as well as formal gardens and phoney classical ruins (constructed on the PM's orders) that have come to be known as King's Follies.

Farther into the park is Meech Lake and its conference centre, where Prime Minister Brian Mulroney and provincial premiers came up with the failed Meech Lake Accord in 1987. In the winter, Gatineau Park is a favoured cross-country skiing venue. For park information, call the visitor centre, (819) 827-2020.

Percé Rock and Bonaventure Island

At the far (far) eastern tip of the Gaspé Peninsula, 800 kilometres northeast of Quebec City on Highway 132, lies one of Canada's best-known natural attractions. Synonymous with the Gulf of St. Lawrence, the **Percé Rock** looms just 85 metres off the coast; its fossil-encrusted mass is estimated to weigh more than five million tonnes.

Despite its distance from major cities, the area has become a mecca for bird-watchers: Percé and nearby Bonaventure Island are important nesting sites for many migratory sea birds—Bonaventure supports one of the largest rookeries of gannets in the world. As well, the area is increasingly popular as a whale-watching site.

Some parts of both islands are classified as federal wildlife sanctuaries and are off-limits to visitors, but much of the area is a small provincial park, **Parc de l'Île-Bonaventure-et-du-Rocher-Percé**. Park staff conduct regular nature tours on both Percé and Bonaventure

Local Knowledge

The Gaspé Peninsula (or Gaspésie) is a huge and ancient land mass that juts into the St. Lawrence, and exploring its rugged outdoors and small, hardy towns can comprise a vacation in itself. Inland on the peninsula are four large parks, including **Forillon National Park**, a wonder of limestone cliffs and beaches that culminates in Cap Gaspé, the eastern tip of the peninsula. Call (418) 368-5505. The communities of the Gaspésie, meanwhile, are like something straight out of a distant, maritime past. Most of them are located along the craggy coastline, and although the remote area was largely unsettled until the 1800s, it has a long history as a fishing and whaling centre for Norse, Portuguese and Basque mariners. Traditionally, many peninsula towns are English-speaking, although the anglophone presence in the Gaspésie has steadily declined in recent years.

Island, and there are hiking trails, picnic areas and (for those who can stand the chilly St. Lawrence waters) swimming is allowed. A ferry runs regularly during the summer to Bonaventure Island, and there is plenty of accommodation in the town of Percé. The park is open only from June to October (winters on the Gaspésie are notoriously harsh). Call (418) 782-2240 for park information.

Skiing

In Eastern Canada, at least, skiing in Quebec is as good as it gets. There are two mountain ranges winding through the southern half of the province, the Laurentians and the Appalachians. Combined with an annual average snowfall of 10 feet, that makes for some great skiing opportunities, one of the reasons that more than a million slope aficionados visit Quebec every year. And it is really the only province east of Alberta where people go for ski vacations.

There are four main skiing areas. The best known and closest to Montreal are the **Laurentians** (or the Laurentides), which actually begin in the city but run north to some of the finest skiing in Canada. The area—just 60 kilometres north of Montreal—is the most popular

Off the Beaten Path

Its distance from major cities puts it at a disadvantage, but if you're willing to go far and wide looking for great skiing, then consider a visit to **Ste-Anne-des-Monts**, way out on the northern shore of the Gaspé Peninsula, which juts into the Gulf of St. Lawrence in eastern Quebec. The area (not to be confused with Mont Sainte-Anne, near Quebec City) has some of the highest peaks in the province, and it is the only place east of the Rockies where you can heli-ski. Plus, the season is really long—often running into June.

resort centre in the province, and it is home to such well-known peaks as Mont Blanc, Mont Gabriel and Mont Tremblant (at 3,000 feet, the highest peak in the Laurentians).

South of Montreal towards the US border, the **Eastern Townships** also boast some good skiing thanks to their position in the Appalachian Mountains. The most popular resorts here are Owl's Head and Mont Orford. Around Quebec City—in fact, just 40 kilometres east—is **Mont Sainte-Anne**, the largest resort in Eastern Canada, with 50 trails and some radical slopes. Farther east, close to the town of Baie St-Paul in the **Charlevoix** region, is the appropriately named Le Massif, which boasts the highest vertical drop (2,500 feet) in the province.

The Least You Need to Know

➤ Montreal, Quebec's largest city and host to Expo 67 and the 1976 summer Olympics, is a multicultural, cosmopolitan metropolis rich in history and culture.

➤ Quebec City, where the British defeated the French on the Plains of Abraham in 1759, is the only walled city in North America, a world heritage site and a must-see for visitors to the province.

➤ Three-quarters of Quebec is wilderness, and offers outdoor activities in more than 35 parks and wildlife reserves, as well as the best skiing in Eastern Canada.

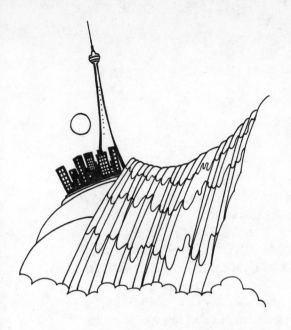

Chapter 11

Ontario

In This Chapter

➤ Getting to know Toronto, Canada's largest city

➤ Exploring Ottawa, the nation's capital

➤ Other Ontario attractions

➤ Ontario out-of-doors

Welcome to Ontario

The industrial heartland of Canada, Ontario is the country's most populous province. For visitors, the main attractions are its cities. Toronto, the nation's largest city, is one of the world's most ethnically diverse metropolitan areas, and although it remains the economic and cultural centre of English Canada, it has largely shed its conservative, somewhat arrogant past to offer travellers a wealth of culture and entertainment. Ottawa, Canada's capital, is Ontario's second tourist destination, rich in history and political power, as well as museums, galleries and festivals. But beyond its cities, Ontario—a large province where most of the population lives in its southern third—also boasts a host of outdoor activities in its parks, its many lakes and its resort areas. From the bustling streets of Toronto to the scenic splendour of the north, Ontario has it all.

Toronto

As the largest city in the country, Toronto is the economic and cultural centre of English Canada. It used to have a reputation as a waspish, stodgy place, the home of early-closing bars, conservative people and a buttoned-down business community. Not anymore. While it's still Canada's main financial and commercial centre, Toronto has managed to unshackle itself, becoming one of the world's sleekest, most culturally diverse, alluring cities. Walking around its clean, safe neighbourhoods, you will find a sometimes startling array of cultures and languages—along with top-notch theatres, shopping, and outdoor activities, happening nightspots and thousands of restaurants and cafés. No place in Canada offers as much to do. For business travellers in town for a few days or for tourists determined to get to know the place, Toronto provides a unique urban experience—and one that is changing all the time.

Toronto Past and Present

For centuries before European settlement, the area now known as Toronto—a natural harbour on the northwestern shore of Lake Ontario—served as a way station along land and canoe routes used by native Canadian Hurons. With the rise of the fur industry in the 18th century, French traders set up a small store and, around 1750, a smaller fortified post around what is now Toronto's Exhibition Grounds.

When British forces invaded in 1759, the fort was destroyed, and the area once again reverted to a mere stop for fur traders. Following the American Revolution, however, Loyalists (who still claimed allegiance to the British crown) flooded into Canada from the United States. Many settled along Lake Ontario in a region that, in 1791, became the province of Upper Canada. The province's first governor, John Graves Simcoe, laid out the town of York in 1793, and it soon became Upper Canada's capital.

Only 700 people lived in the area when war with the United States broke out in 1812. But the War of 1812 turned out, in some ways, to be the best thing that ever happened to Toronto. Twice sacked by American forces, the town became the focus of pro-colonial sentiment, and a wave of British immigration came to York following the war. By the mid-1830s, it had a fast-growing population of 9,000. In 1834, it incorporated as the city of Toronto—a Huron word believed to mean the "place of meeting."

In the coming years, that name would prove particularly apt, as Toronto became an important political and economic centre in the life of a fledgling country. Upon Canadian Confederation in 1867, Toronto was made capital of the new province of Ontario. Steamboat, railway and road-building activity boomed, and the city established itself as an industrial powerhouse, growing to more than 150,000 people by the beginning of the 20th century. As Canada expanded, Toronto became a commercial and industrial hub. By the First World War, it was next only to Montreal in size and influence, and the Second World War only enhanced its manufacturing status. By the early 1950s, its population passed one million.

By the Way

William Lyon Mackenzie was Toronto's first mayor, but he is more famous for his part in the Upper Canada Rebellions of 1837, when he led an armed revolt against the local government. Loyalists, though, easily squashed Mackenzie's movement, and the rebellion ended in confusion. After a decade-long exile in the United States, the fiery Scot returned to Toronto and resumed his journalistic and political careers. He died in 1861 in his home on Bond Street, now a historic site and museum.

Much of the reason for Toronto's cultural renaissance in recent years is its status as a mecca for immigrants from all over the world. Although before the Second World War immigrants to Toronto were primarily of British ancestry, by the 1960s Italian, Germans, Greeks and Portuguese were flooding into the area, followed in the '70s and '80s by immigrants from the West Indies, Southeast Asia and the Indian subcontinent. The influx of non-Anglo-Saxon residents has changed the face of the city. Toronto is now home to more than 80 ethnic groups, who together speak some 100 languages. By and large (and unlike many North American cities), all those different ethnic groups get along. The multicultural mix they've brought to Toronto has made it a feast of sights, sounds, smells and tastes unrivalled by most places its size.

Until recently, the metropolitan region was governed by separate local municipalities, including the City of Toronto and the suburban

Thanks to its size and power, Toronto has attracted more than its share of insulting nicknames: Muddy York, the Big Smoke and Hogtown among them. Lately, some non-Torontonians have taken to calling the city the Centre of the Universe, snidely making fun of Torontonians' alleged propensity to look down their noses at anyone from outside Toronto. Most people from the city, though, have heard all the names—and don't care. And given their justifiable civic pride, they're just as likely to take the name-calling as a compliment.

areas of North York, Scarborough and East York. In 1997, however, the provincial government, in a stated effort to cut costs and eliminate the duplication of services, amalgamated the six disparate municipalities into one so-called mega-city. The move was unpopular among many residents, especially downtown Torontonians, who see themselves as distinct from suburbanites. (If you feel like a heated political argument while in town, just mention the word "mega-city" to a local. You're bound to get a reaction.)

In the 1990s, Toronto surpassed Montreal as Canada's largest city: in fact, its population of nearly three million rivals that of Alberta. And it is arguably the country's most culturally active city—another distinction formerly held by Montreal. Toronto is the world's third-largest theatre centre (after London and New York), with major Broadway-style productions playing throughout the year. The city is home to the third most active video and film production industry in North America, boasts nearly 20,000 retail stores, and can offer gourmands the food and hospitality of its more than 4,000 cafés and restaurants. And Torontonians take pride in the fact that their city is routinely ranked by American and international magazines (such as *Forbes*) as being among the Top 10 best places in the world to live.

The Greater Toronto Area, which includes outlying cities and towns, has more than four million residents and takes up more than 5,000 square kilometres of southern Ontario. Its borders are roughly defined by the communities of Oshawa in the east, Richmond Hill to the north and, to the west, Oakville. Much of that area is taken up by typical sprawl and tracts of suburban residential development. In recent years, suburban governments began a laudable effort to develop city centres and more walkable, interesting civic areas. But for visitors, most places of interest can still be found in and around the central city.

Canada by Web

Useful World Wide Web sites, with general information on Toronto and links to other, informative pages:
ttp://www.tourism-toronto.com
http://www.boatfarm.on.ca/ontario/ontario.htm
http://www.toronto.com
http://www.city.toronto.on.ca

Getting There

By air: Toronto is served by two airports. The major one is Pearson International Airport, about a 20-minute drive (in good traffic) west of downtown, and accessible by three major highways. Its three terminals handle flights from across Canada and around the world, with more than 35 airlines offering regularly scheduled flights. From within Canada, Air Canada operates out of Terminal 2, while Terminal 3 serves Canadian Airlines, the other major domestic service. Call Transport Canada Airport Information for more details, (905) 676-3506. Toronto City Centre Airport, located on the western tip of the Toronto Islands, is just a short ferry ride from downtown. This smaller facility serves mostly corporate and private flights, but also handles regularly scheduled flights from such local area airlines as Air Ontario, Trans Capital Airlines and Grand Aviation. Call (416) 203-6942 for more information. **By Rail:** Canada's national passenger rail system, VIA Rail, serves Toronto from Union Station, located in the south part of the city's financial district near the famous Royal York Hotel, and is within walking distance of several major attractions, including SkyDome and the CN Tower. The station is also right on the public transit subway line. An effective—and often overlooked—way to get to Toronto. **By Bus:** Domestic and cross-border bus routes converge at the Toronto Bus Terminal at 610 Bay St., in the heart of the downtown near the Eaton Centre, a vast shopping complex. Call (416) 393-7311 for fares and schedules. **By Car:** Several major routes, most of them well maintained and well marked by signs, lead to Toronto. The major east-west route, which runs across the north end of the city, is Highway 401; the Queen Elizabeth Way, which locals call simply the QEW, enters Toronto from

Local Knowledge

Located south of many Canadian cities, Toronto has comparatively mild winters and warm summers, similar to the climate in the northeast United States. The months of July, August and September tend to be hottest, with temperatures in the high 20s, while in winter months the thermometer usually hovers just below freezing. The best times to visit are early summer (June to mid-July) and early autumn (mid-September to October).

the west along the shore of Lake Ontario, then turns into the Gardiner Expressway as it approaches downtown. The major north-south arteries into the city are Highway 400, which merges with Highway 401 from the northwest; Highway 404, which runs from Newmarket to the northeast and then turns into the Don Valley Parkway, giving access to downtown; and Highway 427, which runs south from Pearson International Airport to link up with the QEW. A word of warning: the highways leading into and out of Toronto are some of the busiest in the world, and few drivers observe the posted speed limit of 100 km/h. So drive with care.

Getting Around

Toronto is laid out in a grid pattern, meaning that most of the streets run either north-south or east-west. If you're driving (and armed with a decent road map), finding your way through Toronto should prove easy. There are also a large number of taxi companies serving the area, which provide usually dependable (but sometimes kind of frightening) transportation in and around the city.

But the best way to experience Toronto is to leave the car at home. For one thing, there's the traffic: on weekdays, at any given time, streets in downtown Toronto are often jammed with cars and trucks. And during rush hours (from 7 to 9 a.m. and from about 4 to 7 p.m.), getting around in a vehicle can be downright tedious.

One of the joys of Toronto is that it is a city made up of neighbourhoods most of which can be easily walked from one end to the other.

Local Knowledge

Since the mid-1990s, Toronto area telephone numbers have been designated by two area codes, 416 and 905. Roughly, numbers in the central city have the 416 code; the outlying areas to the north, west and east carry the 905 code. For most calls between the two codes, long-distance charges do not apply.

Getting to those areas without a car is made easy by a clean, safe and efficient public transit system, operated by the Toronto Transit Commission (locals simply call the system the TTC). It's an interconnecting pattern of subway, bus and streetcar services that comprise more than 6,000 kilometres of routes serving just about every corner of Metro Toronto. And it's fairly cheap: a couple bucks for a one-way adult fare, and even less when you take advantage of full-day passes and family deals. Small wonder that Toronto has the second-highest public transit ridership in North America. If you're visiting, do as the natives do, and take advantage of it.

Exploring Toronto's Neighbourhoods

If you really want to get the most out of a visit to Toronto, get to know its neighbourhoods. Together, they offer a rich panoply of sights and sounds—not to mention tastes—and they reflect the ethnic flair that makes Toronto so distinct. All of them are reachable by public transit, and they're easy to explore on foot. For shopping, restaurants, entertainment and night life, each offers a unique experience to be savoured.

Yorkville

Back in the 1960s and early 1970s, Yorkville (just north of Bloor and west of Yonge streets, near the Bay subway stop) was *the* hangout for hippie culture in Toronto, attracting musicians, artists and just plain druggies—the flower children of their day—from across Canada and the United States. Among other notables who came to Yorkville because it used to be a cheap place to live, rocker Neil Young and folk artist Joni

Local Knowledge

If Toronto has a "main street," it's Yonge, which locals will never tire of telling you is the longest road in the world, running 1896.2 kilometres north from the shore of Lake Ontario. Yonge Street is also a good landmark to use while walking around downtown, since a subway line runs under it and it divides Toronto into east and west districts. Besides some fine theatres, restaurants and the **Eaton Centre**—a vast indoor shopping complex with more than 300 stores—Yonge Street itself has little to offer tourists, beyond strip joints, X-rated bookstores, vagrants and record shops. But take a look around anyway: it's the closest thing Toronto has to New York's Times Square.

Mitchell started out here in the '60s, before moving on to greater things.

Times have changed. And although Yorkville is still a place to find the hip and the trendy, its denizens are more likely to be wearing Armani and Gucci than bell-bottoms and love beads. Upscale and maybe a little snooty, the area offers dozens of shops and restaurants, laid out in cozy blocks of former row houses and tenement buildings, or in the rambling Hazelton Lanes shopping mall, which marks the western edge of Yorkville along Avenue Road. Clothing stores are the order of the day here, with garments from the hip and happening to the ultra-chic and haute couture. All of them are fairly pricey.

The same could be said for the restaurants, which offer top-notch cuisines from France, Switzerland, South America and the Far East. At night, Yorkville is a favourite place for a stroll—but not a quiet one, especially in the summer, when the area's nightclubs are packed to the doors with gawkers, hangers-on and people who just want to see and be seen. If you like fashionable, Yorkville's your place.

Nearby, just a few minutes' walk along Bloor Street, the **Royal Ontario Museum** (or ROM, for short) offers some less materialistic pleasures. Canada's largest public museum, the ROM (near the Museum subway stop) is home to a spectacular dinosaur exhibit, a weird and sometimes frightening mock bat cave, and one of the most extensive

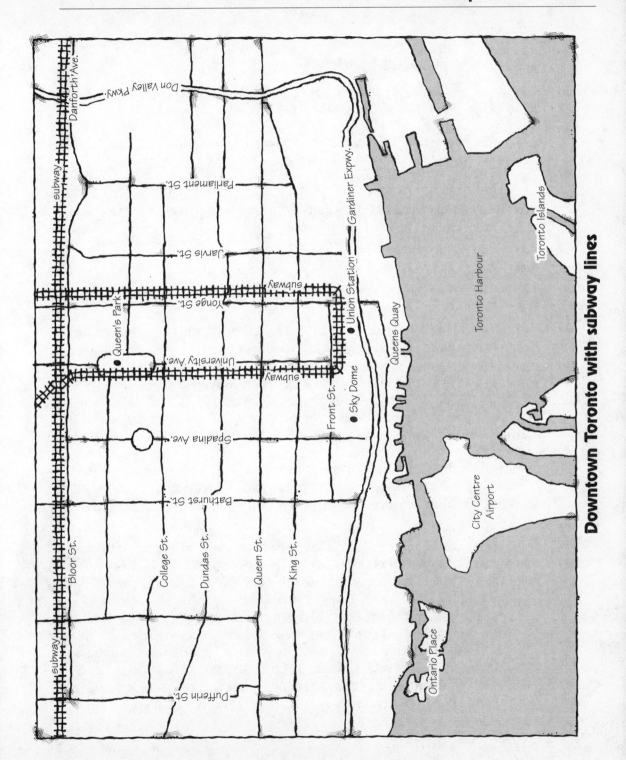

Downtown Toronto with subway lines

Canada by Web

Before visiting the Royal Ontario Museum, check out its excellent World Wide Web site, which features a virtual tour.
http://www.rom.on.ca

collections of ancient Chinese art and artifacts in the Western world. Open seven days a week, the ROM also offers tours, workshops and lectures, as well as special exhibitions. For more information, call (416) 586-5551.

Chinatown

There are actually a number of Chinatowns in Toronto—at least three downtown and several more scattered throughout the suburban area. But the best-known and easiest to get to runs along Dundas Street west of University, then north along Spadina Avenue to College Street. (By TTC, walk or take a streetcar west from the St. Patrick station, or take a streetcar south from Spadina station.) Every day of the week, the streets of Chinatown are alive with the hustle and bustle of one of the largest Chinese communities in North America. And if you block out the sight of the CN Tower to the south, you might actually pretend you are standing in a street in Hong Kong, complete with street vendors, Chinese grocers and the sing-song of Cantonese in the air.

While there is some shopping in Chinatown, what tourists will really want to do here is eat. One of the best places in Toronto to get a quick, nutritious and cheap lunch—check out the so-called noodle houses for the best deals—Chinatown is also home to upscale restaurants that take traditional East Asian cuisine to new heights. On weekend mornings, dozens of establishments serve up dim sum, a tasty and varied smorgasbord of dumplings, stewed meats and sweet desserts that is part brunch, part performance art, as harried-looking wait staff push around carts stuffed with savoury delights. Usually, it's a good bargain to boot—much more economical than brunch at most hotels or North American-style eateries. There is also a substantial Vietnamese element

Local Knowledge

When eating in Chinatown, you will be presented with an array of cuisines. The bulk of Chinatown fare is *Cantonese*, a cuisine that brought North Americans the familiar tastes of sweet-and-sour sauce and egg rolls, but also emphasizes savoury noodle dishes and fresh seafood prepared with minimal seasoning. If you go to a *Szechuan* (or *Sichuan*) restaurant, be prepared for the heat that this spicy, meat-heavy cuisine specializes in. *Vietnamese* cuisine, by contrast, tends to offer more subtle flavours, with delicate soups, meats and salads.

in Chinatown, reflected in the burgeoning (and very good) restaurants that have popped up there since the 1970s.

If you're in the mood for food for the soul, nearby you will find the **Art Gallery of Ontario** (on Dundas west of University Avenue, on the east edge of Chinatown). Known locally as the AGO, Toronto's largest gallery has on display more than 18,000 works of art, including an important collection of Henry Moore sculptures and many works from the Group of Seven. Admission to the permanent collection is pay what you can; temporary exhibitions are specially ticketed. For more information, call (416) 979-6648.

The Danforth

With its active Greek community, Danforth Avenue between the thoroughfares of Broadview and Pape (by subway, get off at Broadview, Chester or Pape stations) brings flavours of the Mediterranean to Toronto. Noticeably more downscale than Yorkville or Queen Street West, but frequented more by Toronto's literati and a film producer or two, the Danforth is a place for locals who still make it a habit in summer months to put on their Sunday best and take a leisurely stroll along the street. Most of the eateries offer traditional Greek fare, although in recent years pizza parlours, pubs, nouveau Greek establishments and a bit of haute cuisine have entered the fray.

Off the Beaten Path

Just west of Spadina Avenue, north of Dundas, is one of the funkiest little areas in the city. **Kensington Market** is an eclectic neighbourhood of outdoor markets, butchers, green grocers, cheese shops and second-hand clothing stores, with just enough dilapidation and down-scale bonhomie to make it a fave spot for the young and trendy. Sometimes the bargains don't bear up to close scrutiny, but from the huge selection of organic foods to the top-notch bakeries and coffee houses, Kensington epitomizes Toronto's ethno-cultural mix.

Shopping here is haphazard, consisting primarily of run-of-the-mill clothing stores and small artisans shops, but the pace is different: more leisurely, less concerned with appearances than other areas. And few Toronto pleasures rival sitting on the patio of a Danforth restaurant on a summer day, sipping a cold beer or a piney retsina and watching the world go by.

Queen Street West

The heart of all that's trendy in Toronto can be found on Queen Street West, an area that was once merely bohemian and has now become fashionable. Running west from University Avenue (by subway, walk or take a streetcar from Osgoode station), the Queen West area is home to a few upscale restaurants, bars and hip fashion boutiques. The emphasis here is on *youth* and the music scene, since Queen West is probably the most active area in the city for live bands. In recent years, the area has attracted some chain restaurants and mall-type clothing stores (much to the chagrin of locals), but it's still trendy enough that you can feel out of place if you're not wearing black.

South of Queen, on the east-west streets of Richmond and Adelaide, a string of nightclubs caters to the party crowd. The bars seem to come and go with each passing year, and they tend to attract a younger, under-40 crowd of upwardly mobile professionals and sometimes-rowdy university students. If this is your scene, be prepared to wait—most of the nightclubs on Richmond and Adelaide also feature long lineups.

Local Knowledge

Toronto is famous for being the safest city of its size in North America. But that doesn't mean visitors should not take the same common-sense precautions they would anywhere else. There *are* parts of the city where tourists, especially when alone, would probably prefer not to find themselves stranded. At night, the area east of Yonge, particularly Church and Jarvis streets and especially on weekends, are havens for prostitution. Further east, the area between Parliament and River streets south of Gerrard is probably best avoided. If you're unsure of where you're going, just ask: most Torontonians will be happy to help out.

The Theatre District

To call the King Street West area (off University to Peter Street, take the subway to St. Andrews station) the Theatre District is a bit of a misnomer, since Toronto's very active theatre industry is spread out throughout the city. Still, the King West area is home to the **Princess of Wales** and other theatres, which mount such Broadway plays as *Miss Saigon*, *Les Miserables* and, more recently, *Rent*.

Here you will also find **Roy Thomson Hall**, home to the Toronto Symphony Orchestra and a prime venue for classical, dance and the occasional pop performance. As well, the **Second City** comedy revue—a venerable Toronto institution, and every bit as popular as its Chicago and Detroit counterparts—relocated to the Theatre District in late 1997.

On King and Front streets, just east of Yonge, are the **St. Lawrence Centre for the Arts**, the **O'Keefe Centre** and the **Canadian Opera Company**, home to fine theatre and opera. And just a five-minute walk north stand the elegantly restored **Elgin and Winter Garden** and **Pantages** theatres, sites of vaudeville and silent movies from 1913 and 1928. With the advent of talking pictures in the 1920s, the Winter Garden became Toronto's premier movie palace, opening *Gone with the Wind* and *The Wizard of Oz*—it's the last operating double-decker theatre in the world. Restored using thousands of pounds of raw bread dough to clean 28 layers of paint from its original hand-painted walls, the Winter

149

Garden is a splendid historic site to tour, even for those tepid about the-atre. Call (416) 314-2871 for tour tickets. Just up the street at **Massey Hall**, an historic concert hall with world-renowned acoustics, you'll find pop, jazz and blues—Charlie Parker, B.B. King and Charlie Musselwhite have all played there.

Within easy walking distance to the south are two of Toronto's best-known attractions, the **CN Tower** and **SkyDome**. At a height of 533 metres, the CN Tower is the tallest free-standing structure in the world, and dominates the Toronto skyline. Visitors can take a glass-walled elevator up to the tower's observation deck, providing an unpar-alleled view of the city. At $12 per adult, the elevator ride is vastly overpriced, but you should do it at least once in a lifetime. The Tower also features a simulator theatre, outdoor mini-golf, a video arcade, a laser-tag arena, and a nightclub, as well as a revolving restaurant (what would the world's tallest building be without one?). Call (416) 360-8500 for more information.

SkyDome is the home of the two-time world champion Toronto Blue Jays and to the Canadian Football League's Toronto Argonauts. If the Jays are having a good year, it's often hard to get a ticket on short notice, so make sure you purchase them ahead of time. On the other hand, even if the Argos are having a good year, you'll likely be able to buy good seats at the gate for a football game: Torontonians are notori-ous for not paying much attention to their CFL team. Tours of SkyDome are also available.

Little Italy (College Street West)

The street signs along College Street west of Bathurst (take a streetcar west from Queen's Park station, or the bus south from Bathurst station) will tell you that you are in Little Italy, where historically Toronto's large Italian population had its cultural focus, but the area might just as well be called "Little Portugal" or "Little Queen Street West." Much of the ethnic element here is indeed Portuguese, with eateries offering spicy roast chicken and other delights. By day, College Street West (you'll rarely hear natives call it Little Italy) is a residential-commercial area with little to distinguish it. But when the sun sets, it comes alive.

In the 1990s, College West became one of Toronto's trendiest nightspot areas, although it's not as appearance-oriented as Queen

Street West. The restaurants, nightclubs and billiard parlours cater to a slightly older, more casual crowd of urban professionals who prefer conversation to loud music. You'll find literati there, and some of the best espresso in the city. And compared with Yorkville, some of the restaurants and bars offer real bargains for a fun night out. It gets a little more crowded with every passing year, but for now College West remains one of Toronto's best kept secrets.

Harbourfront and the Toronto Islands

Toronto in the 1970s and 1980s began a waterfront beautification program, turning what used to be docks and warehouses into a tourist and residential area taking advantage of Lake Ontario's natural beauty. The result is **Harbourfront**, a mall and outdoor shopping area that runs along Queen's Quay, south of the Gardiner Expressway (take the Harbourfront RT streetcar from Union Station subway stop). It's a favourite spot for a pleasant stroll on summer days, thanks to a wide boardwalk that runs along the lakeshore, and at night there are dramatic productions, occasional concerts and special events. There is also a large shopping complex, the **Queen's Quay Terminal**, which offers upscale goods at what some would call exorbitant prices. It is also home to Toronto's **Premier Dance Theatre,** which features performances by avant-garde and classical dance troupes from across Canada. Call (416) 973-4000.

From here you can get to the **Toronto Islands**, which sit in quaint splendour just an eight-minute ferry ride away from the foot of Bay Street. The islands are perhaps the most tranquil setting in all of Toronto—thanks largely to the fact that there aren't any cars here. By foot or on a bike (available for rental), exploring the islands is a great way to spend the day, enjoying the view of Toronto's skyline at sunset, meandering through the park setting or having a picnic.

For the kids, Centre Island's amusement park has a turn-of-the-century Ontario theme, with 30-plus rides and attractions including a miniature train and pony rides. The rides cost about $2 each, but otherwise admission to the park, open from May to September, is free.

Ward's Island has secluded sun bathing and an eccentric mélange of micro-sized, beguiling islander homes and reposeful streets wonderful for meandering through on an afternoon.

Off the Beaten Path

It's a bit of a hike from downtown, but if you've got time and a penchant for quaint shops, mid- to upscale restaurants and a more sedate nightlife, check out the **Beaches** area (Queen Street east of Woodbine; take streetcar east from Queen station). Once a largely residential and resort district, the area now attracts visitors and natives who want to get away from the hectic pace of the city. Ironically, the Beaches in summer (the best time to go) can get downright crowded. Its lakeside boardwalk is usually jammed with strollers and roller-bladers during the day, and the nightclubs and restaurants flow over with customers in the evenings. More conservative than Queen Street West and more laid-back, the Beaches make for a nice day-long summer outing.

Other Toronto Attractions

Kids and adults alike will find something fun to do at **Ontario Place**, a 96-acre park built on three man-made islands in Lake Ontario (by TTC, take streetcar south from Bathurst station). With gorgeous landscaping and intriguing little nooks and crannies—not to mention more than a few Canadian geese—Ontario Place has areas for picnicking, an IMAX theatre, a vast children's playground, pedal-boats for rent, and myriad bars and restaurants. It's a great place to watch Canada Day fireworks, and also boasts a large, open-air concert venue with major rock and pop acts throughout the non-winter months. Open seven days a week from May to September; call (416) 314-9900 for information.

Further north, the **Ontario Science Centre** (at Don Mills and Eglinton; take bus north from Pape subway station, or east from Eglinton station) is a vast and architecturally futuristic building that features more than 800 hands-on exhibits on everything from electrical conductivity (a hair-raising experience) to the inner workings of computers. At less than $8 for adults and $3 for kids, it's an entertaining bargain. Open year-round; call (416) 429-4100 for information.

For sports fans, the **Hockey Hall of Fame** (a short walk to the east of Union Station) has the world's largest collection of hockey memorabilia and displays. Once banished to the far reaches of the Canadian National Exhibition grounds in the city's west end, the Hall of Fame recently moved into its slick new venue in BCE Place—and put itself back in the limelight. A must-see for hockey afficionados. Open year-round; call (416) 360-7735 for information.

It might seem kind of wacky—a museum devoted to footwear—but the **Bata Shoe Museum** (across Bloor Street from St. George subway station) is surprisingly entertaining and informative. The building, designed by famed architect Raymond Moriyama, is unique in itself, and inside you'll find such oddities as Elvis Presley's loafers and sandals from ancient Egypt, as well as an extensive collection of native American footwear. Open year-round; call (416) 979-7799 for information.

If you've got time and weather permitting, plan on spending a day at the **Metro Toronto Zoo** (Meadowvale Road north of Highway 401), which spreads out over 710 acres in east Metro and is home to more than 5,000 animals from all over the world. The zoo is laid out into six geographic regions, all interconnected by scenic pathways, and dotted with pavilions showing off the plants and flowers indigenous to the animals' habitat. Open year-round, but hours vary; call (416) 392-5900 for information.

If you're walking in the Spadina or Dupont areas, you are bound to notice a large castle looming over midtown Toronto like a spectre from a different age. **Casa Loma** (at the north end of Spadina Road, at Davenport) is one of the quirks of Toronto history, built between 1911 and 1914 by industrialist, financier and military officer Sir Henry Pellatt. Behind its imposing stone facade are 98 rooms (many still elegantly furnished), an 800-foot tunnel, a glorious stable area and a few secret passages to explore. The castle is now popular for tourists and for Toronto's burgeoning film industry: the movies *Maximum Risk*, *Extreme Measures* and *Johnny Mnemonic* were filmed in part in Casa Loma's hallowed halls. Open year-round; call (416) 923-1171.

Events and Festivals in Toronto

There's always something happening in Canada's biggest city, but a few annual events have become Toronto traditions. **Caribana** is the wildest party of the summer. Held in early August, the celebration of Caribbean culture and dance—including a glittering parade, elaborate costumes

Out of the Way

North of the city, about a half-hour drive from Toronto off Highway 400, **Paramount Canada's Wonderland** is a gigantic theme park, with over 125 rides and attractions, along with a live concert venue and a water playground. Open May to October; call (905) 832-7000. A little further to the west is the **McMichael Canadian Art Collection**, featuring the works of the renowned Group of Seven set amidst the picturesque woodlands near the town of Kleinburg. Open year round, but hours vary; call (905) 893-1121 for information.

and steel bands—regularly draws almost a million people to the city every year.

Just a little more staid is the **Canadian National Exhibition**, or the Ex, as it's known to Torontonians. Technically, it's an agricultural fair (and one of the world's oldest and longest), but over the past 110 years the Ex has become as much a carnival as a place to show off livestock. Exhibits, special events and concerts round out the Ex experience, held from late August through Labour Day in the Exhibition Grounds in the city's west end.

In early September, the stars come out to attend the **Toronto International Film Festival**, considered by the glitterati to be one of the most important movie-fests in the world, where you can literally watch hundreds of hours of celluloid entertainment (if you've got the stamina). Call (416) 968-3456 for listings/tickets.

A more down-home experience is offered by the **Royal Agricultural Winter Fair**, held every November at the Exhibition grounds. It is home to the International Royal Horse Show, livestock and agricultural competitions—and the obligatory sculptures in butter. Call (416) 345-1839 for information.

Ottawa, a Capital Excursion

Beyond Toronto, Ontario offers travellers a wealth of other unique urban experiences. Leading the pack is Ottawa, national capital of

Canada and one of the country's most popular tourist destinations. Along with Hull—its Quebec neighbour across the Ottawa River—the city boasts a wealth of historical attractions amid stately Parliament Buildings and world-renowned galleries, theatres and museums.

Ottawa Past and Present

Born of trees and water, Ottawa is nestled amid a geographically varied area of woodlands, rivers and hills. Like many other communities in the valley formed by the Ottawa River, the area had long been settled by Algonquian native Canadians before the arrival of Europeans, for whom the river and its tributaries formed the most convenient access to the Canadian interior from the St. Lawrence River. From the 1600s to the 1800s, the valley was the main thoroughfare for fur traders operating out of Montreal. By the early 19th century, Hull (then called Wrightsville) had established itself as an agricultural community, giving rise to a burgeoning timber trade, but the land on the other side of the Ottawa River remained largely unsettled.

That changed in 1826 with the arrival of Lieutenant-Colonel John By and his band of Royal Engineers. By was the officer in charge of the construction of the Rideau Canal, a 200-kilometre-long waterway linking the Ottawa River with Lake Ontario at Kingston, and he set up a

Local Knowledge

Built amid the national-security anxiety caused by the War of 1812 with the United States, the Rideau Canal was an impressive feat of engineering and plain hard work. Over five summers, more than 2,000 men—many of them Irish labourers—sweated it out in the muddy, mosquito-infested bogs and forests of the Ottawa Valley. (In fact, many of them died of malaria.) But the military applications of the canal were never tested, and the Rideau, even though some commercial operations ferried passengers and cargo along it during the 19th century, never made money. Today, it is used almost exclusively by pleasure-boaters in the summer, and in winter is best known as one of the world's largest skating rinks.

base camp at the mouths of the Rideau and Gatineau rivers. Within a year (the canal was completed in 1832), a thriving community of tradesmen, labourers and engineers had sprung up on the site of Bytown, as the canal-builder's HQ came to be known.

For much of the rest of the century, timber was king in the Ottawa area. From the 1830s on, the lumber trade to Great Britain was the main focus of economic activity in Bytown, which had all the hurly-burly character (and lack of sophistication) of frontier towns in the American West. By 1860, thanks to the natural water-power surrounding it, Ottawa (the city got its new name in 1855) was one of the largest timber-milling centres in the world.

In the meantime, a new industry had come to the remote town: government. Although construction of the Rideau Canal and the booming lumber operations had made Ottawa a force in the national economy, by mid-century it still was nowhere near as powerful as Quebec, Montreal or Toronto. And yet, in a move that no doubt shocked just about everybody, Queen Victoria declared in 1857 that, henceforth, the muddy, rugged outpost would be the permanent capital of the Province of Canada. (Before that, the legislature had alternated between Quebec City and Toronto every four years.) At Confederation in 1867, Ottawa became the capital of the Dominion of Canada.

Since then, Ottawa has done pretty well by being the seat of national government—if not, perhaps, in terms of popularity elsewhere, then at least in terms of urban beautification and development. Today, with its parks and freely accessible public spaces, Ottawa is a cosmopolitan city of about 300,000 people; along with Hull and surrounding communities, the national capital region lays claim to being the fourth-largest urban area in the country, with a population topping one million. For the tourist, most areas of interest lie within the city of Ottawa's downtown core, which is dominated by the Parliament Buildings and other government edifices, and is also home to a thriving commercial district of office towers, shops and restaurants.

Despite years of civil-service cutbacks and spending reductions at the federal level, government is still the No. 1 employer in the area, although in recent years the high-tech industry has boomed, earning Ottawa the nickname "Silicon Valley North." The second-largest employer in Ottawa is, not surprisingly, tourism—thanks to the four million or so visitors who visit the capital every year.

By the Way

How did the remote town of Ottawa end up as Canada's capital? When choosing a home for a permanent capital, advisers to Queen Victoria recommended Ottawa because it would offend nobody. Rivalries between Toronto and Quebec ran so high, they warned, that selection of either could lead to political instability (if not outright revolt) in the losing city. So Ottawa became capital more or less by default—a decision fully in keeping with that most Canadian of attributes, compromise.

What they find there is a pristine little city stuck just about in the middle of nowhere.

Getting There

By air: Ottawa's Macdonald Cartier International Airport is one of the busiest air terminals in Canada. A main stop in the Ottawa-Montreal-Toronto corridor, the airport lies in the southern end of the capital region, but is only a 20-minute cab ride from downtown Ottawa. The municipal public transit system also serves the airport, as do shuttle buses operated by the major downtown hotels. Call (613) 998-1427 for information. **By rail:** VIA Rail runs regular trains to Ottawa, and the station is on Tremblay Ave. near downtown. **By car:** From the east, Highway 417 is the major route between Montreal and Ottawa, and from the west Highway 7 is the most direct route from Toronto (although most commuters will take Highway 401 from Toronto and then up highways 16 or 31 north to Ottawa). From Quebec, Highway 148 enters Ottawa from the northeast, and from northern Ontario Highway 17 approaches the capital from the northwest. Roadways into the capital are clearly marked: just follow the maple leaf signs.

Getting Around Ottawa

If you stay downtown (as you should), the most efficient and enjoyable way to see the city is by foot. From the Parliament Buildings to

Confederation Square to By Ward Market is an easily walkable distance; you can even make it across the bridge to Hull on foot (if you're feeling energetic and the weather is amenable). On the other hand, public transportation in the Ottawa-Hull region can be confusing, with a different bus company serving each side of the river. (Passengers can transfer between OC Transpo, serving Ottawa-Carleton, and the STO, serving the Quebec side of the Ottawa River, along Rideau and Wellington streets in Ottawa).

Taxis are available either at designated stands in the downtown area or by ordering ahead, but they tend to be on the expensive side. If you rent a car or take your own vehicle (as many tourists do), buy a good road map of the area—there are plenty of one-way streets and complex intersections (locals have taken to calling Confederation Square, where Wellington, Sparks and Elgin streets meet, "Confusion Square"). And traffic can be, well, a nightmare, especially during rush hours. So if you can manage it, plan on walking.

Exploring Ottawa's Neighbourhoods

Thanks largely to the presence of the federal government and to a municipal structure that has carefully preserved and maintained its historical and political sites, the capital is home to the architecturally significant (and well-maintained) public institutions in the country. Not as overwhelming as Toronto nor as bustling as Montreal or Vancouver, Ottawa offers historically or culturally minded tourists—not to mention political junkies—plenty to do and see.

Parliament Hill

Granted, it is not really a neighbourhood per se, but Parliament Hill might just as well be. It is the natural place for any tour of Ottawa to begin, and it is surrounded by some of the city's prime attractions.

Canada by Web

Some good general sites on Ottawa:
http://www.city.ottawa.on.ca
http://www.ottawakiosk.com
http://www.ottawa.com

Located north of Wellington Street between Bank and Elgin, and bounded on the north by the gently curving Ottawa River, this is where it all happens in Canadian federal politics. Dominating the landscape are the **Parliament Buildings.** At the moment, the three Gothic stone buildings—West Block, Centre Block and East Block—that comprise Canada's Parliament don't look like much: their stone

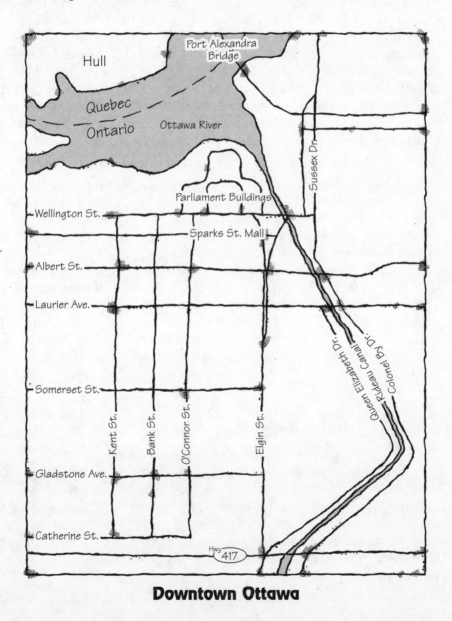

Downtown Ottawa

facades are currently undergoing extensive structural renovations, and they are likely to be covered in their latticework of scaffolding until beyond the year 2000. But there is a wealth of history and fascination within the buildings' walls.

The grounds of Parliament Hill are always open, and guided tours of the **Centre Block**— dominated by the 90-metre-tall **Peace Tower** on its southern face—are available every day of the year except Christmas, New Year's Day and Canada Day. The Tower itself is one of the main attractions. Completed in 1927 (five years after the completion of the then-new Centre Block, the original building having been largely destroyed by fire in 1916), the tower has 63 massive bells in its carillon—which can be heard across the city and into Quebec when they play on a clear day. The tower is also home to the **Memorial Chamber**, a tribute to Canadians who died at war.

The main draw of Centre Block, however, is the **House of Commons**, where the seats of power in Canada plump themselves—the room, dominated by the colour green, houses more than 300 seats for members of Parliament, along with a public gallery and a press area. (Members of the public can arrange to view the House in session by contacting their local MP well before their visit to Ottawa.) Less evocative, perhaps, is the **Red Chamber**, where the Senate sits. But for architectural splendour, few buildings in Ottawa can rival the **Parliamentary Library**. The only area of Centre Block to escape the 1916 fire relatively unscathed (although it did suffer extensive damage to its books and other holdings in a 1950s blaze), the library remains a wonder of detail in its wood carvings, furnishings, and in-the-round style.

Local Knowledge

When the Parliament Buildings were originally commissioned back in the 1850s, the original budget for their construction was just over $1 million. But by the time they were completed—after a series of labour strikes, numerous cost overruns and a Royal Commission to figure out what was going wrong—the final price tag came in at more than $3 million. Government over-spending, it seems, is hardly a modern phenomenon.

The West Block of Parliament is closed to the public, but the **East Block**—the only building on the Hill that survives extant from pre-Confederation days, and substantially restored in the early 1980s—is open for guided tours daily during the summer months. Inside, visitors will find four rooms of historic importance: the Governor General's Office, over the main west entrance, occupied by Canada's heads of state until the late 1920s; the office of Sir John A. Macdonald, Canada's first prime minister; another room commonly called the Prime Minister's Office, restored to its 19th-century appearance and not occupied by a PM since Pierre Trudeau in 1976; and the Privy Council Chamber, where until the late 1970s every Cabinet met to make the *real* decisions about the country.

If you skip the guided tours, the grounds of Parliament Hill still offer plenty of pomp and circumstance. One such spectacle is the **Changing of the Guard**, a 30-minute ceremony performed at 10 a.m. every day during the summer months (weather permitting) by scarlet-clad members of the Governor General's Foot Guards and the Canadian Grenadier Guards—complete with military music. Afterward, take in the historically evocative statuary that dot the Parliament Hill grounds, including likenesses of famous prime ministers—Sir John A., John Diefenbaker, William Lyon Mackenzie King, Sir Wilfrid Laurier—and an impressive (and famous) statue of Queen Elizabeth II on horseback.

Off the Beaten Path

Any tour of the Parliament Hill grounds would be incomplete without a visit to two of the area's quirkier sites. In the northwest corner, just before you get to the steep escarpment down to the Ottawa River, is a little enclave that serves as a home base to the perhaps hundreds of cats that live in and around Parliament. Maintained by a local citizen, it is little more than a hut and a scattering of food dishes—along with dozens of cats, who recline in both the summer heat and the chill of winter. To the east, and just above the round Parliament Library, is the so-called Fire Bell—a cracked remnant of the original Centre Block that fell to the ground when the building's main tower collapsed in the fire of 1916.

(The horse, by the way, was Canadian-born.) In front of the Peace Tower, too, is the **Centennial Flame**, an ever-burning tribute installed on the Hill in 1967 as part of Confederation celebrations.

Just east and down the escarpment from Parliament Hill, on the west side of the Rideau Canal near the locks where it meets the Ottawa River, is the **Bytown Museum**, one of the region's smallest and most charming museums. Laid out more like an old curiosity shop than a museum, the Bytown features slices of daily life in Ottawa from the early 19th century, with a fine array of period costumes, toys and furniture, as well as lots of information on Colonel By. Call (613) 234-4570 for information.

Up the hill to Wellington Street and just east of the Rideau is a well-known Ottawa landmark, the **Chateau Laurier Hotel**, a magnificent railway hotel renowned for its large, ornate front lobby. I've always found the lobby somewhat overrated, but do check it out even if you can't afford to stay at the Laurier—it has become something of a common meeting place for tourists, and it's a pleasant place for a quiet sit-down during a long day of walking. Nearby is the **Canadian Museum of Contemporary Photography**, built underground in an old tunnel that used to connect the Chateau Laurier to a nearby rail station. Call (613) 990-8257 for information.

Across Wellington Street, where it intersects with Elgin and Sparks streets, is **Confederation Square**, whose main feature (besides being a common meeting-place for visitors) is the National War Memorial. The large statue was erected in 1932 to honour Canadians killed in action during the First World War. Immediately to the south is the **National Arts Centre**, the most important theatre in the Ottawa area, and one of the most important in the country. Home to a fine orchestra and an impressive physical structure in itself, the NAC regularly features touring shows and troupes, both English and French, from across Canada. Call (613) 947-7000 for show times and tickets. To the south, just on the other side of the Mackenzie King Bridge from the NAC, is **Confederation Park**, home to summer concerts and all-around lazing about in downtown Ottawa during the warmer months.

Directly south of Parliament Hill, running east-west between Elgin and Bank streets, is the **Sparks Street Mall**, a pedestrian-only boulevard lined with office towers, but also home to many stores and restaurants. In the summertime, in particular, the mall can be a crowded venue for strollers, and it is one of the most active commercial and dining areas in the city. But one gets the impression that its business owners were hit hard by the recession of the early 1990s, and the area is beginning to look, well, a little decrepit. Yet if you're walking through downtown Ottawa, it is a pleasant enough refuge from traffic.

The Byward Market Area

One of the oldest parts of town, which sprang up during the heady pioneer days of Bytown back in the late 1820s, is the Byward Market. And in a city that is too often a bit stodgy, the market area is also among Ottawa's liveliest. Located in the shadow of Parliament Hill, Byward runs west of Sussex Drive and north of Rideau Street, and parts of it (marked with historical signs) are still home to local produce growers and vendors, peddling fresh fruits and vegetables as they have done for more than a century. But the Byward has become a fashionable district in itself: its old rowhouse-style buildings (some of the oldest in Ottawa) now house trendy restaurants, funky clothing stores and (more recently) quite a few nicknack stores aimed at spendthrift tourists. Year-round, too, the area is a favourite for nightclubbers of all sorts, with down-scale clubs featuring jazz and rock (including the nearly famous Zaphod Beeblebrox) dotting the market landscape, and generally catering to the younger crowd.

Near the market area proper, east across Mackenzie Avenue, are more edifying diversions. Chief among them is the **National Gallery of Canada**, at the corner of Sussex Drive and St. Patrick Street. There is no mistaking it: a stunning, modern creation of steel and glass, the National Gallery stands out for its architectural splendour and sheer visual impact.

And what's inside is just as impressive. With seven galleries devoted to visual arts, plus two reserved for photographs, prints and drawings, the National offers art lovers a day-long (or even longer) trip through the art of Canada and the world. Its Canadian collection is, arguably, unrivalled in this country, featuring the works of the Group of Seven, Tom Thompson and Emily Carr, and the Contemporary Gallery houses one of the most significant modern art collections in Canada. Admission is free. Beyond its permanent offerings, the National often plays host to special exhibits. Call (613) 990-1985 for more information.

Near the National Gallery is the **Canadian War Museum**, which

Local Knowledge

If you visit the National Gallery, be sure to visit the Contemporary Gallery and check out *Voice of Fire*, American artist Barnett Newman's simplistic painting of three vertical stripes in blue, red and blue. The work is as well known for its price as for its artistic value: when the government-supported National bought it in 1989 for a whopping $1.5 million (U.S.), the purchase set off a storm of controversy. Some modern-art afficionados think *Voice of Fire* is a masterpiece; others say it a colossal waste.

features a glimpse of Canada's military past with exhibits that feature (among other things) a real Sherman tank and a somewhat scarily accurate re-creation of a First World War trench. Call (819) 776-8600 for information.

For money buffs, further along Sussex Drive is the **Royal Canadian Mint**, which offers guided tours through its large gold-refining and minting operations. Call (613) 993-8990 for more info.

Rockcliffe Park

If you've got some time in Ottawa and are in the mood for a little rich-and-famous gazing, a sojourn through Rockcliffe will fit the bill perfectly. Situated along Sussex Drive on the other side of the Rideau River from Ottawa proper, Rockcliffe is actually a self-governed village with its own set of rules. There are plenty of important and impressive houses to see, not the least of which is 24 Sussex Drive, the official residence of the prime minister ever since Louis St. Laurent in 1951. In Rockcliffe, too, is the house of software magnate Michael Cowpland, an opulent creation of gold, glass and brick on Soper Place road. His former home, on Buena Vista Road, is even more garish—and even more of a draw for local sightseers.

The Glebe

Urban and hip, the oddly named Glebe is primarily a residential district, but strollers can find plenty of diversions in this neighbourhood. The

Local Knowledge

The Rockcliffe neighbourhood used to be a favoured destination for tour buses to show off the palatial homes and groomed gardens of the area's moneyed politicians, businesspeople and ambassadorial crowd—until the local council banned the buses from operating in Rockcliffe after residents complained. If you want to see it, you'll have to drive yourself or, alternatively, walk. But beware: its meandering streets have no sidewalks.

Local Knowledge

Ottawa's department of community services has set up a Heritage Programmes Unit, which conducts walking tours of some of the city's more interesting neighbourhoods, including Sandy Hill, the Glebe and the Byward Market. Call (613) 244-4474 for more information.

area (actually, a village unto itself) is located in the south end of Ottawa, between Lansdowne Park and the Queensway, and its main thoroughfare is Bank Street. Trendy is the byword here, and the atmosphere is something akin to Queen Street West in Toronto. Catering to the yuppie crowd, many stores in the Glebe have a multicultural (and somewhat overpriced) flavour. Fashion boutiques (both upscale and second-hand) and international gift shops, along with coffeehouses and some fine restaurants, can be found along Bank Street, and the area is a local mecca for laid-back nightlife (folk music is big in these parts!).

Sandy Hill

History buffs will want to take a stroll through this old Ottawa neighbourhood, second only to Rockcliffe in the opulence of some of its homes. Traditionally, Sandy Hill—between the Rideau Canal and the Rideau River, on the east end of the city south of Rideau Street—was the neighbourhood chosen by the political elite in the post-Confederation era, right up until the early part of the 20th century. Here you'll find **Laurier House**, the Ottawa residence of Prime Minister Sir Wilfrid Laurier in the early 1900s, later occupied by another PM, William Lyon Mackenzie King; the house, maintained in period style by the federal Department of Canadian Heritage and located near the corner of Chapel Street and Laurier Avenue, is open to visitors. East on Laurier, behind an imposing iron fence, is **Stadacona Hall**, once occupied by Sir John A. Macdonald, Canada's first prime minister. Today, it is owned by the Sultan of Brunei.

Other Ottawa Attractions

It's not even in Ottawa, but one of the major tourist attractions in the area is the **Canadian Museum of Civilization**, on the Quebec side of the Ottawa River in Hull. The site of the CMC is impressive in itself: designed by native architect Douglas Cardinal, the ancient Manitoba limestone of the museum's rolling structure takes up more than one million square feet, set on the picturesque shores of the river on a 24-acre lot. From the lush parkland that surrounds the museum, there is a great view of the Parliament Buildings directly across the Ottawa. The best way to get there (if the flesh is willing) is to hoof it across the Alexandra (or Interprovincial) Bridge, a stunning vista for both the river and the cities of Ottawa and Hull. (Here's a hint, though: watch out for the cyclists!)

Opened in 1989, the museum on its lower level offers exhibitions about Canada's First Nations peoples, their history and culture. On the main level can be found an art gallery and special exhibitions hall, as well as Cinéplus, a movie theatre of truly spectacular proportions that typically shows films of geographic or historical interest. The showstopper of the CMC, however, is on its upper level, in Canada Hall. Here, full-scale buildings, period furniture and often-stunning lighting effects re-create four major periods in the history of Canada, from early Norse adventurers to the towns and military outposts of the 19th century. Fascinating in both its expanse (more than 30,000 square feet) and its detail, Canada Hall makes the Canadian Museum of Civilization well worth the short trip to Hull. Call (819) 776-7003 for information.

Children, in particular, will get a kick out of two other Ottawa attractions. Located in downtown Ottawa at Bank and Macleod streets, the **Canadian Museum of Nature** is an old building that houses world-class dinosaur and bird exhibits, as well as a geology section that includes a "multimedia" tour of time. Call (613) 566-4700 for details. For a more interactive experience, visit the **National Museum of Science and Technology**, on the outskirts of the city (take the St. Laurent exit off the Queensway). The NMST's focus is on learning through doing, and gives energetic kids an opportunity to burn off calories—and use their brain cells—in exhibits about automobiles, computers, marine history and more. Call (613) 991-3044.

Ottawa Events

Living in the national capital means that Ottawans enjoy the benefits of a bustling civic life. And nowhere is that more evident than in the number—and lavishness—of the many festivals and celebrations going on year-round. Among the most popular, however, is **Winterlude**, an annual celebration of the cold season—and in Ottawa, it gets pretty cold! One of the largest winter festivals in the country, Winterlude runs for three weekends in February, and at its centre is the Rideau Canal, transformed in winter into what natives boast is the world's longest skating rink. (At 8 kilometres, it probably is.) The festival features sporting events and ice-slides, as well as an international ice-sculpture competition. Call (613) 239-5000 for details.

In the spring, Ottawa comes alive with colour for the annual **Tulip Festival**, when the city is almost literally blanketed with bright flowers, especially in the Major's Hill Park area south of the National Gallery. Held every May, the festival is a big draw for green thumbs—and for tourists who simply want to see Ottawa at its prettiest. Call (613) 567-5757 for information. Finally, if you are visiting Ottawa in the summer, try to squeeze in a trip to Parliament Hill on **Canada Day**. Nationally televised every July 1, the Parliament Hill firework displays and concerts for Canada Day are among the most impressive in the country. And what better place to be than the nation's capital—and one of its most interesting cities—on Canada's birthday?

Other Ontario Must-Sees

Niagara Falls

For decades now, Niagara Falls has epitomized tackiness. From the 1920s onwards, tourists flooded to the American and Canadian sides of the Niagara River to play and to take in the area's natural beauty—and what seems like a million cheap motels, along with cruddy souvenir shops and seedy amusement parks, sprang up to trap tourist dollars.

But the fact is, the Canadian side—a city of about 75,000 about an hour and a half southwest of Toronto by car, just off the Queen Elizabeth Way highway—has always been a little (emphasis on "little") more upscale than Niagara Falls in New York. Recently, too, Niagara Falls, Ont.—though it may not be a world-renowned honeymoon destination any more—has started to pick up, with better hotels, more and better tourist attractions, even a good restaurant or two.

And no matter what the blight around them, no one can argue with the beauty and the awesome power of the falls. In fact, there are two falls in Niagara: the less dramatic ones on the American side, and Horseshoe Falls—the real star of the city—on the Canadian side. In itself, Horseshoe Falls makes a trip to Niagara worth the trouble. While the American cataract (which is higher than its Canadian neighbour) pours out a measly 14 million litres of water per minute, Horseshoe Falls churns over a whopping 155 million litres per minute—making it the world's largest waterfall by volume. When Horseshoe is illuminated—as it nightly is by Niagara parks staff—it creates one of the greatest light shows on the planet, and it is particularly spectacular in the winter.

With commendable foresight, the Ontario government way back in 1887 established Queen Victoria Park all along the Canadian side of the Niagara River right up to the falls. In the warm months, it is a long expanse of green, and the Niagara Parks Commission (one of the city's largest employers) sees to it that the park is festooned with flowers—hundreds of thousands of daffodils, tulips, magnolias and roses, depending on the season. Strolling along the boardwalk in Queen Victoria Park is the best way to see the awesome beauty of the falls—except, of course, for the *Maid of the Mist*, a boat and Niagara Falls legend that has been taking sightseers (weather permitting) from the American falls to the base of the Horseshoe Falls since 1846.

Too much of the rest of town is taken up with the aforementioned tourist traps, particularly a strip of downtown that features an unnatural selection of wax museums, video arcades and '60s-era "thrill rides." The strip, of course, is part of the charm of Niagara Falls, but if you go, be prepared to spend more money than you'd think—and be prepared to be disappointed.

Several other local attractions, however, have helped to offset the cheese factor. Among them are the **Niagara Parks Botanical Gardens**, a 100-acre horticultural school about 6 miles north of the Canadian falls, which boasts renowned displays of ornamental trees and shrubs. The gardens are also home to a recently built **Butterfly Conservatory**, an 11,000-square-foot facility (complete with walking trails) that houses one of the continent's largest and most exquisite collections of live butterflies, which are allowed to roam free throughout the conservatory. More natural wonders (although perhaps more confined) can be found at **Marineland**, an amusement park and exhibition stadium that features performances from trained killer whales and other sea mammals.

Although kids may like those attractions, many adults will probably get a bigger kick from one of the city's newest attractions, **Casino Niagara**, a fully licensed gaming establishment that, since its opening in 1996, has become one of Niagara Falls' largest employers and has helped revivify the once-decrepit downtown core. A big draw for gamblers and partyers from the other side of the US-Canadian border, the 96,000-square-foot casino offers every popular game of chance (except craps, which is illegal in Canada). But even though it is definitely more upscale than the old amusement rides and sideshows that have made Niagara Falls into Canada's undisputed champion of cheese, the casino does share one thing with them: there, as elsewhere, you pays your money and you takes your chances.

For more information on these and other attractions, call the Niagara Falls Visitor and Convention Bureau, at (800) 563-2557.

Niagara-on-the-Lake and Stratford

Niagara-on-the-Lake is best known as the site of the annual **Shaw Festival**, the only regular staging of plays by George Bernard Shaw in the world. The Shaw runs every year from May to about the end of October, and its many plays are staged in three venues: the lavish 1970s-built Festival Theatre, the charming Royal George Theatre specializing in musical comedies, and the Court House Theatre, in the same historic building where the festival got its start back in 1962. If the witticisms of Shaw are not your cup of tea, the festival has expanded its playbill to include works by the Irish playwright's contemporaries, including (most recently) Arthur Conan Doyle and Oscar Wilde, all performed by one of the finest dramatic ensembles anywhere. For ticket information, call (800) 511-SHAW.

Stratford is a mecca to thousands of theatregoers not only from the rest of the province, but across Canada and around the world. Located about 100 miles west of Toronto on Highway 7, near London, Stratford is a quaint little place, with tree-lined avenues, old houses and the wide main street that so characterizes southwestern Ontario railway towns.

But the big draw, of course, is the **Stratford Festival**, an annual celebration of Shakespearean drama that since its 1951 launch has truly put this town on the national map. Renowned as perhaps the finest classical stage company in North America, the Stratford Festival, which runs from May to November, has produced some of Canada's most famous actors, including Christopher Plummer, William Hutt, Martha Henry, Kate Reid and (who could forget?) William Shatner—yes, Captain James T. Kirk got his earthbound start here.

Ontario: Towns of interest and outdoor attractions

In recent years, the festival has moved away from staging only Shakespeare's works (in fact, the first non-Shakespearean play ran at Stratford in 1954), and includes many more modern works—a move that seems to have only enhanced its performances and popularity. Even if the classics of stage aren't your thing, it would be worth giving the Stratford Festival a chance. You haven't seen Shakespeare unless you've seen his plays live, and the Stratford company breathes life into what too many people consider to be merely dusty old tomes. For ticket information, call (800) 567-1600.

Outdoors Ontario

Mention Ontario, and most Canadians will probably think of the big cities, like Toronto, and urban sophistication that have come to define the country's most populous province. But the open secret about Ontario is that it also offers some of the country's most beautiful back country, and plenty of possibilities to explore the great outdoors.

Its myriad provincial parks offer access to often-picturesque geography, as well as to the varied flora and fauna that thrive in ecosystems ranging from the verdant hills of the south to the pristine, remote wildernesses of the north. For sportsmen and women, Ontario is virtually dotted with lakes and waterways, making for perfect camping, hiking and fishing spots.

Algonquin Provincial Park

Algonquin is Ontario's oldest and largest provincial park, comprising more than 7,700 square kilometres of forests, lakes and rivers, about three-and-a-half hours north of Toronto by car. The closest cities are Pembroke to the east, Huntsville in the southwest and North Bay— known as the Gateway to the north—to the northwest. In the busy camping season, Algonquin Park could almost lay claim to being a community unto itself, as campers flock to its woods and streams—and more than 2,500 lakes—every summer, as they have for much of the time since Algonquin was established way back in 1893.

There is plenty to see and do in Algonquin Park, and really two ways to experience its wonders. The least arduous route is to stick to the Parkway Corridor, a stretch of Highway 60 that runs directly through the southern half of the park, and offers the most up-to-date camping

Canada by Web

If you're planning a trip to Algonquin, check out the Ontario Ministry of Natural Resource's Web page for the park:
http://www.algonquinpark.on.ca

For information on other provincial parks, try the ministry's excellent parks Web site:
http://www.mnr.gov.on.ca/MNR/parks

facilities for tent or trailer on or near the main highway. Most of the park's 1,500 campsites are in this area. Along this 56-kilometre stretch of road, you will find the Algonquin Visitor Centre, which has a bookstore, exhibits about park animals and plants, and an ongoing exhibition of native Canadian art. Here, too, just inside the east gate, is the Algonquin Logging Museum (featuring a re-created camboose camp) and the Algonquin Gallery, an exhibition of wildlife art from around the world.

The more difficult—but also more rewarding—way to see Algonquin is to dive right in and explore the park's vast interior for anywhere from a few hours to a few days (or more). For backpacking, there are three major trail systems, each offering loops ranging in length from 6 kilometres (about an hour's walk, for most hikers) to 88 kilometres—best explored over couple days. The real joy of Algonquin, however, is canoeing, and with more than 1,500 kilometres of canoe routes in the park's interior, it's no wonder that a canoeing trip in Algonquin has become an annual ritual for thousands of southern Ontarians.

Either by foot or by canoe, you are bound to run into at least some of the permanent denizens of Algonquin, which is home to more than 260 bird species, 40 species of mammal and (you have to look hard for these) 20 species of reptiles and amphibians. The park is also home to a thriving moose population, a few wolves and more than its fair share of black bears—about 2,000 of them, or one for every 3 square kilometres. They are particularly attracted to campground areas, drawn by carelessly stored food items or improperly disposed garbage. Here's some common-sense advice: DO NOT FEED OR APPROACH THE BEARS. They may look friendly, and may have no fear of cars or people, but there

Local Knowledge

Algonquin is a very busy park, drawing more than 300,000 people every summer. That usually means that campsites are packed—even in the interior, visited by some 40,000 every year—and campgrounds are usually full on summer weekends. Park authorities warn that visitors should reserve a campsite (for a small fee) well ahead of their arrival. For more information, call (705) 633-5538.

have been enough attacks in recent years to prove that getting intimate with a bear, however cuddly they seem, is a really bad idea.

Point Pelee National Park

One of the most frequently visited parks in Canada, Point Pelee National Park sits on the southernmost point in Canada, a slim spit of land that juts tentatively into Lake Erie for 10 kilometres. Located near the southwestern Ontario town of Leamington, Point Pelee also boasts one of the warmest climates in the country, and its situation in the midst of all that water has created an oasis for plant and animal life that is unique in North America.

This park is—quite literally—for the birds, as it lies beneath the major migratory routes for many avian species. More than 350 different birds have been identified among its marshes and grassy beaches, and nearly 100 species nest in the park. There is also a host of unusual plant species—including the prickly pear cactus, rare in Canada—and animal life that ranges from deer and raccoons to mink and coyotes. The Woodland Nature Trail, winding for 3 kilometres, is the most popular walk in the park, and gives a good overview of the sights and sounds. Other trails include a boardwalk through marshland, and a path along the southern tip of Pelee that is hard by the shores of Lake Erie. There is no camping allowed in the park itself (although several campgrounds are nearby), but bicycles and canoes are available to rent for those who would rather pedal or paddle. If you go, be sure to bring a good pair of binoculars to get a close-up view of the winged wonders Point Pelee has to offer. Call (519) 322-2371 for information.

173

The Trent-Severn Waterway

There are plenty of well-known cottage and weekend-getaway areas in Ontario, including the Thousand Islands in the East, Muskoka in central Ontario, and the shores of Georgian Bay. But the Trent-Severn Waterway stands out for the way it mixes natural beauty with a real taste of Ontario life.

Winding its way from Trenton on Lake Ontario to Port Severn on Georgian Bay, the waterway has 43 locks (including two of the world's tallest hydraulic lifts) over its nearly 400-kilometre route, and passes through such pristine-sounding lakes as Stoney, Sturgeon, Balsam and Lovesick (a personal favourite), and also through the big water of Lake Simcoe. Along the way, boaters can stop at small cities and towns like Peterborough, Lindsay, Bobcaygeon, Fenelon Falls—places that, while providing all the modern conveniences, still embody something of the rural, agrarian roots that are Ontario's past—and take in the sights of rich farms, rolling woodlands and stark rock outcroppings in the Canadian Shield.

You can see much of the waterway by car, but the best way is by boat, even though it can become awesomely busy on the Trent-Severn's lakes, especially on summer weekends. A number of private outfits rent (even to inexperienced boaters) houseboats that can carry upwards of eight or ten passengers, and it takes about a week to travel the full waterway. But you don't have to: the best trip is from the

By the Way

Trivia buffs travelling the Trent-Severn Waterway might want to make a stop in **Campbellford**, a historic little town at Lock No. 11 (by car, halfway between Ottawa and Toronto on Highway 30). Its claim to fame: the designer of the toonie, Brent Townsend, is from there. Billing itself as "The Home of the Two-Dollar Coin," Campbellford also boasts a 20-foot replica of the coin, and its Polar Bear Winter Festival is named for the animal included in Townsend's design. You could say Campbellfordians are loony for the toonie.

heart of the waterway (about an hour-and-a-half's drive northeast of Toronto, in the Bobcaygeon area) to Georgian Bay, which can be accomplished in three or four days.

The Bruce Trail

For hard-core hikers and backpackers, the Bruce Trail represents both a wonderful opportunity to see Ontario and a major challenge. The Bruce is a cleared and marked footpath that runs all the way from Queenston Heights Park near Niagara Falls north to Tobermory—over 750 kilometres in all, cutting along the Niagara Escarpment, a jut of raised land classified by the United Nations as a World Biosphere Reserve. (Horseshoe Falls, in fact, tumble over it.)

Maintained by the Bruce Trail Association, a collection of local camping clubs, the trail runs through both private and public lands, and passes through such communities as Grimsby, Orangeville, Collingwood and Owen Sound. It also traverses some of the most picturesque countryside in the province, particularly the Caledon Hills northwest of Toronto. Because of its length, many hikers break up the Bruce Trail jaunt into single- or multi-day trips, taking advantage of its well-maintained campsites.

The northern terminus of the Bruce Trail is a major tourist site in itself. Nestled on a natural harbour on the spit of land separating Georgian Bay from Lake Huron, **Tobermory** still maintains a commercial fishery and is the main departure point for the Chi-Cheemaun ferry that runs to Manitoulin Island. The Tobermory area is rich in maritime history—it was a major port of call for Great Lakes ships from the late 19th century on—and it is home to two of Canada's newest national parks: **Bruce Peninsula** and **Fathom Five**.

The Bruce Trail runs through the former park, which offers stunningly spectacular views of Georgian Bay and the unique geology that comprises the Bruce Peninsula. Fathom Five, meanwhile, is Canada's first national marine park, established in 1987 to preserve both its rare underwater ecosystem—it is located at the confluence of cooler water from Georgian Bay and warmer water from Lake Huron—and its many shipwrecks. Flowerpot Island is one of Fathom Five's most popular features. Accessible only by boat, Flowerpot has some outlandish geological features thanks to its limestone bedrock and the forces of erosion, and visitors can explore its largest cave and the outcroppings of rock that give the island its name. Most of the rest of the park is underwater, and while it can be seen by boat, the clarity of Fathom Five's water and the inherent attraction of its shipwrecks makes it a prime spot for scuba diving. Park facilities are set up so that any level of diver, from novice to expert, can find something to explore under water. For information, call (519) 596-2233.

Quetico Provincial Park

One of Ontario's most remote—and beautiful—parks, Quetico is fast growing in popularity. Located northwest of Lake Superior, near the northern Ontario town of Atikokan 160 kilometres west of Thunder Bay, Quetico offers visitors dramatic vistas of rock outcroppings, lush northern forests and a rich variety of plants and animals. For drive-in camping, the Dawson Trail Campground has more than 100 campsites, some of them with electricity, and there are interpretive hiking trails along the road leading to the ground. But the real adventure of Quetico can be experienced only by canoe—the way that early French fur traders travelled through these parts on their way to the West.

Canoeing through Quetico will take you to some of the most remote and pristine wilderness in Eastern Canada, but park officials maintain more than 2,000 back-country campsites and will provide visitors with a detailed (and waterproof) map of the park's vast interior. In Ontario outdoors circles, Quetico is regarded as the real thing—and it's lately become almost trendy among eco-tourists and adventurous campers. For information and reservations, call (807) 597-2735.

The Least You Need to Know

➤ Toronto, the capital of Ontario, is best known as a financial centre and for its bustling street life, but tourists should take time to explore the multicultural flavour of Canada's largest urban area by getting to know its neighbourhoods.

➤ The nation's capital, Ottawa, offers a wealth of educational and informative attractions, including Parliament Hill, the National Gallery and (in Hull, Que.) the Museum of Civilization.

➤ Other interesting places in Ontario include Niagara Falls, Niagara-on-the-Lake and Stratford.

➤ Ontario wilderness areas include Algonquin Park, the Bruce Trail and Quetico Park.

Part 4
Western Canada

There's more to the West than you might imagine—cities spring up throughout the vast tracts of prairie beauty for which Western Canada has always been known. Rich in history and full of reminders of a pioneer past, this area of Canada offers many museums perfect for any tourist. Manitoba's capital, Winnipeg, home to 60 per cent of the province's residents, boasts many attractions. Saskatchewan's reputation as Canada's largest grain producer certainly rings true, as silos dot the horizon and 12,000 tons of grains are harvested there each year.

Alberta's Edmonton is home to the West Edmonton Mall, the world's largest shopping centre. Meanwhile, Vancouver in British Columbia is a fast-growing metropolitan centre, with its laid-back style and nature-loving people.

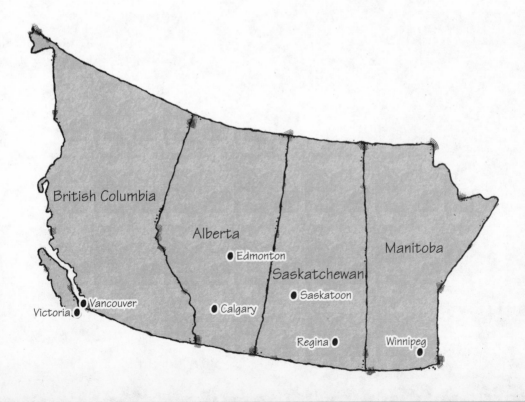

In fact, nature is the big draw in Western Canada, where millions of tourists flock every year to camp, hike and fish. There is certainly plenty to see out-of-doors in the West, from the remote plains of northern Manitoba and Saskatchewan to the splendour of Alberta's Rockies and the magnificence of the BC coast, where mountain and ocean meet.

Manitoba

Welcome to Manitoba

Manitoba is a land of transitions and connections. This is where the East ends and the West begins, where (economically, at least) the manufacturing powerhouse of Ontario gives way to the agrarian breadbasket of Canada. Those two influences are evident throughout Manitoba, but nowhere more than in Winnipeg, the historical conduit between East and West thanks to its importance as a hub for the national railway system.

In fact, all many visitors ever see of Manitoba is Winnipeg, one of the most ethnically diverse cities in Canada, home to a thriving cultural community and with deep roots in the history of the West. Beyond Winnipeg's borders, however, the province takes on a decidedly different aspect—farmland, prairie, huge tracts of forest and sparsely populated near-Arctic lands. Between the bustle of its capital and the beauty of its outdoors, Manitoba offers visitors a study in contrasts.

Canada by Web

The government of Manitoba has an excellent site devoted to the province's main attractions, including an explorer's guide:
http://www.gov.mb.ca/itt/travel

Winnipeg

Lying near the geographic centre of Canada about 100 kilometres north of the US border, Winnipeg is known as the Gateway to the West, the place where the forbidding rocks of the Canadian Shield turn into the rolling expanse of the Prairies. Winnipeg is Manitoba's largest city, with a population of 600,000, and home to about 60 per cent of the province's residents. Deeply rooted in the history of Manitoba and of Canada, it is nevertheless a thoroughly modern place, substantially re-built from the 1960s on, and it offers all the amenities and diversions of any big city. Winnipeg is by no means the prettiest town in Canada, but it is an ambitious place, bent on urban revivification and boasting per-haps the most active cultural community in the Prairies.

Winnipeg Past and Present

The confluence of the Assiniboine and Red rivers was a meeting place for indigenous Canadians long before the arrival, in 1738, of the French ad-venturer Pierre Gaultier de La Verendrye, who along with his two sons was instrumental in opening up the west to the fur trade. La Verendrye is credited with being the first European to establish a permanent structure at the Forks (as the meeting of the two rivers is known), with the building of Fort Rouge on land that would later become the city of Winnipeg. After the fall of New France in 1763, the area became a stopping point on fur routes of the rival North West and Hudson's Bay companies, leading to often violent conflicts between the mixed-race Métis, who depended on the North West, and the Scottish immigrants imported into the bur-geoning Red River Colony by the Hudson's Bay Co.

Winnipeg itself got its start in 1863, when Henry McKenney set up a general store on the fur-runners' trail leading to Fort Garry—a place that would later become the intersection of Portage and Main, which is still the centre of the city. After Confederation four years later, the Red River Colony was destined to fall under Canadian jurisdiction, opening up the

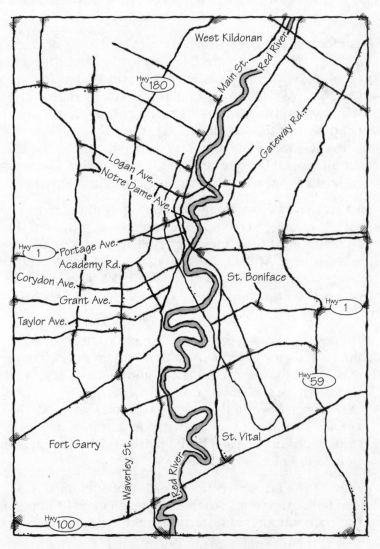

Downtown Winnipeg

area to further settlement by Anglo-Saxon immigrants. But the prospect met strong resistance from the then-majority Métis who, under the leadership of Louis Riel, organized a national committee in 1867 and later seized the Hudson's Bay outpost of Fort Garry. Skirmishes between Canadians and Métis ensued, culminating in the execution of Canadian surveyor Thomas Scott by Riel's forces in 1870. Still, Riel and the French-speaking Métis were instrumental in negotiating the *Manitoba Act*, which made the territory a province of Canada in July 1870.

Incorporated as a city in 1873, Winnipeg (the name derives from *win-nipi*, the Cree word for "murky water") remained a relatively unimportant trading centre until the building of the Canadian-Pacific Railway in 1885. As a major rail conduit for the wheat trade, Winnipeg boomed in the late 19th century, attracting immigrants from Eastern Canada and all over the world; by 1921, the city was home to nearly 200,000 people, more than 100 times its population in the 1870s. The railroad itself shaped the city, dividing the North End's working-class Slavs and Jews from the wealthy and powerful Anglo-Saxons.

That economic disparity and ethnic segregation contributed in 1919 to the Winnipeg General Strike, when 30,000 workers downed tools in a failed effort to secure collective bargaining rights and better working conditions. At the behest of big business and local politicians, federal troops occupied the city in June of 1919, after police forcefully put down a workers' demonstration on so-called "Bloody Saturday," in which 30 people were injured and one man killed.

In subsequent years, ethnic and economic tensions largely subsided, although the city's basic pattern of formerly distinct neighbourhoods remains. Today, Winnipeg is a cosmopolitan place, and the ethnic diversity that was once a cause for bitterness is now one of the city's main virtues. Beyond the Anglo-Saxon majority, there are large Ukrainian, Polish and native Canadian communities, as well as the more recent additions of Asian immigrants, and St. Boniface still boasts a large population of francophones.

Winnipeg remains the economic centre of Manitoba, with strong export and manufacturing industries. It has maintained its importance as a rail and air transportation hub, and it is still the headquarters of Canada's grain industry. Thanks to a fierce civic pride, the city has also developed a thriving cultural community, and it is home to the world-renowned Royal Winnipeg Ballet, the Manitoba Theatre Centre and a burgeoning

Local Knowledge

Besides immigration and the railway, the other great force that has shaped modern-day Winnipeg is the Red River, notorious for its floods. The most devastating came in 1950, after which much of the city had to be rebuilt. To prevent that sort of destruction from happening again, Premier Dufferin Roblin's government oversaw the construction of the Winnipeg Waterway, a floodway that many locals derided as "Duff's Ditch." They weren't laughing in 1997, however, when the ditch helped save Winnipeg from one of the Red River's worst floods, which drowned the rest of southern Manitoba but left the capital city relatively unscathed.

film production sector. It's a college town, as well, home to the University of Manitoba and the University of Winnipeg. And in 1994, Winnipeg won the honour of hosting the 1999 Pan-American Games.

In recent years, city officials and local businesses have gone about rebuilding many of the older districts, especially Portage Avenue and The Forks—transformed in the 1980s from a vast, ugly rail yard into Winnipeg's most popular tourist attractions. Considering that the Forks is where the city got its start, that seems altogether appropriate.

Getting There

By air: Winnipeg International Airport is just 7 kilometres west of downtown, and serves regularly scheduled flights from both major carriers from departure points across Canada and the United States. Call (204) 983-8410. **By bus**: The main regional bus terminal is on Portage Avenue, on downtown's west side. Call Grey Goose, (204) 783-8840, or Greyhound, (204) 786-8891, for information. **By rail:** The Winnipeg railway station is on Main Street, downtown, and VIA Rail runs regular trains to and from Churchill, Toronto and Saskatoon. **By car:** The Trans-Canada Highway (Highway 1) runs east-west through the heart of Winnipeg, becoming Portage Avenue downtown. Route 6 is the major entry from the northwest, while Highway 59 runs south to the US border with Minnesota.

Local Knowledge

Square in the middle of Canada, Winnipeg is known for extreme temperature fluctuations: hot, dry summers and long, cold winters. The average high temperature in July soars to 26.1 degrees Celsius, while in January the average high drops to -13.2. That may not seem cold by comparison to other Canadian cities—but in the dead of winter, there are few places on the planet that seem as cold as the corner of Portage and Main in downtown Winnipeg.

Getting Around

Winnipeg's most popular sites are largely within walking distance of one another, and you can easily see most of the city's attractions on foot. To get your bearings, the main thoroughfares are Portage Avenue and Main Street. Streets typically run north-south, avenues run east-west, and address numbers begin from the Red River, which runs north-south, and from the Assiniboine, which goes east-west. For the suburbs and for getting quickly around the city centre, **Winnipeg Transit** runs a cheap and fast bus service throughout the city, including buses from the airport to downtown hotels. Call (204) 986-5700.

Exploring Winnipeg

The basic pattern of Winnipeg's cityscape, determined by the distinct ethnic communities and by the railway, largely remains today, although it has been affected by extensive rebuilding after the 1950 flood and successive (sometimes ill-conceived) attempts at urban renewal and beautification. The Portage and Main area is still the heart of the city, and it is surrounded by administrative buildings and shopping centres. To the south, The Forks area has been substantially redeveloped, becoming a major tourist and entertainment complex. On the other side of the Assiniboine from downtown, Osborne Park is the grunge capital of Winnipeg, while the suburb of St. Boniface still bears the marks of the area's French and Métis heritage.

Portage and Main

Near the banks of the Red River, the intersection of Portage Avenue and Main Street is the historical centre of Winnipeg. It was here, way back in the 1860s, that Henry McKenney started up the general store on a spot that would later become the hub of city life. At the intersection itself, however, there is little of real interest, and a naggingly durable skid row nearby has been a Portage and Main landmark for decades. Still, much of the area has been redeveloped in recent years, and now the intersection is surrounded by shops, restaurants and tourist attractions.

Head north on Main Street and you'll enter the so-called **Exchange District**, a block of former warehouses and commercial buildings. Today, its cobblestone streets are home to stores and eateries, and on weekends a bustling flea market occupies the district's core. At Main and Rupert is the Manitoba Centennial Centre, a large complex that houses two of Winnipeg's prime attractions.

The **Manitoba Museum of Man and Nature** lays claim to being one of Canada's finest interpretive museums, and it is laid out into interactive and entertaining galleries. The most popular is the Nonsuch Gallery, which features a replica of a 17th-century fur trader's boat. There are also exhibits exploring astronomy, urban culture, polar bears and insects. The Manitoba Planetarium is adjacent to the museum. Call (204) 956-2830 for information. The Centennial Centre also houses the **Concert Hall**, where the Royal Winnipeg Ballet, the Manitoba Opera and the Winnipeg Symphony Orchestra perform throughout the year. Call (204) 949-3999 for tickets and show times.

Two other performance houses are also in the Exchange District. The **Manitoba Theatre Centre** has two stages; it specializes in regional works and hosts the Winnipeg Fringe Festival in July. Call (204)

Canada by Web

Exhaustive listings of Winnipeg's attractions can be found at:

http://www.mbnet.mb.ca
http://www.tourism.winnipeg.mb.ca

By the Way

By the Way

Winnipeg's Exchange District gets its name from the city's turn-of-the-century heyday, when its population soared and it became known as the Gateway to the West. As the main conduit for the agricultural plenty of the West, Winnipeg became a vital commodity-trading centre, earning it a reputation as the "Chicago of the North," and between 1880 and 1920 a number of stock and commodity exchanges popped up north of Portage Avenue. Hence the name of the Exchange District—which now has more theatres than stock exchanges.

942-6537. Nearby is the **Pantages Playhouse Theatre**, an old Vaudeville house built in 1914 that now offers a variety of local and touring entertainment in its 1,475-seat hall. Call (204) 986-3004.

The rest of Portage Avenue is a busy shopping and commercial district whose several malls and concourses are linked by indoor walkways, producing a welcome respite from winter cold and summer heat. Portage Place (393 Portage Ave.) boasts an **IMAX Theatre** (seemingly an obligatory addition to any Canadian city these days), with regularly changing films playing on its humongous screen. Call (204) 956- IMAX. Further west on Portage, where it meets Memorial Boulevard, the **Winnipeg Art Gallery**, shaped like the prow of a gigantic ship, sticks out for its stark modern architecture. The gallery is reputed to hold one of the world's best collections of Inuit art, and it features the works of individual artists in its mezzanine area. Call ahead, (204) 786-6641, to find out what's on when you're there.

The Forks

Until a few years ago, the historic Forks area on the south end of Main Street was a bit of an eyesore. But now, the old railway yards have been redeveloped into a sprawling, 56-acre park which has become Winnipeg's most-visited attraction. Two old railway buildings have been transformed into shopping complexes: the **Forks Market** specializes in fresh produce and meats, as well as food kiosks, while **Johnson Terminal** houses boutiques and restaurants. Near the river is an outdoor amphitheatre and a skating rink. Boat tours of the Assiniboine and Red are available. Call (204) 957-7618.

For youngsters, the **Manitoba Children's Museum** is probably The Forks' most entertaining attraction. Billed as the only museum of its kind in Western Canada, it specializes in hands-on exhibits, which

Out of the Way

Less than 10 kilometres west of the city centre along Portage Avenue is **Assiniboine Park**, an oasis of greenery that comprises 290 acres of walking paths, duck ponds and gardens. A popular spot for locals on summer weekends, the park also houses a conservatory, which features works by local artists in its gallery, and the **Assiniboine Park Zoo**, which has more than 1,250 animals, including polar bears, Siberian tigers and snow leopards. Call (204) 233-8972. Farther west is the **Living Prairie Museum**, a small field area that preserves some of the only virgin prairie in the area. Admission is free. Call (204) 832-0167.

are half education and half pure fun. The most popular is All Aboard, a gallery featuring a 1950s vintage diesel engine and a 1910 passenger car, which traces the importance of the railway. Other interactive galleries include a look at life in an oak tree (where kids can dress up in raccoon and bear costumes) and a "live" TV studio where older children can videotape their own programs. Call (204) 956-1888.

Osborne Village

South of downtown on the other side of the Assiniboine River, five blocks of Osborne Street comprise Osborne Village, a residential and commercial strip that is a favourite hang-out for Winnipeg's large student population. The Village is Winnipeg's most densely populated neighbourhood, its atmosphere hovering somewhere between trendy and bohemian. The city has recently undertaken a redevelopment of the area—including the construction of a bell tower to create the illusion of an old village square—so some of its grunge is slowly being wiped away. The area is known for its cheap eateries, but recently some finer cafés and restaurants have sprung up along Osborne, which also has plenty of craft shops, clothing boutiques and bookstores. If you're into contemporary music, it's also a happening night spot, although the Village's clubs and bars tend to cater to a young crowd.

Across the Assiniboine but still on Osborne Street, be sure to stop by the **Manitoba Legislative Building**, which contains the

By the Way

A Winnipeg landmark, the Golden Boy atop the Manitoba Legislative Building, was designed to symbolize "Freedom Forever" and "Equality for All." But the 4-metre-high youth had a long, arduous journey to his prominent perch. The statue was cast in 1918 at a foundry in Paris, which was bombed during the First World War. After that, the boy languished in the hold of a troop ship for two and a half years before he finally arrived in Winnipeg—in plenty of time for the opening of the Legislative Building in 1929.

provincial government offices and legislative chamber. Built in 1920, the building's ostentatious neo-classical trappings draw oohs and aahs from fans, and gags from critics. Built of local Tyndal stone, the building features sculptures that tend to be big and allegorical (don't miss the two life-size buffaloes inside), topped off by the Golden Boy, which perches atop the legislative building's dome. You can do a self-guided tour of the building on weekdays, and guided tours can be arranged in advance. Both are free. Call (403) 945-5813.

St. Boniface

A suburb that joined Winnipeg in 1972, St. Boniface is the traditional centre of French culture in Winnipeg, and it still has the largest French-speaking community in Western Canada. A largely residential and commercial district, it's across the Red River from downtown, and most of the places of interest (besides a few good French restaurants) are scattered along Taché Avenue, which runs near the river; the Promenade Taché, just off the avenue, provides a good view of downtown Winnipeg.

Walking along the promenade, you'll come across the huge facade of the **St. Boniface Basilica**, a Romanesque cathedral that was built in 1908. Tragically, a fire destroyed much of the church in 1968, but the facade survived, and now it serves as the front of the new basilica. Inside, in a nod to the community's Métis roots, the cathedral has been formed into the shape of a giant teepee. Outside in the old cemetery (even older than the original cathedral) is the burial place of Métis leader Louis Riel, whose body was transported here after his execution in Regina in 1885.

Across from the basilica, the white and green **St. Boniface Museum** is the oldest building in Winnipeg. Built in 1846, it was originally a convent for the Grey Nuns, but later was used as a school and

Local Knowledge

Louis Riel was instrumental in the negotiations that led to Manitoba joining Confederation in 1870. But his contribution to Canadian history did not end there. By 1885, after a brief exile in the United States and a nervous breakdown, Riel had moved from the Red River Colony to Batoche, Saskatchewan. Convinced that he was a prophet acting on the will of God, he amassed a small armed force and declared a provisional government, leading to two months of skirmishing with the North-West Mounted Police in a conflict that became known as the North-West Rebellion.

For his part in the revolt, Riel was sentenced to death and hanged in Regina on November 16, 1885—an event that alienated Quebec, always sympathetic to the Métis, from the governing federal Conservative party and set voting patterns in French Canada that largely remain to this day. After the execution, Riel's body was shipped to Manitoba and buried in St. Boniface, a suburb of modern-day Winnipeg.

orphanage. The museum concentrates on the French-Canadian and Métis peoples who helped settle the area, and on the missionaries who served their spiritual needs. With Métis and religious artifacts and trinkets, the museum uses a *tableau vivant* style to trace the history of the Red River Colony and the area's French-language community up to the First World War. Call (204) 237-4500.

Festivals and Events in Winnipeg

Winnipeg is an ambitious cultural centre, and the number of festivals the city stages, both in winter and summer, bears witness to its civic pride. The city has a healthy music scene (famous exports include the Crash Test Dummies), and music is the focus of Winnipeg's most popular summer fests. At the end of June, the city plays host to the **Jazz Winnipeg Festival**, a week of concerts staged downtown. Call (204) 989-4656. The **Winnipeg Folk Festival** is held annually in mid-July, about 40 kilometres outside the city at Bird's Hill Provincial Park. The largest event of its kind in North America, the four-day festival draws acts from around the world, and features a wide range of musical styles, from Celtic to Cajun. Call (204) 231-0096.

Winnipeggers make the most of their cold winters with two popular ice-bound festivals. **Rivertrail**, held from mid-January to late February, is a celebration of the Red and Assiniboine rivers that features skating, snowshoeing, dog-sled rides and outdoor entertainment, focused in and around the Forks area. In February, St. Boniface honours its French-Canadian past with the **Festival du Voyageur**, Western Canada's largest winter festival. Street parties, outdoor entertainment, snow sculpture competitions and sleigh rides characterize the 10-day affair. Call (204) 237-7692 for information.

Out and About in Manitoba

Manitoba is a huge province, stretching over 650,000 square kilometres from the US border to its northern reaches. Of that land mass, however,

Manitoba: Outdoor attractions

only a little over one-tenth is suitable for agriculture; the rest is made up of forests, freshwater lakes and streams, and forbidding sub-arctic zones in the north. Not surprisingly, then, the vast majority of Manitobans—95 per cent—live in the south, and of them two-thirds live in Winnipeg.

For travellers, modern-day amenities and attractions outside of the capital are few and far between. Chances are—unless mining and farming are your things—you won't find much of interest in Manitoba's other communities and outlying regions. The exception is the number of possibilities Manitoba holds for outdoor adventures. With plenty of lakes and streams—the third most of any province—it boasts more than 100 provincial wilderness and recreation parks. Manitoba is a too-often-overlooked retreat for campers, fishers and backpackers from elsewhere in the country. If you go, plan on long drives between Manitoba's intriguing outdoor locations—some of them you can't even reach by car.

Whiteshell Provincial Park

Only about 100 kilometres east of Winnipeg along the Trans-Canada Highway, Whiteshell is among the most popular—and largest—of Manitoba's many provincial parks. Comprising an area of more than 2,500 square kilometres, Whiteshell has 200 lakes. It is a popular spot for fishing—particularly for walleye, northern pike and lake trout. In fact, a quarter of all fishing lodges in Manitoba lie within the park's borders, so you can easily arrange first-class accommodation and guides.

The northeast is still largely a remote wilderness, but the southern and western parts of the park have camping, swimming and fishing facilities. Falcon Lake is a resort town within the park, and it has a shopping centre, a mini-golf facility and an 18-hole golf course, and Manitoba's largest sailing club. The park has hundreds of kilometres of trails, including the 60-kilometre Mantario wilderness trail, and is a favoured site for mountain biking, horseback riding and boating in the summer, snowmobiling and cross-country skiing in the winter.

The natural attractions include the Alfred Hole Goose Sanctuary, where some 200 Canada geese nest during the summer; Pine Point Rapids, north of Betula Lake; and West Hawk Lake, at 111 metres the deepest in the province, and believed to have been created by a meteorite. The park also features a wildlife natural history museum with exhibits on the animals (including black bear, moose, deer, and beavers) that inhabit Whiteshell.

The Manitoba Escarpment

Two of the province's most popular parks are situated on the Manitoba Escarpment, a stretch of geologically distinctive rock that rises above the surrounding plains. The result is a variety of forest ecosystems, from deciduous woodlands of maple and oak to boreal tracts of spruce and balsam.

Just south of the town of Dauphin in southwestern Manitoba, about 200 kilometres west of Winnipeg, is **Riding Mountain National Park**. The park features roads through each of the forest types, as well as hiking trails along which visitors can get a closer look at the flora and fauna, which include a small, well-tended herd of plains bison in a grassland area on the eastern edge of Lake Audy. Another attraction is the abundance of so-called "prairie potholes"—tiny, deep lakes created by retreating glaciers. Call (204) 848-7275.

The big draw at **Duck Mountain Provincial Park**, 100 kilometres northwest of Dauphin, is Baldy Mountain, in the southeast corner, which at 831 metres is the highest point of land in the province. Hiking trails on the mountain lead up to the summit and an observation tower, where you can get a spectacular view of the surrounding boreal and deciduous forests. Others come to Duck Mountain for the fishing—the fabled muskellunge lurks in some of its dozens of lakes, and arctic char inhabit the park's northern reaches. The Blue Lakes (East and West) are renowned for their clarity, and you can see the bottom even at depths of 12 metres. From the Blue Lakes Campground, visitors can arrange boat rentals, pick up groceries or take a swim by the beach. Call (204) 542-3482.

Local Knowledge

Riding Mountain National has plenty of inviting lakes and streams. But take care: some of its lakes are infested with a parasitic flatworm which causes an annoying and painful skin irritation called "swimmer's itch." So before you dive in, check with park staff.

Spruce Woods Provincial Heritage Park

If you're driving west along the Trans-Canada Highway from Winnipeg before you get to Brandon, turn south along Highway 5 and you'll find some of Manitoba's strangest natural wonders in **Spruce Woods Provincial Heritage Park**. The park is best known as the home of the Spirit Sands, a 5-square-kilometre tract of desert surrounded by prairie. The Sands, a fabled place among local native tribes, features dunes as high as 30 metres, and is home to snakes, cacti and Manitoba's only lizard, the northern prairie skink.

The rest of the park is made up of prairie and forests, and is pock-marked by strange-looking blue-green ponds, the most well known of which is called the Devil's Punch Bowl. Guided hikes and horse-drawn covered-wagon rides can be arranged through the park visitor services centre. Lakeside camping is available in the park's south end. Call (204) 827-2543.

Churchill

The town is nothing much to look at. It's cold even in the summer and the bugs make life miserable. But Churchill, on the southwest shore of Hudson Bay, is an increasingly popular spot for nature watchers and eco-tourists. The only way to get to the town of 1,100 is by plane or by rail. The most relaxing method is by VIA Rail, which runs thrice-weekly services from Winnipeg along the old Hudson Bay Railway line, completed in 1929 and, for a time, an alternative grain-shipping route to the East. The 1,600-kilometre trip takes two nights and a day.

Once an important outpost for the Hudson's Bay Company, the town of Churchill is surrounded by sites of historical interest, including the partly restored **Prince of Wales Fort**, built in the 1770s to protect company traders from the French, and now a national historic site. Call (204) 675-8863 for information. But the major reason people travel all that way is the wildlife. Churchill is known as the polar bear capital of the world, one of the few places where people can get up close and personal with the giant white animals in their natural habitat. The best viewing time is October and early November (dress warmly!), as the bears venture out onto the ice in search of seals.

Besides the bears, the area is also home to beluga whales (best seen from June to August) and seals (from spring to September), and is on migratory routes for more than 100 bird species. Bird Cove, south of Churchill and accessible by trails, is one of the best places for watching the gulls, ducks and geese that frequent the shore, and you can see the wreck of the nickel-carrying ship the *Ithaca*, which foundered during a windstorm in 1961.

If you go, don't miss the Aurora Borealis—the Northern Lights in Churchill are reputed to be spectacular. Visitors can arrange boat tours and guides through local outfitters in town. To the southeast is **Wapusk National Park**, a fairly new park that is still constructing its facilities. Call (204) 848-7275 for information.

The Least You Need to Know

➤ Winnipeg, the capital of Manitoba, is an ethnically diverse city with large French, Ukrainian and Polish populations.

➤ Winnipeg's Exchange District and The Forks are home to Winnipeg's major attractions, including theatres, shopping and museums.

➤ Popular outdoors destinations are Whiteshell Provincial Park, the parks of the Manitoba Escarpment and Churchill in the province's far north.

Chapter 13

Saskatchewan

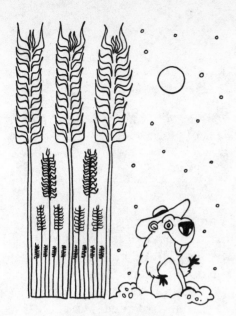

In This Chapter

➤ Things to do in Regina and Saskatoon

➤ Out and about in Saskatchewan

Welcome to Saskatchewan

The closest many Canadians ever get to Saskatchewan is 30,000 feet or so, the distance from the ground to the airplane in which they are flying. Jetting on to the better-known cities and mountainous regions to the west, they look through their windows and down upon Saskatchewan's plains, and one word goes through their minds: wheat. In part, of course, the commonly held conception of Saskatchewan as a relatively uninteresting breadbasket is true: the province is far and away the largest grain producer in Canada, harvesting more than 12,000 tons of wheat every year. And even from the ground, driving along the Trans-Canada Highway through Saskatchewan is probably one of the world's most, well, *uniform* experiences.

Once you get off the highway or the plane, however, the misconceptions start to fall away. For one thing, nearly two-thirds of

Canada by Web

Saskatchewan Tourism operates an informative Web site listing all the province's major points of interest: **http://www.sasktourism.com**

Saskatchewan's million people live in urban areas, not farms. The two largest, Regina and Saskatoon, are thoroughly modern cities, although still evocative of their not-too-distant pioneer past. And then there is the physical variety. More than a tenth of the province's 650,000-square-kilometre area is taken up by freshwater lakes and streams. In the southwest are some of the highest places east of the Rockies, and to the north are arboreal forests teeming with wildlife and opportunities for outdoor excursions. Saskatchewan will probably never be able to

Saskatchewan: Major cities and outdoor attractions

compete with Alberta and British Columbia for tourist dollars. But for those in search of out-of-the-way (and not too busy) travel experiences, that surely is one of the province's main attractions.

Getting There

By air: Saskatchewan's two major cities are the main points of arrival and departure for air travellers. The airport in Regina, the provincial capital, is about 5 kilometres west of the city centre, and handles flights by both Air Canada and Canadian Airlines. Call (306) 777-0898. Saskatoon Airport, north of the city centre, also services both major airlines. **By rail:** There is no rail service to Regina, but VIA Rail operates trains to Saskatoon from Winnipeg to the east and Edmonton to the west. **By car:** Saskatchewan has an extensive highway system. The Trans-Canada Highway (Highway 1) runs east-west through Regina; Highway 6 runs south to the US border, and the major Regina-to-Saskatoon route is Highway 11.

Getting Around

If you are limiting your stay to either Regina or Saskatoon, you can probably get by without a car. Most of the few major attractions in either city are reachable on foot, and both cities run public transit buses. If you have a car, you can wrap in a tour of Saskatoon and Regina in a couple days. As the crow flies, Saskatoon is about 235 kilometres northwest of Regina, and driving between the two only takes a few hours. By bus, the Saskatchewan Transportation Co. runs scheduled motorcoach services from Saskatoon, Regina and other communities to points throughout the province. Call 1-800-987-7776.

Regina

Part of the Prairies' desolate appeal is the way that man-made structures—small towns, grain elevators, silos—stand in such stark contrast to their seemingly uniform surroundings. Saskatchewan's capital, Regina, is no exception. Built on top of a flat alluvial plain with basically no arboreal life, Regina rises out of the prairie like an oasis of tree-lined streets, modern buildings and pleasant gardens. The city was founded in 1882, thanks to the Canadian Pacific Railway's desire for a base on the Wascana Creek, and to the North-West Mounted Police (later the Royal Canadian Mounted Police), which set up its headquarters here. In 1883, Regina (named after Queen Victoria) was made capital of what were then the North-West Territories, a distinction it maintained after the creation of Saskatchewan as a province in 1905.

Regina lies in the heart of some of the most fertile wheat-growing land in the country, a fact that has defined much of the city's economic life. The city has also benefited from its political importance, and (even though Saskatoon is larger) it is the major commercial and financial centre of Saskatchewan. Regina's importance as an agricultural and economic hub has attracted some immigrants, largely Germans, Ukrainians and Scandinavians, although most of the city's 180,000 residents were born there.

Visitors to Regina will no doubt end up at some point in the **Market Square** complex, which occupies 24 blocks of the downtown. The square has Regina's tallest buildings, including the distinctive twin towers of McCallum Hill, and its interconnected strips of stores and boutiques comprise the city's main shopping district. Elsewhere downtown is a memorial to the days when the life of the city revolved around the railroad. The old VIA Rail station at the corner of Broad Street and Saskatchewan Drive no longer handles train traffic, but is still a money-making enterprise: the big square building has been renovated into a casino, which is now the province's biggest tourist attraction. The full-service gambling establishment, **Casino Regina**, is open year-round. Call 1-800-555-3189.

For those wary of losing their shirts, the most popular place to hang around is **Wascana Centre**, a 2,300-acre green space that is one of the biggest urban parks in North America. Built around the man-made Wascana Lake, the park takes up much of the southeast corner of the city. Guided nature walks of the park are available if booked 24 hours in advance; call (306) 522-3661. Wascana also contains many of Regina's most interesting places. In the heart of the park, overlooking the lake, is the **Saskatchewan Legislative Building**, constructed between 1908 and 1912 in a style meant to evoke English Renaissance and French Louis XIV architecture. Outside are carefully manicured gardens, and inside you can take a tour of the building's rotunda, its six small art galleries and the oak-panelled legislative chamber. Call (306) 787-5357.

The **Royal Saskatchewan Museum**, at the corner of Albert and College, features an interesting First Nations Gallery and an Earth

Sciences exhibit, as well as a dinosaur display on Scotty the Tyrannosaurus Rex (discovered by a school principal in Eastend, Sask.). The museum's life sciences gallery, recently destroyed by fire, was due to open in June 1998. Call (306) 787-2815. In Wascana Centre, too, is the **Saskatchewan Science Centre**, with 80 hands-on exhibits that kids should enjoy, and an IMAX mega-theatre. Call 1-800-667-8497.

One of the city's premier art galleries, meanwhile, is on the corner of Albert and 23rd in the park. In the late 1950s, the **MacKenzie Art Gallery** was instrumental in promoting the so-called Regina Five, a group of local artists whose bold abstract works caused a stir when they toured the nation in 1961. Today, the gallery houses a good collection of historical and modern Canadian art, and is also home to the city's most popular theatrical attraction, *The Trial of Louis Riel*, based on transcripts from the 1885 treason trial of the self-styled Métis "prophet" who led the North-West Rebellion. Call (306) 522-4242. On Lakeshore Drive is the **Saskatchewan Centre of the Arts**, where the quite good Regina Symphony Orchestra has its permanent home (call 1-800-667-6300).

West of the city centre, just within walking distance, is the **RCMP Centennial Museum** on Dewdney Avenue, beside the RCMP barracks. The official museum of Canada's national police, the facility explores the history of the force from its 19th-century beginnings to its (rather troubled) present. Here, too, visitors can take in the Sergeant Major's

Out of the Way

East of the MacKenzie Gallery in Wascana Centre sits a piece of Canada's past. And political junkies will get a kick out of the **Diefenbaker Homestead**, a small wooden house where the only prime minister from Saskatchewan, John G. Diefenbaker, spent part of his boyhood. Born in Ontario, Diefenbaker (1895–1979) moved with his family to the North-West Territories and then lived in several prairie towns before settling in Saskatoon in 1910. The homestead in Wascana Centre was moved from Borden, Sask., in 1967, and features Diefenbaker family memorabilia and turn-of-the-century artifacts, giving a sense of the rural pioneer influences that helped shape the populist political tenets of the Chief, Canada's Conservative prime minister from 1957 to 1963.

Canada by Web

Virtual tours and travel info for Regina and Saskatoon can be found at:

Discover Regina—**http://www.saskweb.com/~tregina**
City of Saskatoon—**http://www.city.saskatoon.sk.ca/tourism**

Drill Parade on weekdays, and from July to mid-August the colourful Sunset Retreat Ceremonies, which revolve around the lowering of the flag. For museum information, call (306) 780-5838.

Two annual festivals in Regina pay tribute to the city's agrarian heritage. **Buffalo Days**, running from the end of July to the first week of August at Exhibition Park (off Dewdney Avenue West), feature midway rides, livestock exhibits and concerts, as well as a parade. Call (306) 781-9200. Around the first week of December, the city plays host to the **Canadian Western Agribition**, the second largest agricultural show in North America. Call (306) 565-0565.

Saskatoon

Situated on the banks of the South Saskatchewan River, Saskatoon is the province's largest city, with a population of about 200,000. The city was started by Ontario colonists back in 1882, but it didn't really get off the ground until the construction of a railway to Regina a decade later. In the subsequent years, it became an important railway hub, and its livelihood increasingly depended on the boom-and-bust of the province's farm economy.

From humble beginnings, Saskatoon boomed as immigrants, largely from Eastern Europe, came to the city in the early part of the 20th century, and in the post-Second World War period their numbers have been enhanced by immigrants from other countries. As a result, Saskatoon is probably the Prairies' most culturally diverse city, home to substantial Ukrainian, Hungarian, Indian, Pakistani and Chinese communities, along with a growing aboriginal population. (A welcome side effect of that diversity is an abundance of different cuisines in

Saskatoon, and locals boast that the city has more restaurants per capita than any place in the world.) It's a mix that seems to work, and Saskatoon's residents have a fierce, probably justifiable civic pride.

On the other hand, Saskatoon has never really garnered a reputation as a tourist site, and most places of interest to visitors can be found in and around the river, which lends the city a pastoral charm despite the modern buildings looming by its banks. The best way to see Saskatoon is along the **Meewasin Valley Trail**, a well-groomed, 19-kilometre stretch that runs along both sides of the South Saskatchewan River.

At the head of the trail is an interpretive centre, with maps and films tracing the history of the area. Call (306) 665-6888. Nearby you will find the **Ukrainian Museum of Canada**, with exhibits on the history of Ukrainian-Canadian culture and a much-praised display of the community's folk art; group tours—which include a Ukrainian buffet—are available. Call (306) 244-3800.

By the Way

In 1882, John Lake arrived on the banks of the South Saskatchewan in the hopes of setting up a "dry" community—he was, after all, a surveyor working for the Temperance Colonization Society of Toronto. Lake probably got the name for the colony from *misaskwatomin*, a Cree word for the edible, sweet berries that grew abundantly in the area. These days, visitors to the city will likely be thankful that Saskatoon berry pie is still a delicious part of the local cuisine—and just as thankful that teetotaling isn't.

Also along the river is the **Mendel Art Gallery**, the city's best, which houses local businessman Fred Mendel's good collection of works by Emily Carr, Lawren Harris, David Milne and other Canadian artists, as well as a gift shop and civic conservatory. Call (306) 975-7610.

Across the river, the University of Saskatchewan campus is home to several small natural sciences museums, but its biggest attraction is the **Diefenbaker Canada Centre**. The centre's mandate and exhibits are broad-based, exploring the history and achievements of Canada, but its tribute to the fiery Dief (who is buried on the university grounds nearby) is the main draw. Call (306) 966-8384.

The river setting of Saskatoon is used to good effect every July and August, when the waterway's banks play host to the **Shakespeare on the Saskatchewan Festival**. Staged in two tents near the Mendel

Gallery, the acclaimed festival is known for its inventive interpretations of the Bard's works. Call (306) 653-2300. Another important summer event is the **SaskTel Saskatchewan Jazz Festival**, an 11-day string of mostly free concerts at venues throughout Saskatoon's downtown. Call (306) 638-1211.

Three Saskatoon-area attractions give a sense of the area's rich (and often difficult) frontier history. On the south end of the Saskatchewan River (less than 10 kilometres from downtown) is the **Western Development Museum**, dedicated to preserving Western Canada's past. Exhibits include large displays of early vehicles and farm machinery, but the most interesting is a re-creation of "1910 Boomtown," with more than 30 buildings (including a church and pool hall) meant to evoke the experiences of Saskatchewan's European settlers. Call (306) 931-1910.

Five kilometres north of Saskatoon on Highway 11, **Wanuskewin Heritage Park** gives a glimpse of even earlier times. A large and ambitious complex, the park explores 6,000 years of native Canadian history, with 19 archeological sites connected by trails and walkways. The interpretive centre houses a theatre, an art exhibit and an archeological lab, as well as a restaurant that specializes in aboriginal cuisine. Call (306) 931-6767.

Further afield, about 90 kilometres northeast of Saskatoon off Highway 225, is **Batoche National Historic Park**, featuring the remains of the village of Batoche, where Louis Riel and his Métis forces had their base in the North-West Rebellion of 1885. The visitor centre has displays explaining Métis culture and the events of Riel's battles with territories authorities, and along the park's pathways and trails you can explore the old church, cemetery and the grave site of Gabriel Dumont, Riel's commander-in-chief. Open May to October; call (306) 423-6227.

Out and About in Saskatchewan

When it comes to attracting outdoors types from out of province, Saskatchewan definitely plays third fiddle to its mountainous fellow westerners, Alberta and British Columbia. Part of the reason is that it has a reputation for being a flat expanse of farm fields and prairie—but that only applies in part of the province. Elsewhere, Saskatchewan has an abundance of lakes and streams, as well as many good parks and, yes, even a few hills.

Canada by Web

For information on Saskatchewan's parks, see:
http://www.gov.sk.ca/serm/WWW/PARKS

Its relative unpopularity as an outdoor adventure place is good news for those willing to go off the beaten path and explore areas where many others have never thought of treading. If it lacks towering mountains, Saskatchewan also lacks the crowds that clog up other provinces' outdoors. And if you check out its more popular and interesting wilderness areas, you'll soon find that there's more to Saskatchewan than wheat fields and combines.

Prince Albert National Park

Near the geographical centre of Saskatchewan more than 200 kilometres north of Saskatoon, Prince Albert National Park is a 3,875-kilometre wilderness area with myriad lakes and streams at the confluence of two characteristic northern ecosystems. Here, aspen parkland to the south gives way to the boreal forest that covers much of northern Canada, and the result is a rich mix of wildlife. In its grassy southwestern corner, the park is home to a small herd of wood bison, while on its northwestern edge, on Lavallee Lake, is a breeding colony for the rare white pelican. And throughout the park, there are wolves, bear, moose, fox and a host of other species.

For visitors, the town of Wakesiu has a nature centre and a beach (very busy), and the park's major car-oriented campsites (more than 400 of them, in all). For more adventurous souls, Prince Albert has many hiking trails both short and long, and it's a good place to explore by water—canoes are available for rental at several marinas throughout the park. For information, call (306) 633-5322.

Meadow Lake Provincial Park

West of Prince Albert National Park along Highway 55, this is one of Saskatchewan's most popular vacation spots. Tucked firmly in the

By the Way

Grey Owl, one of Canada's most colourful and vocal spokesmen for wildlife preservation, was also one of Prince Albert National Park's most famous residents. Born Archibald Stansfield Belaney in Hastings, England, in 1888, he came to Canada as a teenager and soon adopted what he interpreted as the lifestyle of its aboriginal peoples. In 1931, seven years before his death, he and his Mohawk wife, Anahareo, moved to Prince Albert park, where he wrote several books—including *Pilgrims of the Wild* (1935) and *Empty Cabin* (1936)—that helped to popularize the notion of preserving wilderness areas. Visitors to Prince Albert can still visit his cabin on the shores of Ajawaan Lake, also the site of Grey Owl's grave.

Local Knowledge

Bug alert! Northern Saskatchewan may not be home to many people, but insects—most noticeably the biting kind—seem to love its forests, lakes and streams (not to mention the masses of human food that come to visit every summer). If you go, bring plenty of insect repellent.

northern boreal forest, Meadow Lake Provincial Park comprises 1,600 square kilometres running roughly along the length of the Waterhen River. The lakes are the big draw here—with over 25 of them—and visitors can fish, water-ski, swim or just lie around on one of the park's many sandy beaches. There are over 900 campsites in Meadow Lake park, offering facilities ranging from the rustic to full-scale resort accommodations. For park information, call (306) 236-7680.

Cypress Hills Interprovincial Park

If you thought Saskatchewan was just plain flat, think again. Cypress Hills Interprovincial Park, on the Alberta border south of the

Trans-Canada Highway, sits on a plateau that soars to 1,392 metres above sea level—the highest elevation between Labrador and the Rocky Mountains. Cypress Hills was Canada's first interprovincial park, and responsibility for maintaining its 18,400 hectares are shared between Saskatchewan and Alberta.

Thanks to its unique elevation and climate—the Cypress Hills are more humid than the surrounding plains, and their soil is fed by many underground springs—the park is home to a rich abundance of flora and fauna. Its stands of lodgepole pine are unique to Saskatchewan, and 13 species of orchid survive in its mixed, rolling woodlands. Elk, mule deer, bobcat and moose are just a few of its animal inhabitants.

The park is divided into two blocks: the western portion, which is wilderness, and the centre block, which contains most park facilities. On the Saskatchewan side are 450 campsites and 250 private cottages, as well as the Cypress Hills Four Seasons Resort, which offers hotel accommodations. The Alberta portion of the park has similar camping facilities, and both sides have ski hills and restaurants. For information, call (306) 662-4411.

Southwest of the park is **Fort Walsh National Historic Site**, a

Out of the Way

If you want to get a sense of how the prairie used to be—before modern-day agriculture dug it up—pay a visit to **Grasslands National Park**, two tracts of relatively undisturbed land southwest of Regina at the US border. Comprising 140 square kilometres, the park is home to a varied ecosystem where sage, cacti and wildflowers flourish, and where mule deer and pronghorn antelope graze. It is also home to the black-tailed prairie dog, a species that can be seen in its natural habitat nowhere else in Canada.

The most dramatic physical sight is the Frenchman River Valley, carved out by a glacial stream, and bordered by 70-Mile Butte, which soars 100 metres into the air. Still in its infancy, the park offers few amenities and no serviced campsites—but it's a good place to catch a glimpse of more or less virgin prairie while you still can.

partial reconstruction of a North-West Mounted Police fort and trading post built in the 1870s. The Cypress Hills area had long been a wintering area for aboriginal tribes, and in the last part of the century was one of the few remaining bison-hunting areas. In 1873, a group of American and Canadian wolf hunters slaughtered 36 Assiniboine natives—an event that came to be called the Cypress Hills Massacre—and it spurred on the creation of the North-West Mounted Police. Fort Walsh, near the site of the massacre, was one of the new force's first outposts. At the historic site, costumed staff lead visitors through the history of the Cypress Hills, and guided tours are available. Call (306) 662-3590.

The Least You Need to Know

➤ The best attractions in Regina, Saskatchewan's capital, are in Wascana Centre, a large urban park.

➤ Saskatoon, the province's largest city, is a multicultural, pretty place where community life revolves around the South Saskatchewan River.

➤ Saskatchewan's many outdoor attractions include Meadow Lake Provincial Park, Prince Albert National Park and Cypress Hills Interprovincial Park.

Chapter 14

Alberta

In This Chapter
➤ Exploring Calgary and Edmonton
➤ Alberta's great outdoors

Welcome to Alberta

It is the westernmost of the Prairie provinces, where grasslands and agricultural riches give way to the Rocky Mountains, soaring to heights of over 11,000 feet and marking a natural divide, with British Columbia to the west. The Rockies are the main reason tourism is one of the top four industries in a province well known for its others—oil, natural gas and agriculture.

Complementing that natural splendour are Alberta's cities: Edmonton, the provincial capital and the Gateway to the North, and Calgary, home of the Stampede and the heart of cowboy culture. Both cities are forward-looking places, perhaps to a fault, as they are constantly being renewed and rebuilt. The consistent factor, though, is the desire to build and to move on, born out of the pioneers and entrepreneurs that settled the province. Alberta these days is a prosperous and

By the Way

So you don't like mountains, couldn't care less about museums? All you want to do is shop? Well, shopaholics take note: Alberta is the only province without a provincial sales tax. The GST, unfortunately, still applies.

By the Way

The early days of Edmonton were tough slugging—and not just for Edmontonians. When the Klondike Gold Rush began in 1897, the town attempted to capitalize on the fever by billing itself as an alternate route to Dawson. The luckiest of those who tried the route, instead of the more-travelled Chilkoot Trail through Alaska, lived to regret it and ended up settling in Edmonton. Scores of others died on the way.

modern place, but in some ways it will always be on the edge of the frontier.

Edmonton

The capital of Alberta and the province's largest city, Edmonton has long been regarded as the Gateway to the North. In many ways, it still sits on the edge of a frontier. To the south are the sprawling farmlands of central Alberta, while north of the city begin the trackless wilds of northern Alberta—and beyond. Even today, Edmonton has a kind of frontier atmosphere, rising above the valley of the North Saskatchewan River like some remote outpost of modern skyscrapers and manicured parks.

The rugged surroundings, however, belie the fact that the capital is home to some of Western Canada's best cultural institutions, and is a thriving, bustling metropolis. Edmontonians are remarkable boosters of their home town—how else could they dub it the "City of Champions?" Likewise, Edmonton inspires in visitors to the city few mixed opinions: people either love it or hate it.

Edmonton Past and Present

The valley where Edmonton sits has probably been inhabited for thousands of years, but the first European settlers—fur traders—arrived in 1795, and by the early 1800s Fort Edmonton was the most important hub in the western fur trade. It took nearly another 75 years—and the construction of a rail link to the north side of the river—before real settlement outside the fort began in earnest.

Selected as the capital of the newly created province of Alberta and an increasingly important transportation centre, Edmonton and nearby

Strathcona (on the south side of the river) boomed in the early part of the 20th century—and then declined again during the First World War. Until the Second World War, the city lived and died by the fortunes of agriculture, making it a true boom and bust town.

The Second World War brought another boom, since Edmonton was strategically placed for northern military operations, and the discovery of oil at Leduc in 1947 really got the ball rolling. Young men from across the country and around the world headed to snare lucrative jobs in the oil fields near Edmonton. What they found, in the early going, was a pretty insignificant meat-packing town. But as it established itself as a centre of oil refining and (later) natural gas transport, it became one of the fastest-growing cities in Canada.

Despite being hit hard by recession in the 1980s, Edmonton has grown fairly continuously ever since the 1950s. The downtown core has been rebuilt so often that it's hard to find the old buildings (there are still a few there) among the gleaming office towers of the petrochemical and financial giants. The growth has broadened Edmonton's layout, and the formerly separate community of Strathcona has been swallowed up—as has much of the surrounding fertile countryside. At more

Local Knowledge

The federal government's selection of Edmonton as the provincial capital in 1905 was a blow from which many Calgarians never fully recovered. In fact, that and the economic competition between the two cities created one of the longest-standing (and most vocal) civic rivalries in Canada. For years, the hostilities have been largely confined to sports, as residents of Alberta's two largest cities argue over which city had the best CFL team (Edmonton's Eskimos or the Calgary Stampeders) or the best pro hockey team (the Oilers or the Flames).

Considering the rivalry, Edmonton's dubbing itself the "City of Champions" is a pretty clear dig at its neighbour to the south. On the other hand, Edmonton pretty much deserves the nickname: its beloved Oilers have won five Stanley Cups (to Calgary's one), and the Eskimos have captured more Grey Cup championships than any other team in the Canadian Football League.

than 670 square kilometres, Edmonton's area is the second largest of any Canadian city, and the majority of its 860,000 residents live in the many bedroom communities that surround the core. As a result, on week nights and especially during the winter, the streets of downtown Edmonton can seem like barren places, indeed.

On the other hand, against the sprawl so typical of other North American cities, Edmonton has worked hard to retain green spaces, and

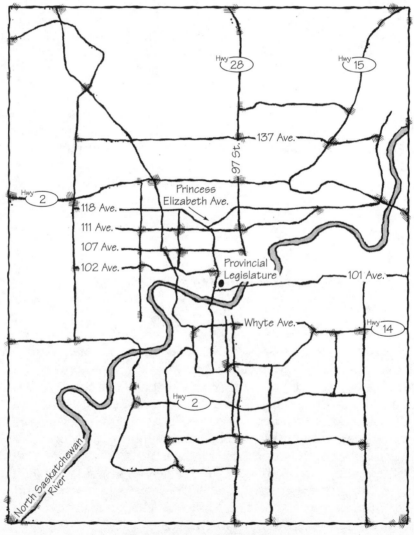

Downtown Edmonton

Local Knowledge

The northernmost capital in Canada, Edmonton is a
pretty cool place: in July, the average temperature is
only about 17 degrees Celsius, while in January the average is -15. You may hear some people claim that the winters don't
seem that cold, that an abundance of sunshine and lack of humidity
take the edge off Edmonton's icy chill. Still, if you visit the city in
the cold months, it's a good idea to pack an extra sweater and wear
that thick parka. The it's-not-that-cold camp may well be right, but
why take a chance?

it is home one of the largest "urban forest" areas in the world. As well,
the city (with the help of the provincial government) has fostered an
active arts and cultural community, and it is home to some of the best
theatre and concert venues in the country. Its annual events, meanwhile, particularly the Edmonton Folk Festival and the International
Fringe Theatre Festival, are world renowned both for the audiences and
the entertainers that attend them.

When Edmontonians are in the mood—and they often are—they
know how to let loose.

Getting There

By air: Edmonton International Airport is a very good, modern facility
that serves flights from across Canada and around the world. It's located
29 kilometres from the city centre. Cab rides to downtown cost nearly
$30, but shuttle-bus services are available for a little over $10, one way.
Call (403) 890-8382 for airport information. **By rail:** Edmonton lies on
VIA Rail's sole cross-Canada route between Saskatoon and Jasper. Trains arrive at and depart from the station on 104th Street, downtown under the
CN Tower. **By bus:** Greyhound runs buses to Edmonton from throughout
North America; call 1-800-661-8747. The regional carrier, Red Arrow, runs
between other Alberta cities and Edmonton. Call (403) 424-3339. **By car:**
The major east-west route through Edmonton is the TransCanada
Yellowhead Highway (Highway 16); the main access from Calgary, nearly
300 kilometres to the south, is Highway 2, the Calgary Trail.

Getting Around

Most of the downtown attractions in Edmonton are easily reachable on foot, and navigating the core is easy: numbered streets run north and south, numbered avenues run east and west. But to see the rest of the city (and you will want to, particularly the West Edmonton Mall), you'll need an alternative means of travel. Cabs are fairly expensive, but the city's public transit system is cheap and efficient. It combines bus services and a light-rail system (LRT), which runs from the University of Alberta in the south to Commonwealth stadium in the north, and bisects the city core. The LRT has only 10 stops, but there are patches of city you don't need to visit anyway and it's a quick mode of transport. Outside of peak periods, public transit is free within the downtown area.

A Guide to Edmonton

Edmonton is made up not so much of neighbourhoods as areas, and although within each area you can easily walk around, you'll have to take a car or public transit to travel between them. Economic and tourist activity tend to focus in two widely dispersed areas, the downtown and the West Edmonton Mall. (It might seem strange to describe a mall as, in some ways, a "neighbourhood," but wait till you see it.)

Street life, meanwhile, is a notoriously scarce commodity in Edmonton, replaced by largely indoor spaces like urban malls and office towers. Still, the city is clean and safe, and if you're looking for happening avenues and interesting walks, there are a few places, like Old Strathcona, that you can try.

Canada by Web

Two good sites give information on and links to Edmonton's major attractions:

http://www.infoedmonton.com
http://www.cs.ualberta.com/UAlberta/Edmonton.html

Downtown

Edmonton's city centre, roughly built around Sir Winston Churchill Square, is the focus of government and business activity. Its office buildings house more than 2,000 businesses, but it is also the site of the city's major hotels, more than 200 restaurants and lots of shopping opportunities—eager for business, now that they have to compete with the humongous West Edmonton Mall on the outskirts of town. An indoor climate-controlled pedway links the major buildings and malls, and you can cover more than half the downtown area walking along its above- and below-ground walkways.

Worth looking at is **City Hall** (on Churchill Square), a remarkable eight-storey glass pyramid built on the grounds of the old municipal building in 1992. Its outdoor wading pool is a skating rink during the winter, and tours are available. Call (403) 496-8200. Surrounding it is Edmonton Civic Centre, a six-block-square area of interconnected public buildings. Here you will find some of the city's major cultural attractions.

The **Citadel Theatre** is Canada's largest regional theatre company, and it has been a stalwart of Edmonton's cultural community

Out of the Way

South of the Civic Centre and Jasper Avenue at 100 Street is one of the few historic buildings still standing in the downtown area. The **Hotel Macdonald**, built in 1915, has long been the city's most cherished place to stay. From here you can pick up the **Heritage Trail**, a historic fur trader's route that has been fancied up—red brick sidewalk, historical streetlights—and provides good views of the river to the south.

It will take about 30 minutes walking along the trail before you get to the **Alberta Legislature Building**, an imposing sandstone structure built between 1907 and 1912 in classical-revival architectural style. There's a reflecting pond on its 13-hectare grounds, as well as greenhouses to the south. Free guided tours run every 30 to 45 minutes. Call (403) 427-7362.

since 1965. It has five theatres, seating more than 2,000 people, and is home to regular performances of contemporary and classical works, performed largely by Edmontonians. The theatre complex houses a restaurant, lounge, an indoor park—even a waterfall. Call (403) 425-1820.

Just to the north is the **Francis Winspear Centre of Music**, opened in 1997 and home to the Edmonton Symphony Orchestra, which performs more than 100 concerts every season. Call (403) 428-1414. Also on the square is the **Edmonton Art Gallery**, which houses a renowned exhibit tracing major Canadian art movements and also hosts touring and temporary exhibitions. Call (403) 422-6223.

Around the City Centre

It can't compete, in either size or energy, with the better-known districts of Toronto and Vancouver, but running along 97 Avenue north of 105 Street is Edmonton's traditional Chinatown. A compact three-block area, "old" Chinatown is today occupied by the Pacific Rim Mall, as well as some small shops and restaurants. The "new" Chinatown is south of here, running along 102 Avenue to 95 Street, where it meets Jasper Avenue—its west side is marked by the distinctive Chinatown Gate, near Churchill Square. West and north of new Chinatown is the so-called **Avenue of Nations**, extending along 107 Avenue from 95 to 116 streets. The multicultural hub of Edmonton, the area comprises stores and restaurants with an international flair—Chinese, Italian, Polish, Ukrainian, Japanese and Latin.

Local Knowledge

If you want a break from the office buildings and malls of downtown Edmonton, it isn't far away. The North Saskatchewan River winds through the heart of the city, and the valley has been preserved as the longest expanse of urban parkland in North America. At over 7,400 hectares, it offers nature trails, concession stands and boat rentals, and there are more than 95 kilometres of cycling and walking paths. Maps and brochures are available at the **River Valley Centre**, and walking tours are available. Call (403) 496-7275.

Strathcona

It used to be a city unto itself, but today Old Strathcona, running along Whyte Avenue south of the river, is firmly a part of Edmonton's civic life. The area is home to some of the oldest buildings in the city, some of which date back to the 1890s when the railroad arrived in Edmonton, and many have been restored. Along and around Whyte Avenue are more than 70 restaurants, cafés and pubs, and the knick-knack stores and clothing boutiques in the area are as trendy as any Edmonton has to offer.

There are a few tourist-oriented attractions here, mostly of historical or specialized interest. They include **the Old Strathcona Model and Toy Museum**, an eclectic display of old playthings—call (403) 433-4512—and the **C&E Railway Museum**, housed in a re-creation of the town's old railway station. Call (403) 433-9739.

The West Edmonton Mall

It's hard to talk about the West Edmonton Mall without using the phrase "world's largest" in every sentence. Why fight it? With over 800 stores and services, and costing more than a billion dollars to build, the West Edmonton Mall, in the city's west end, is the world's largest shopping centre. With numerous rides and attractions, it is also the world's largest indoor amusement park. And if that weren't enough, it is home to the world's largest indoor lake. It's kind of like Las Vegas under one roof, and some critics attack the mall as tacky, excessive and low-brow.

Out of the Way

On the south side of the river is a nice retreat from the city—particularly on chilly winter days. The **Muttart Conservatory**, at 9626 96A Street, comprises three glass pyramids on the banks of the North Saskatchewan, and under them is a fine collection of tropical and other plants that thrive in its climate-controlled atmosphere. The conservatory is home to thousands of orchids, and stages different floral displays throughout the year, depending on the season. Call (403) 469-8755.

But there is no doubting its popularity, and it has indisputably revived Edmonton's tourist industry—drawing more than nine million visitors a year. You can easily spend a whole day there, or even two.

Of course, the mall has all the shops and department stores you'd expect in a shopping centre the size of more than 100 football fields. But it's the amusement rides and other attractions that really set the West Edmonton Mall apart. In the middle of it is the Galaxyland Amusement Park, the world's largest (here we go again) indoor midway, whose centrepiece is the 14-storey "Mind-bender" roller-coaster. Just to the southwest is the Ice Palace, a glass-domed rink with a skating surface the size of an NHL arena.

On the west end is the Deep Sea Adventure zone, an indoor lake where a life-size replica of Columbus's *Santa Maria* is permanently docked. You can climb into one of four real submarines here, and get a glimpse of the fish and other marine life (including dolphins) with which the lake is stocked. To the south, the 5-acre World Waterpark features a beach, picnic areas, whirlpools, volleyball courts, rapids, 16 water slides, and (of course) the world's largest wave pool—heated uniformly to a balmy 30 degrees.

But wait, there's more! For adults, the mall houses a bingo hall and the Palace Casino, a dinner theatre, a Yuk-Yuk's Komedy Kabaret and Red's, an entertainment complex within an entertainment complex, with a bowling alley, brew pubs and billiard tables. If you just can't get enough of the mall's wonders, you can stay over at the 350-room Fantasyland Hotel, in the southwest corner. The oddity here is rooms decked out according to various exotic themes: African, Arabian, Roman, Victorian Coach, Polynesian, Hollywood and Truck—whatever that is.

All in all, the West Edmonton Mall is a place like no other. After a day or two there, you may have a hard time deciphering what's real from what's imitation. Either way, it could ruin you for malls for the rest of your life.

Edmonton Festivals and Events

Edmontonians are justly proud of the many festivals staged in the city throughout the year, and they go at them with a vengeance. **Klondike Days Exposition**, held in July, is a 10-day event in honour of the Gold Rush era, with street performances, competitions and a midway. More renowned is the **Edmonton Folk Music Festival**, held every

August in Gallagher Park near the Muttart Conservatory. One of the best music fests in North America, it isn't restricted to folk performers, but also pays homage to blues, gospel and rock. (Elvis Costello, my personal fave, performed there recently.) Call (403) 429-1899. Following the folk festival in August, the **Fringe Theatre Event** is the largest celebration of alternative theatre in North America. It's held over 10 days, in the Old Strathcona part of town. Call (403) 448-9000.

Calgary

Like Edmonton, Calgary has been built on agriculture, natural resources and the transportation links so vital to the livelihood of the West, and it too has been raised on the shores of a river, the Bow. But in other ways, Alberta's second largest city has plenty to distinguish it. It's a sprawling place with some dramatic scenery, where woodlands, water and the majesty of the Rockies in the background mix to create a distinctive urban landscape. Downtown, much of it is shiny and new, with towering skyscrapers and glossy urban spaces that highlight the city's many cultural attractions. But it is still a city devoted to maintaining its agricultural, frontier past—most clearly as the home of the annual Calgary Stampede. A place where commerce meets the cowboy way, Calgary is a city like no other.

Calgary Past and Present

The valley of the Bow River, where modern-day Calgary stands, has been inhabited since ancient times. Native Canadians first traversed the valley 12,000 years ago, and successive tribes of aboriginals came to the area in search of bison well into the 19th century. Although European fur traders were active here in the 1700s, it was bison and booze that determined the course of its early settlement by whites.

In the 1860s, American and native hunters followed ever-receding herds of bison to the Bow Valley, and whisky traders followed, setting up outposts from which they bartered illicit alcohol for pelts. The illegal whisky trade was a major factor in the formation of the North-West Mounted Police, and in 1874 the new force established at the Bow and Elbow rivers a military post, later called Fort Calgary.

Like so many other Western communities, Calgary, incorporated in 1893, grew up around the police outpost, but by the turn of the century it had become an important centre for the cattle industry and the burgeoning farming sector. The population increased tenfold by 1911. In 1914, another boom was set off when oil was discovered at the Dingman No. 1 well in Turner Valley, just a few kilometres to the southwest. Already an important transportation hub thanks to the rail lines that radiated from the city core, Calgary became an oil town. The first refinery was built in 1923, and like Edmonton, Calgary benefited from the Leduc oil discovery of 1947. Oil, of course, meant money, and Calgary soon became the leading financial centre of southern Alberta, a position it still holds today.

Depending largely on one industry, the city was hurt badly by recession in the '80s and '90s, but has since recovered. Today, its citizens have the highest per capita income in Canada, and its cultural and high-tech sectors are playing an increasingly significant role in Calgary's economy. And the city has one of the lowest unemployment rates of any Canadian metropolis. Immigration from within and from outside Canada has strengthened the cultural mix: its Anglo-Saxon contingent has fallen from more than half to about a quarter of the population since the 1950s.

Still, Calgarians are largely a conservative lot, both in politics and morals. Part of the reason, clearly, lies in their city's hard-bitten frontier past. But just as likely, Calgarians' conservatism is a side effect of living in such a prosperous, self-reliant city. In Calgary, a city on the move, the unofficial motto is "Can do."

By the Way

The first Calgary Stampede rodeo was held way back in 1912, and by all accounts it was a great success. Crowds (such as they were—about 14,000) were electrified in particular by a character named Tom Three Persons, who put on a stunning bronco ride aboard Cyclone, and prize money totalled $16,000. After a hiatus for the First World War, the Calgary Stampede has been thrilling audiences every July ever since 1923. Only the stakes have changed. These days, the 10-day event attracts a million visitors to Calgary—and prize money totals half a million dollars.

Getting There

By air: Calgary's modern airport is located about 10 kilometres north of town, and handles flights from both major domestic airlines and from around the world. Call (403) 292-8400. **By rail:** The railway is no longer a major passenger route from Calgary, but a scenic tour, operated by the Great Canadian Railtour Co., still runs three trains a week in the summer to Vancouver, with a stop in Banff. It's expensive—well over $500—and takes two days, but a good way to see the Rockies. Call 1-800-665-7245. **By bus:** Greyhound and other bus services run regularly scheduled routes between Calgary and other Canadian and American destinations. The bus terminal is a 30-minute walk from downtown, and not very interesting, so take a taxi or public transit. **By car:** Calgary is located on the Trans-Canada Highway (Highway 1), which cuts through the city as a four-lane thoroughfare. The main road to Edmonton in the north is the Calgary Trail, Highway 2, which is the Macleod Trail south of the city and extends to the US border, nearly 200 kilometres away.

Getting Around

Just about everything you will want to see in Calgary is located downtown or near downtown, so the best way to tour the city is to walk. In the winter, however, that can get pretty cold, so consider using the clean, cheap transit system—the C-Train, a kind of bus/rail system, is free in its downtown stretch; otherwise, it's less than $2 a ride. Call (403) 262-1000.

Walking downtown is made easier by the Plus 15 system, a network of elevated, enclosed walkways that connect most of the major buildings and shopping centres (and give the city core a distinctively futuristic appearance). If you still want to tour the city by car, the streets

Canada by Web

For information on Calgary tourist attractions and good descriptions of the city, check out:
http://www.calexplorer.com

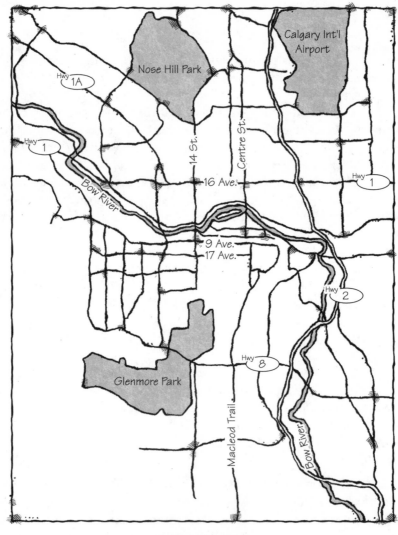

Calgary area

are laid out according to a grid pattern, but most of them are one way and it would be a good idea to buy a detailed road map.

Exploring Calgary

For its size, Calgary is a bustling city, and during the warmer months the carefully manicured gardens and malls of downtown are alive with

Local Knowledge

Most of the winter in Calgary, situated in the land-locked heart of southern Alberta, is, to say the least, cold. But once in a not-too-great while, a breath of fresh air hits the city and makes it positively come alive. By a process too complicated to explain here, warm, dry Chinook winds occasionally descend on the city from the Rockies, an event often presaged by dark clouds in the western sky. When it hits, the fabled Chinook can raise temperatures by as much as 10 degrees Celsius, and snow on Calgary's streets can evaporate overnight. Of course, you can't plan your trip around the appearance of the rather unpredictable winds. So if one happens to hit when you're there in the dead of winter, count yourself lucky.

activity. In the winter, it's a different story, as much of urban life takes place indoors and along the Plus 15 system of walkways. Some points of interest are scattered around the city's far-flung suburbs and older neighbourhoods, but the compact, sleek downtown contains most of the city's major attractions.

Downtown

The centre of Calgary is roughly bound by the Bow River on the north and 9th Avenue on the south. There is no mistaking where the downtown begins, even from a distance, thanks to the looming presence of the **Calgary Tower**, 55 storeys high, on the corner of 9th and Centre Street. Opened in 1968, it houses the tourist information centre and an obligatory revolving restaurant, but its main attraction is the view it affords of the rest of the city below. The tower was used as the model for the torch used in the 1988 Winter Olympics, and looking at it from outside you can see the resemblance. Call (403) 266-7171.

Just east of the Calgary Tower is one of the city's prime attractions, the **Glenbow Museum**. The museum is world renowned, and houses the country's best collections of First Nations and Western Canadian artifacts, as well fine exhibits on native and pioneer history. The Glenbow is usually a stopping place for fine touring exhibits, as well, and its

Out of the Way

On the west end of downtown, at 11th Street West and Stephen Avenue, the **Science Centre** offers hands-on, interactive exhibits about everything from dinosaurs to astronomy, and there is also a small observatory in the centre's odd-looking concrete edifice. Kids will probably love it. Call (403) 221-3700.

three floors are housed in one of Calgary's most impressive edifices. Hours vary; call (403) 268-4204.

Nearby, a pleasant place to relax is **Olympic Plaza**, site of the medal presentations during the 1988 Games, and now a scenic public square. A popular spot for office workers to lunch, the plaza is the focal point of downtown open-air concerts and other events year-round. Facing Olympic Plaza is the **Calgary Centre for the Performing Arts**, home to the Calgary Philharmonic Orchestra and Theatre Calgary, among other performing arts companies. Call (403) 294-7455.

Most of the downtown west of 1st Street West is comprised of office towers and interconnected malls, which provide plenty of shopping and eating opportunities for visitors. The easiest, though least interesting, way to explore them is by using the Plus 15 system. An alternative is walking along the **Stephen Avenue Mall**, a stretch of pedestrian-only, cobblestoned road that runs west from the Olympic Plaza. There are many restaurants, bars and shops along the avenue, catering mostly to the office crowd. The main attraction for visitors here is to see a rare bit of old Calgary. The not-quite-majestic sandstone buildings are among the oldest in the city. Civic boosters call the area historic; others may find it a little seedy.

North of the Mall, in the glossy, not-at-all-seedy TD Centre, are the **Devonian Gardens**, 3 acres of indoor horticulture on the fourth floor of a downtown office and shopping complex. The gardens boast running streams and a waterfall, trees and lush flower beds, and an interesting system of walking paths. Admission is free, though donations are accepted. Call (403) 268-5207.

Chinatown

Calgary is home to a tiny but durable Chinese population which numbers only about 2,000, most of whom are descendants of railway workers who came here in the 19th century. Chinatown occupies a small parcel of land north of downtown and south of the Bow River around Centre Street, and there are plenty of restaurants and unique shops that give the area a distinctive Asian flavour. The focal point of the community is the **Calgary Chinese Cultural Centre**, designed by mainland Chinese workmen in the pattern of the Temple of Heaven in Beijing. Incorporating many elements of classical Chinese architecture, the centre's decorative paintings include more than 500 dragons and phoenixes. Admission is free. Call (403) 262-5071.

Just to the west of Chinatown is the **Eau Claire Market**, a fairly new warehouse-style building that houses specialty food shops, craft stores, restaurants and gift shops. Thanks to activity in the market, the surrounding area has recently started to offer increasingly upscale boutiques and eateries. North of it, easily reachable on foot across a bridge, is **Prince's Island**, an urban park area in the middle of the Bow River. It's a popular retreat from downtown, suited to picnicking and jogging.

Kensington

For a while now, what there is of counterculture in Calgary has been focused in and around Kensington, a trendy neighbourhood northwest of downtown about 20 minutes' walk from Prince's Island. Along Kensington Road, there are plenty of bars and restaurants, and it is one of the city's most active places for nightlife and music. It has become increasingly gentrified, but still thrives with its own characteristic energy. And it's the big centre for New Age shops and seminars in buttoned-down Calgary.

Other Calgary Attractions

If you're in town for a few days, you may want to check out a couple of attractions in Calgary's southeast end. **Fort Calgary**, on 9th Avenue SE,

Local Knowledge

Kensington's first-place position as a restaurant spot is now being challenged by an increasingly trendy district, in the south of the city along 4th Street southwest. If you're looking for a place to eat in Calgary, the area offers Caribbean, bistro and even Mongolian fare.

is the site of a North-West Mounted Police outpost built in the 1870s, only a few remnants of which remain. Filled with photographs and artifacts that evoke the area's troubled frontier days, the fort's visitor centre is staffed by interpreters in period costume. Call (403) 290-1875.

Farther east is St. George's Island, home to the **Calgary Zoo**, the second-largest in Canada. Built in 1920, it contains more than 400 animal species, including gorillas, giraffes and polar bears, and takes pride in ingeniously displaying them within faithfully re-created "natural" habitats. The zoo area is dotted with botanical gardens, and also features a Prehistoric Park, with 27 life-size models of dinosaurs. Call (403) 232-9300.

Events and Festivals in Calgary

The big daddy of Western events is, of course, the **Calgary Stampede**, held every July. Attracting millions of visitors, the Stampede fills up the city with festivals, street parties and exhibitions, as well as a huge, colourful parade. Over the 10-day event, Calgary is where cowpokes—

Out of the Way

Sports buffs and armchair athletes ready to try the real thing should definitely visit **Canada Olympic Park**, site of the luge, bobsleigh, ski-jumping and freestyle skiing competitions during the 1988 Winter Games. Tours of the site, which is still used as a training facility, guide visitors through the major events and characters of the '88 Olympics, and the COP is home to the world's largest museum of the Games, the **Olympic Hall of Fame**.

The big draw, though, is the opportunity to try out the sports on your own. In the winter, you can take a run at the luge or the bobsleigh, and you can also try your luck in the summer at ski-jumping and bungee-jumping, which are of course not Olympic sports—yet.

and cowpoke wanna-bes—come home to graze, and it creates a party atmosphere like no other. But the rodeo events, most of which take place at Stampede Park south of downtown, are taken deadly seriously by the best bronc-busters, ropers and steer-wrestlers in the world, who compete for prize money totalling half a million dollars.

The Stampede tends to overshadow other civic events, which include the **Calgary International Jazz Festival** in June and the **Calgary Winter Festival**, with the usual assortment of outdoor activities, in January. As well, for less rough-and-tumble horseplay than the Stampede, visitors might want to head out to **Spruce Meadows**, southwest of the city, which is Canada's finest and best-known equestrian facility. In June, it plays host to the national championships, followed by the North American in July and the Spruce Meadows Masters in September. Call (403) 254-3200.

Alberta: Outdoor attractions

Out and About in Alberta

Most tourists go to Alberta in the first place not to see Calgary or Edmonton, but to get *out* of the city—and into the Rockies. They are, not to put too fine a point on it, truly wonderful, a national treasure providing such a wealth of outdoor experiences that you can (and probably should) spend a whole vacation just poking around them. If you don't have time for that, the Rockies in Alberta can easily be seen and enjoyed by car—after all, you can't miss peaks that tower thousands of feet above you, even on a busy highway. If you haven't been to the Rockies, go see what all the fuss is about, because they live up to expectations.

There's more to Alberta than mountains, of course, and if you're willing to depart from the well-beaten path to the mountains, the province has a few other surprises—like dinosaurs.

The Rockies: Banff and Jasper National Parks

Certainly Canada's best-known park area, Banff is also the oldest, formed in 1885. If you visit, you'll also notice another of Banff's distinctions among national parks: it's the busiest. In fact, Banff National Park is one of the biggest tourist attractions in all of Canada, drawing nearly five million visitors a year.

One reason for that is its proximity to Calgary. The park is only a little over 100 kilometres along a stretch of the Trans-Canada highway, a trip that takes about an hour and half on a typical busy day. Another reason for the park's popularity is the number of things you can do there. You can ski (alpine and cross-country), hike, bicycle or even shop for haute-couture.

Banff is really two places. There is the park itself, more than 6,500 square kilometres of stunning mountain vistas and wilderness, and then there is the town of Banff, in the southern end of the park. It's permanent home to about 7,000 people, but the town's lifeblood are the millions of people who pass through. It's a trendy and desirable little place, with surely the most spectacular main street in Canada—thanks to the mountain towering over it. There are plenty of places to stay, too, including the famous Banff Springs, an 800-room hotel with a gorgeous golf course, more than a dozen restaurants and 50 shops.

Just outside the town is one of the park's main attractions, the **Cave and Basin National Historic Site**. The site contains the hot

Local Knowledge

The town of Banff is a pretty spot, and chances are you'll end up spending at least a couple of hours there if you visit the park or if you're going skiing. But while you're there, keep an eye on how much money you spend. The town's shops and restaurants are notoriously expensive. Two of the best bargains in town are the **Banff Park Museum** and the **Whyte Museum of the Canadian Rockies**, widely praised facilities that trace the human and natural history of the park and its surroundings. Call (403) 762-1558 for Banff Park Museum, and (403) 762-2291 for the Whyte.

springs that originally made Banff famous, restored to their turn-of-the-century state. (Visitors are not allowed to take a dip.) The site has an interpretive centre, as well as boardwalk trails along which you can take in the scenery. Call (403) 762-1557.

The park itself is a hugely popular stop for car-camping. There are over 2,400 campsites equipped to handle automobiles, and on summer weekends they can fill up very quickly—you can't reserve ahead of time. For the more adventurous, Banff National has over 1,100 kilometres of trails, many of which are easily accessed along the road routes through the park. On the other hand, some are really arduous and some enter environmentally sensitive areas, and if you want to explore the back country, you should check with park staff. Call (403) 762-1550.

The easiest way to see the park itself is by car, and two picturesque roadways run roughly north-south along its length. **The Bow Valley Parkway** (Highway 1A) is the scenic route north from the town of Banff. The parkway gives some great views of the Bow River that meanders through the mountains, as well as Johnston Canyon. The parkway ends at Lake Louise, another in-park community, but the real attraction is the small, emerald-green body of water from which the town gets its name. **Lake Louise**—the lake, not the town—is maybe the most recognizable feature of the park, a shimmering pool surrounded by towering peaks. You can get there by road, and it's a favourite stop on the bus tour circuit.

Lake Louise (the town, that is) is also an important destination for winter sports enthusiasts, skiers in particular. The ski hills within park boundaries have long been one of its prime attractions, and they offer some of the best high-mountain runs in the world. They are all commercially owned and operated, and offer a complete range of accommodations and services for those who don't feel like roughing it in the bush. The major skiing areas are Lake Louise, Mount Torquay and Sunshine Village.

North of Lake Louise, the **Icefields Parkway** provides scenery that is among the most spectacular in Canada. As it approaches the Continental Divide to the north, the parkway runs beside one glacier after another, and you may spot some of the animals that live in Banff park, including Rocky Mountain sheep and the ever-present marmots.

The Icefields Parkway continues into **Jasper National Park**, 10,000 square kilometres of 11,000-foot peaks and stunning glaciers. The highlight of the park is Athabasca Glacier, just inside the boundaries north of Banff National. Four miles long and flowing out of the Columbia Icefield in British Columbia, the glacier is pocked with thousands of crevasses, so if you don't know what you're doing it's not a great idea to explore them on foot. For the greenhorn, a better plan is to take the snow coach, special buses that can safely manoeuvre on the treacherous ice.

A little less busy than Banff, Jasper National Park has 10 campgrounds with more than 1,500 campsites. There are also, like Banff, commercially run skiing facilities at Marmot Basin, and there are plenty of places for cross-country skiing. Almost as popular is the park's fine network of back-country trails, over 1,000 kilometres in all, which roam through montane and alpine ecosystems. For information, call the park superintendent, (403) 852-6161, or the Jasper Park Chamber of Commerce, (403) 852-3858.

The Badlands: Dinosaur Country

It's a weird-looking area of southern Alberta: a dry, sun-baked land of hills and flats that seem more suited to the surface of the moon than the prairies. Just over 100 kilometres east of Calgary along the Red Deer River, the Alberta Badlands were formed by meltwater from ice age glaciers 14,000 years ago. Today, the Badlands are best known as the most productive dinosaur research territory in Canada. To paraphrase an old Western saying: der's bones in dem dar hills.

The town of Drumheller is the traditional gateway to the Badlands, and some of the area's more peculiar features can be seen along the 50-kilometre Dinosaur Trail, a road that runs northwest from town along the Red Deer River Valley. Near Drumheller is the **Royal Tyrrell Museum of Paleontology**, the area's most popular attraction and a must-see for dinosaur fans. The museum boasts the world's largest collection of complete dinosaur skeletons, displayed in a huge central hall. To get up close and personal, you can take a guided tour—or even join in—on an archeological dig. Call (403) 823-7707.

Still in the Badlands but about 200 kilometres to the southeast is **Dinosaur Provincial Park**, home of the **Field Station of the Tyrrell Museum**, which is also the hub of the park's activities and services. This is active dig country. More than 300 complete skeletons have been found in the park, designated a World Heritage Site by the United Nations. Camping is available during the summer, but the most popular thing to do here is take a bus or hiking tour of the dinosaur dig, where some of the skeletons have been left where they were found. Be sure to call ahead to get a spot on the tours. For park information, call (403) 378-4342.

By the Way

Walking around the Badlands, you might get the sense that you're walking on another planet. The impression will be heightened by Hoodoo Rocks—strange rocks, sometimes a few metres high, that take on weird, fantastic shapes. They are formed from the combined action of wind and water on relatively soft rock. But looking at them, you might swear that they were crafted by an alien artist.

The Least You Need to Know

➤ The biggest tourist attraction in Edmonton, the capital of Alberta, is the West Edmonton Mall.

➤ Calgary, host of the 1988 Winter Olympics, is Alberta's second-largest city, and home to the renowned Glenbow Museum.

➤ Banff National Park is the oldest and most-visited of Canada's parks, and lies south of Jasper National Park.

➤ The Alberta Badlands, east of Calgary, are the site of fascinating archeological digs and the Royal Tyrrell Museum of Paleontology.

British Columbia

Welcome to British Columbia

It's where Canada ends—or begins, depending on your perspective. British Columbia, a jewel of a province, is really two places. The coast, perhaps better known to Canadians because it is home to BC's biggest cities, Vancouver and Victoria, is a land of snow-capped peaks rising above picturesque fjords and inlets, a place where mountain and sea meet. The Interior, meanwhile, is still mountainous, but can be dry and sunny where the coast is rain-soaked. Together, the two landscapes offer a wild diversity of experiences. Small wonder that a big part of the British Columbian lifestyle is enjoying the nature that surrounds its cities and towns.

It used to be that *British* Columbia lived up to its name—the most overwhelmingly Anglo-Saxon province in Canada, founded (or, at least, dominated) by settlers of British ancestry. But that has clearly changed, and today—even though it is Canada's westernmost province—some have taken to talking about British Columbia as the Far East, thanks to its important economic and cultural ties with Asia, on the other side of the Pacific Ocean.

Nowhere are the changes more noticeable than Vancouver, the province's largest metropolis, where different cultures intermix to create a vibrant city that has still been able to maintain its unique atmosphere of ease and tolerance. Whether you're looking to enjoy the great outdoors or one of the world's great cities, British Columbia has it all.

Vancouver

Other Canadians sometimes think Vancouverites are, well, a little smug, always boasting about the city, the weather, the skiing, and on and on. But the truth is, they have plenty of reason to boast. Canada's third-largest city is set amid the natural splendour of mountains and sea—a combination that the locals take full advantage of. More than that, it is an ethnically diverse and energetic modern metropolis, and the most important cultural centre in the West.

That combination of nature and urbanity lures not only tourists but also would-be Vancouverites looking to enjoy one of North America's most laid-back cities on a permanent basis, resulting in Vancouver being Canada's fastest-growing metropolitan region. The Vancouver boom has had its downside—including soaring real estate prices—but the city still enjoys a reputation as one of the most beautiful in the world. And if you don't believe it, just ask a Vancouverite.

Vancouver Past and Present

Even though it is situated on a natural, deep harbour, Vancouver's settlement by whites didn't depend on the sea, but on the railroad. In the

Canada by Web

A complete listing of Vancouver's attractions, along with descriptions of its districts, can be found at:
http://www.discovervancouver.com

By the Way

Born in Illinois, William Cornelius Van Horne was instrumental in the shaping of modern Canada. As an executive of the Canadian Pacific Railway, he is best known as the driving force behind the building of the cross-Canada railroad, and he was instrumental in the completion of the main line between Montreal and British Columbia in the 1880s. Railways were clearly in his blood—he promoted construction of one in Cuba, for instance, in the early 20th century—but Van Horne also had other interests.

For one thing, he started up the CP chain of hotels—still highly regarded—and even helped design Quebec City's famous Chateau Frontenac and the Banff Springs Hotel. His mark on Vancouver, meanwhile, went beyond building the railroad: it was Van Horne who, in 1886, suggested the name for the new city, in honour of the 18th-century explorer of the BC coast, George Vancouver.

1880s, William Van Horne, the colourful vice-president of the Canadian Pacific Railway, decided to extend the line beyond Port Moody to an area of land surrounded by the Burrard Inlet, the Fraser River and the Strait of Georgia. There had been attempts at settling the area years before—they didn't get very far. But where the railway went in 19th-century Canada, people followed. The province incorporated the city of Vancouver in 1886, and the people elected—fittingly, perhaps, given the current price of real estate in the area—W.A. MacLean, a real estate dealer, as its first mayor.

A fire destroyed much of the city in the same year, but the rebuilding proved beneficial for Vancouver, and press attention to the reconstruction efforts helped attract industry. When the Klondike Gold Rush hit in 1897, the city became a major port en route to the North, and until the First World War it enjoyed healthy immigration from Ontario and Britain.

As it became a centre for fishing, lumber and mining, Vancouver gradually surpassed other Western cities—first Victoria, then Winnipeg —in economic importance. By the 1920s, it was the third largest metropolitan area in Canada. In the following decades, Vancouver's resource-based industries were enhanced by its increasing importance as a transportation centre, and by the 1960s it was the most active port in Canada, sending wood, wheat and raw materials to destinations around the world. Today, Vancouver is Canada's gateway to the Far East, and municipal and provincial officials have carefully cosseted the area's ties with Japan and China.

Those links to Asia have helped define Vancouver's history and its character. Chinese immigrants helped build the CPR, and many stayed in Vancouver when it reached its final destination in the 1880s. They were joined in subsequent decades by Japanese, South Asians and other immigrants. In recent years, during the pre-handover period in Hong Kong, a second wave of ethnic Chinese have come to the city, and they have formed one of the most thriving and economically powerful Asian

Local Knowledge

Anti-Asian racism in southern British Columbia has a long and depressing history. Fuelled by misconceptions about Chinese culture, Vancouverites staged anti-Chinese riots as far back as 1887, followed by another in 1907. For decades in the first part of the century, British Columbia was instrumental in maintaining discriminatory head tax laws, which demanded inordinate fees to allow Chinese into the country. Even until the 1930s, the city of Vancouver banned Chinese from owning businesses outside the traditional Chinatown district, and across the province they were not allowed to practice law or pharmacy.

Despite the hardships, the Chinese community in British Columbia has not only survived, but thrived. And with the repeal of the head tax in 1947 (which didn't take effect until the 1960s), a new wave of immigrants came to Vancouver. The latest surge, largely from Hong Kong in the late 1980s and early 1990s, has unfortunately reawakened anti-Asian sentiments among some Vancouverites, who blame Chinese for everything from rising real estate prices to congested roadways. While visiting the area, you may hear (or overhear) such sentiments given voice. Just remember: most Vancouverites would like to keep racist attitudes where they belong—in the past.

communities in North America. Today, Vancouver is one of the country's most multicultural cities.

Vancouver is a prosperous post-industrial city—and still one of North America's most beautiful. The downtown area has been almost completely redeveloped in recent years, a process that is still ongoing—Vancouver is one of Canada's fastest-growing metropolitan areas. But the stunning backdrop of water and mountains has not changed. The Vancouver area's 1.3 million residents live in the midst of a wilderness wonderland, and there are plenty of opportunities for fishing, skiing, sailing, swimming—you name it. Within the city's boundaries, meanwhile, a sophisticated cultural community thrives, boasting museums, galleries and performing arts companies that are unrivalled in the West. And for the wanderer, the history of the place and its geography have made Vancouver into a true city of neighbourhoods, from the bustle of downtown to the laid-back streets of Granville Island. All that, combined with some of the friendliest weather in the country, make Vancouver a must-see stop on any exploration of Canada.

Getting There

By air: Vancouver International Airport is on Sea Island, south of downtown about a 30-minute car ride away. Handling flights from all over the world at its two terminals, it is the second busiest airport in Canada, after Toronto's. For information, call (604) 276-6101. **By rail or bus:** The rail station and bus terminal are in the same complex, at 1150 Station Street east of downtown, which is also served by the public transit Skytrain. VIA Rail runs trains from Edmonton to Vancouver three times a week; all major bus companies have routes to Vancouver. **By boat:** Ferry services from other parts of BC operate out of two Vancouver-area ports, to the south and west of the downtown. Call British Columbia Ferry Corp., (604) 277-0277. **By car:** The main route into Vancouver from the east is the Trans-Canada Highway (Highway 1), which runs 975 kilometres from Calgary and through the Rockies. The main northern entry is the Squamish Highway.

Getting Around

Like most Canadian cities, Vancouver has a cheap and efficient public transit system. It's a little hard to figure out, however, since it has so many elements, including buses, a Skytrain that runs into downtown

Local Knowledge

Vancouver is renowned for its mild winters. The average temperature in January is nearly 3 degrees Celsius, and the city receives less than 55 millimetres of snow in a year. The tradeoff for those balmy conditions: Vancouver receives a whopping 1200 millimetres of rain, almost three times the total precipitation (including snow) in Calgary. Bring an umbrella, or be prepared to get wet.

from the suburbs, and a catamaran-like "SeaBus" that connects to the north part of the city. Call BC Transit, (604) 638-2000. Still, once you get used to it (or pick up a travel guide from the transit authority), public transit certainly beats driving. There are no expressways running through downtown Vancouver—which is a good thing, unless you're in a car, since a trip of a few blocks can quickly seem like hours. The fast growth the city has enjoyed recently hasn't helped the traffic situation either.

A Guide to Vancouver

Greater Vancouver is a sprawling place, one of the (if not *the*) largest metropolitan regions in Canada in terms of area. But getting around to its neighbourhoods is relatively easy by walking and public transit. Much of the economic activity in the city is focused in and around the downtown, but you should try to get out and explore Granville Island, Stanley Park and Vancouver's bustling Chinatown. You can see the bulk of the city's hot spots in a couple days; stay longer if you want to soak up the atmosphere.

Downtown

Downtown Vancouver, roughly centred around Robson Street between Burrard and Granville streets, is where much of the action is. Shops of all varieties, restaurants and bars, offices and malls—downtown Vancouver is a rich and vibrant place. Robson Street, running east-west, is the main drag, and on weekend nights teenagers carry on the great

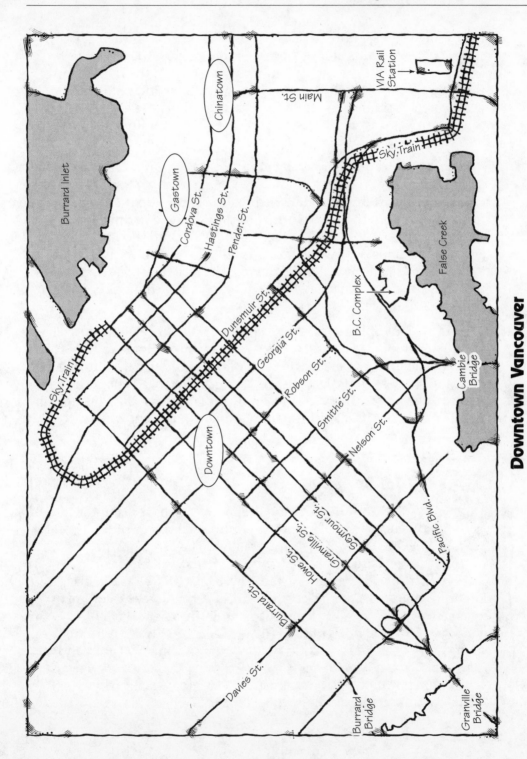

Downtown Vancouver

North American tradition of cruising up and down it in their cars. The shops and restaurants along Robson tend to cater to the tourist crowd. Southeast of Robson Square, a luxurious urban park, the north-south thoroughfare of Granville Street is lined with cafés and nightclubs. Davie Street is similar, a strip of clubs and discotheques, some of them catering to Vancouver's large and thriving gay community.

Vertically impressive, central Vancouver has bloomed with 40-storey office towers and unique architectural sights in recent years, including some of the city's finest hotels. One, the Pan-Pacific, is in **Canada Place**, a building designed to look like a ship on the water-front just north of the downtown core. From here, you can get a good view of the the sea and the mountains that surround the city. There is also a big mall inside, with restaurants and an IMAX big screen theatre; it also serves as the city's convention centre. Like many waterside shopping complexes in Canada (who knows why?), the shops of Canada Place are expensive. Call (604) 666-7200.

At the foot of Robson Street is BC Place Stadium, the world's largest air-inflated dome—it looks like a big marshmallow. Home to the BC Lions Canadian Football League team, the dome is also the site of concerts and special events. Downtown, you'll also want to check out the **Vancouver Art Gallery**, in the old provincial courthouse on Hornsby Street. There's the usual assortment of Canadian art, but what

Out of the Way

The most important museum in Vancouver is to the far southwest of downtown, on the campus of the University of British Columbia. The **Museum of Anthropology**, designed by renowned Canadian architect Arthur Erickson (who also designed the Vancouver Art Gallery), is a collection of spacious halls that trace the history and explore the culture of Canada's Pacific Northwest native peoples. In the Great Hall are more than 30 totem poles of the Haida, Salish, and Kwakiutl tribes, among others. The museum also houses extensive Inuit, African and Asian exhibits, but the showcase is *The Raven and the Beast*, a huge cedar carving by modern Haida artist Bill Reid that weighs in at over 4 tons. For information, call (604) 822-3825.

distinguishes this gallery is a fine collection of works by Emily Carr, the largest in Canada. Call (604) 682-4700.

Gastown

Really an extension of the downtown core, the Gastown district is just a few minutes' walk from Canada Place. The area gets its name from "Gassy Jack" Deighton, who opened a saloon on the shore of Burrard Inlet in 1867, around which sprang up a backwater settlement that didn't really take off until the arrival of the CPR in the 1880s.

For much of this century, Gastown fell into disrepair, a skid row of cheap hotels and warehouses. In the '70s, however, it became the focus of a big urban rejuvenation program, and today firmly caters to the tourist crowd. The buildings—the oldest in Vancouver—have been restored along the old cobblestone streets, and fake gas lamps give the impression of a made-to-order historic district. Still, the area is popular with visitors, and it's home to some of the city's busiest nightspots. In particular, the Town Pump, on Gastown's main drag of Water Street, is an institution in the Vancouver alternative music scene.

Chinatown

Just south of Gastown around Pender Street, Vancouver's Chinatown is one of the largest in Canada—and one of the most active. The community has deep roots in Vancouver: many Chinese came to Canada in the

Local Knowledge

Cambie Street, running roughly north-south through the central city, has long been the economic dividing line in Vancouver. Historically, the well-to-do settled west of it, living on large lots and owning their land. To the east were the poor and working class, whose houses sat on tiny parcels of land and who usually rented rather than owned. The dividing line is less stark than it was in the past, but you can still see signs of it today, particularly along Hasting Street east of Gastown, a poor neighbourhood that is home to a depressingly persistent drug abuse problem.

Local Knowledge

The bars and nightclubs in Vancouver are open late, but don't be surprised if they seem less than active in the wee hours of the morning. Compared with other urbanites, Vancouver locals are notorious for going home early, and many of the nightspots will seem pretty deserted after 10 p.m.

mid-19th century to work on the railroad, and for many decades they and those who followed were not allowed to conduct business outside the traditional Chinatown district. With the recent influx of immigrants from Hong Kong, the area has become the focal point of one of the largest Chinese communities outside Asia. If Asian cuisine is your thing, this is the place to get it in Vancouver. And many gourmets rate its restaurants, especially its Cantonese ones, above those in Toronto—thanks in large part to the wealth of fresh seafood available to Vancouver's cooks.

The main attraction, outside food, in Chinatown is the **Dr. Sun Yat-Sen Classical Chinese Garden**, a 2.5-acre park which, as the name implies, was built in honour of the founder of the first Chinese Republic. Built for Expo '86, the garden cost millions of dollars, and incorporates patterns that attempt to embrace the concepts of yin and yang, balance in all things. Guided tours are available. Call (604) 662-3207.

Stanley Park

Beyond the trendy West End, a coveted residential area for Vancouver's yuppie set, Stanley Park occupies the western end of the city's central peninsula. At nearly 1,000 acres, it is one of the largest urban parks in the world, and it is still quite wild, with heavily forested areas and beaches surrounded by sea on three sides. But it's very busy, especially on weekends, and is a favourite getaway for locals.

The park can be circumnavigated along the seawall, a 10-kilometre trail that will take several hours to walk but provides wonderful views of Vancouver's natural setting. (If you don't want to walk, you can rent a bicycle.) Other trails criss-cross the park, and guided nature hikes are also available at Nature House, on the south side of Lost Lagoon, a former tidal inlet that's now a shallow lake. Along its perimeter, Stanley Park has three popular beaches, named English Bay, Second and Third—all busy spots in summer.

North of Lost Lagoon is a children's zoo and the impressive **Vancouver Aquarium**, its entrance marked by a distinctive native carving. The aquarium houses more than 6,000 marine species, specializing in the sea life of the Pacific Northwest, including stellar sea lions and performing orca (killer whales). Call (604)268-9900.

Granville Island

South of downtown under the Granville Street Bridge, Granville Island was once an industrial wasteland, but enjoyed a substantial redevelopment in the 1970s. Today, the island's industrial past has largely been preserved in its buildings, and the area has become one of Vancouver's most popular places for shopping, eating and socializing. At the centre of it is the Granville Island Public Market, which houses over 50 shops and stalls selling an amazing variety of food—from fish to fudge. Nearby are plenty of galleries, cafés and restaurants, where the laid-back

Out of the Way

If you're in Vancouver for an extended visit, be sure to check out the natural attractions that so define the city's lifestyle. In the winter, **Grouse Mountain**, just 10 minutes north of downtown in North Vancouver, is a quick and easy destination for skiers, with 22 runs and seven lifts. Call (604) 984-0661. In the summer, visit the beaches. Besides those in Stanley Park, the most popular is **Kitsilano** (or "Kits") **Beach**, southwest of downtown over the Burrard Bridge, a favourite hang-out for students from the nearby University of British Columbia.

And if you want a real taste of the lifestyle, go to **Wreck Beach**, on the western edge of the UBC campus. The beach seems to harken back to hippie days, with long-haired denizens braiding their hair, selling or smoking illegal recreational drugs, or just letting it all hang out—literally. On Wreck Beach, clothing is optional.

Local Knowledge

On weekends, parking on Granville Island is a nightmare. Save yourself a hassle and take either public transit or one of the privately operated ferries that run between downtown and the island.

Vancouver attitude is in full form. As well, a Kids Only Market near the island entrance caters to children, and there are a water park and adventure playground to keep the young ones busy.

Out and About in British Columbia

There is so much to do in British Columbia outside of Vancouver that it's difficult to know where to start. You can soak up the historic charm

B.C.: Towns of interest and outdoor attractions

of Victoria, ski the world's best slopes at Whistler, bask in the sunshine of the Okanagan Valley or fish in the Campbell River. Even then, you wouldn't cover everything BC has to offer—but it would be a start.

Victoria

The capital of British Columbia, Victoria used to be the premier city in the province, but it was long ago superceded by Vancouver. Perched on the southern shore of Vancouver Island, about 100 kilometres west of Vancouver, the area was first settled back in 1843 by the Hudson's Bay Co., and boomed during the Fraser River gold rush of 1858. It was the early capital of the Vancouver Island colony, and it has tried hard to maintain its 19th-century charm: Victoria is probably still the most *Victorian* of Canadian cities.

Besides government, tourism is a big industry in greater Victoria, a metropolitan area of 300,000 people. The most popular way to get there is by ferry from Tsawwassen, south of Vancouver; call BC Ferry Corp., (604) 669-1211 in Vancouver, (250) 386-3431 in Victoria. Air commuters, meanwhile, arrive at Victoria International Airport, north of the city, which serves both major Canadian airlines.

You can easily walk around Victoria and catch most of its attractions. The harbourfront area now has a boardwalk system. The first things you'll notice at the top of the inner harbour are the Empress Hotel, built in 1908, and the legislative buildings, completed in 1898. Behind the Empress are the **Crystal Gardens**, once an indoor swimming pool and now a conservatory devoted to exotic and rare animals. Many of the other attractions in Victoria are overtly touristy and try to capitalize on the city's much-vaunted "Old World charm." Most notable

Local Knowledge

There are few more quintessentially Victorian pastimes as taking tea in the Empress Hotel. A Canadian Pacific hotel, the luxurious Empress puts on both regular teas (with scones and crumpets) as well as high teas, the whole shebang of cucumber and cream cheese sandwiches. Make sure you call ahead: (250) 384-8111.

Out of the Way

Even if Victoria isn't your cup of tea (pun intended), it's a good jumping-off point for exploring the natural beauty of Vancouver Island. One of the most rewarding but arduous ways to do that is along the **West Coast Trail**, a 77-kilometre-long path through the wilderness that begins in Port Renfrew, west of Victoria. Originally laid out as a telegraph route in 1891, the West Coast Trail is regarded as one of the most difficult hiking areas in the world, and is located in **Pacific Rim National Park**, a land of rich marine life, dense forest and spectacular scenery.

If you plan on doing the trail, you have to be prepared: trail use is strictly monitored by Parks Canada, and you will need to reserve and obtain a permit. Once you're in, be careful: plenty of tales of broken legs and ankles have emerged from West Coast Trail treks. For more info, call Discover BC, 1-800-663-6000.

is the **English Village**, west of the harbour, which is a re-creation of an Elizabethan town, and which contains Anne Hathaway House, a re-creation of the English birthplace of William Shakespeare's wife.

The Okanagan Valley

In south-central British Columbia a four-hour drive east of Vancouver, the Okanagan Valley stretches for 200 kilometres between the Columbia and Cascade mountain ranges. The Okanagan is widely touted as one of the most beautiful landscapes in the country, a region of low-lying hills and glacial lakes that also enjoys hot, dry, sunny weather. That's made it a prime wine region in Western Canada, as well as a mecca for tourists from Eastern Canada and the United States.

In the summer, they come to explore the quaint villages nestled along the shores of Okanagan Lake, and to enjoy the region's 40 golf courses and winery tours (there are 28 wineries in the valley). In the winter, the Okanagan is a popular spot for skiing, with three ski resorts (Silver Star Mountain, Big White and Apex) located near Penticton, the second-largest community in the valley after Kamloops. Among the favoured spots for hiking and camping is the well-serviced (and

Local Knowledge

The combination of great weather and outdoor activities has made the Okanagan Valley an increasingly popular spot for vacationers, and some BCers complain that it has become far too touristy. Towns like Kelowna and Penticton can be jam-packed with cars and trailers on summer weekends. And many of the tourists are staying: the area has become a breeding ground for the high-security suburban developments called gated communities, which cater in particular to senior citizens from outside the valley.

By the Way

Driving around British Columbia, you'll drive through miles and miles of seemingly pristine forest—and then suddenly come across a great patch of barren land that looks like a bomb hit it. Pockmarked with stumps, the unsightly lands are the result of clear-cutting, a practice whereby loggers take down every tree within a defined area. It's a controversial practice: environmentalists claim that it destroys ecosystems that can never fully recover, all for the sake of making money. The forest companies, meanwhile, counter that clear-cutting allows tracts of forest to recover naturally, much as it would after a fire.

practically bear-free) **Cathedral Provincial Park**, near the town of Keremeos by the US border. Call (250) 371-6400 for information.

Whistler

About 120 kilometres north of Vancouver along Highway 99 is perhaps the best skiing area in BC. The area receives—on average—10 metres of snow every winter. **Whistler** and **Blackcomb** mountains are widely regarded as the best areas in the world for "cruising"—no, not picking up

247

Canada by Web

Information on Whistler, along with snow and weather conditions, is available at:
http://www.whistler.travel.bc.ca

strangers in bars, but long, not-too-strenuous ski runs that seem to go on for hours before you have to hop back on a lift. That's not to say that the area isn't challenging: near the tops of both mountains, there are opportunities for deep-snow powder skiing and a couple of very difficult mogul runs. You can ski both mountains for under $60 a day.

The village itself is a quaint-by-design place at the foot of the mountains, and has an unparalleled array of facilities: more than 75 restaurants, myriad ski and clothing stores, and the most slope-slide lodgings in North America, all within a 10-minute walk of the ski lifts. Everything's expensive, but that's a testament to Whistler's popularity (especially among Japanese skiers). And there's no point complaining that the place is too touristy—it's *for* tourists, after all. And as resort areas go, there are few better.

Campbell River

The fabled Pacific salmon fishery, once a mainstay of the BC economy, is in big trouble thanks to rapidly dwindling fish stocks, and it is still unclear what steps governments will take to restrict sport fishing, historically one of the province's most popular attractions.

Still, a few areas in the province are legendary fishing spots. Perhaps the most famous is Campbell River, a town of about 28,000 on the eastern coast of Vancouver Island north of Victoria. If you're just passing through and want to try your luck, you can rent fishing equipment at the Government Wharf; if you're more serious, a host of charters and guided expeditions are available from local outfitters. There are all kinds of fish in the lakes around Campbell River and in the Georgia Strait, and they include five types of Pacific salmon. But what fishermen from around the world really come here for is tyee salmon in nearby Discovery Passage—huge lunkers that top 13 kilograms.

Out of the Way

About 80 kilometres off the northern BC coast lies some of the most pristine wilderness in the country. The **Queen Charlotte Islands** comprise a 250-kilometre-long archipelago in the Pacific which, unlike most places in Canada, have been untouched by glacial activity. The result is a biologically unique area of abundant wildlife and haunting ancient forests. To get there, you have to fly in to Graham or Moresby islands, home to the Queen Charlottes' largest towns, or take a ferry from the mainland.

The southern section of the islands is now a protected national wildlife reserve, **Gwaii Haanas**, and it is home to a UN World Heritage Site at **Ninstints**, an old Haida village with spectacular totem poles. The wildlife is amazing: huge black bears, eagles, salmon, puffins, sea lions, whales and dolphins. You can get to the park by boat, kayak or plane, but there are no roads and only a few primitive campsites. As well, you have to reserve a visit to the park, and once there you will be watched by Haida Gwaii Watchmen, whose job it is to protect the heritage sites. For info on visiting the Queen Charlotte Islands, call (604) 559-4742.

The Least You Need to Know

➤ Vancouver is British Columbia's largest city and the third largest in Canada.

➤ Victoria, known as the most "British" city in Canada, is on Vancouver Island, which offers some of the province's best fishing and most challenging hiking trails.

➤ Outdoor areas worth visiting are the Okanagan Valley, Whistler Resort and the Queen Charlotte Islands.

Part 5
The North

There is much more than igloos and dogsleds in Northern Canada. Though the North is remote and vast, modern air travel and roads have made getting around easier, and a good dose of determination and excitement will help you to see a part of Canada that many Canadians have yet to conquer. Cost and temperature are big concerns when thinking about heading North, but it will be worth the trip—if not for the cites, then for the fishing and abundant natural beauty you'll be sure to encounter.

Yukon Territory

● Whitehorse

Northwest Territories

● Yellowknife

The Northwest Territories

Welcome to the Northwest Territories

How many times have Canadians heard foreigners ask whether everyone in Canada lived in an igloo? It's a national joke now, but it's doubly ironic, because few (housebound) Canadians ever see the land where there actually *are* igloos.

There is more to the Northwest Territories, however, than ice houses, and the region contains a rich diversity of land and people. Much of the NWT is a vast wilderness, and the territories comprise more than a third of Canada's entire land mass. Spread out across that huge area are only about 60 communities, in which live 60,000 or so people. About a third of the NWT's population are Inuit, whom whites used to call Eskimos, but there are also substantial Dene and Métis populations.

From a visitor's standpoint, the trouble with the NWT is that they are so far away. Modern air travel and the construction of a few roads have made it easier, but the region still is difficult to explore. Then again, that is part of the North's allure—the promise that you will be seeing things that few people have ever seen before.

Politically, the face of the Northwest Territories is about to undergo a major overhaul. In 1992, the Inuit people of the Eastern Arctic voted in favour of ratifying a complex land claims accord with the federal government, under which a new territory would be established. Nunavut—Inuktitut for "our land"—is a two-million-square-kilometre swath of the Arctic that will be under the effective control of the region's native peoples. Nunavut will have its own legislative assembly, modelled after those in the Northwest and Yukon territories, and its largest settlement will be Iqaluit on Baffin Island. When the new territory becomes official in 1999, it will be the first redrawing of the Canadian map since Newfoundland joined Confederation in 1949.

Getting There

... Is half the battle. The Northwest Territories are, to say the least, remote. By road, the distance from Vancouver to Yellowknife, the territorial capital, is nearly 2,600 kilometres; from Edmonton, the nearest major city, it's more than 1,500 kilometres; from Toronto, it's a whopping drive of 4,550 kilometres.

By air: Most of the tourist traffic to the NWT is by air. Although most communities in the region have their own airfields—it's often the only way to get from point A to point B—chances are you will fly into Yellowknife, as 90 per cent of other travellers do. Connections from southern cities, which usually stop over in Edmonton, are very good, and both major airlines offer regularly scheduled flights. **By car:** The Mackenzie Highway and the Yellowknife Highway—two-lane roads that are sometimes paved, sometimes gravel—are the main links between northwestern Alberta and the communities of Hay River and Yellowknife. The Liard Highway runs from Fort Nelson, in northern British Columbia, to the Mackenzie route. The Dempster Highway links up with the Klondike Highway, east of Dawson City, Yukon, and runs to the Mackenzie Delta community of Inuvik. Before you head out, remember the distances involved. And remember, too, that gas stations, restaurants and food supplies can be hundreds of kilometres apart.

Getting Around

The other half of the battle. Although there are some highways, they mostly link up areas in the western territories around Yellowknife and south, and there simply are no roads (except for winter roads that run over frozen lakes) to many communities. You can still see plenty of territory by automobile, but remember there are great distances involved, and you'd better enjoy spending time in your car. On the other hand, almost all communities of more than 100 people have an airfield, and the territories are served by nearly 50 regional airlines. You can book flights from Yellowknife or Fort Smith to most other places you'll want to go. Flying is a good way to see plenty of territory (and even some wildlife, like herds of caribou and muskoxen) in a relatively short period of time. The downside? It's expensive.

Travelling in the territories is a unique experience, but one that you want to prepare for well in advance. Consider in particular two factors: weather and money. Weather in the North tends to extremes, and it's often unpredictable. You may, depending on weather conditions, not get to where you're planning on going, and since so much of getting around the NWT depends on air travel, flight delays are not uncommon.

Which brings up the second factor, money. Everything is more expensive in the North than just about anywhere else in Canada. You'll pay the same amount of money for a ramshackle hut in Pangnirtung as you will for a luxury hotel room in Toronto. (If the weather's bad, you'll still count it a bargain!) The same goes for air travel, which is a very

Canada by Web

Two very good Web sites give thorough information on travelling to the Northwest Territories:
http://www.nwttravel.nt.ca
http://www.arctic-travel.com

Also check out the Nunavut tourism web site:
http://www.nunatour.nt.ca

Local Knowledge

Not to belabour the obvious, but it can get very cold in the North. Average January temperatures in many areas of the Northwest Territories can reach -30 degrees Celsius, and temperatures of -60 are not unheard of. Suffice it to say, it is very rare for tourists to visit except during the summer. And in many areas, particularly the Mackenzie Valley, summers can be quite warm, with an average of about 16 degrees Celsius.

pricey way to get around, but then again you don't have much choice. If your flight is delayed, then you will have to pay for the extra nights' accommodation, plus meals and other expenses. Try to factor that in to the budget for your trip.

As a general rule, the more remote the location you're trying to get to, the more expensive it's going to be—and, as a corollary, the more it will cost you to stay there. The point is, if you're travelling to the North and plan on staying a while, think about time and money. And make sure you have plenty of both.

By the Way

A couple of Yellowknife facts:

- It has the most sunshine of any Canadian city, with more than 1,030 hours a year.
- It is probably the only city with a street called Ragged Ass Road.

Yellowknife

This is usually the first stop on any tour of the Northwest Territories, a city of about 18,000 people on the north shore of Great Slave Lake. The territories' only city, Yellowknife's economy is based largely on its status as territorial capital and on mining—gold was discovered in the area as far back as 1898, and the city is now home to two producing mines. The downtown area is remarkably modern looking, with a 19-storey high-rise at its centre, containing a mall, condominiums and offices. Beyond a cluster of modern office buildings, including a sleek domed legislature and city hall, typical suburban houses sit alongside log cabins and shacks—a testament to the new-ness of the city, but also to the price of housing.

The centre of social activity in Yellowknife is the **Prince of Wales Northern Heritage Centre**, which houses an extensive museum and a cultural centre for local theatre companies, visiting artists and com-munity groups. Most of all, however, the citizens of Yellowknife enjoy a host of outdoor activities: the city is home to an Olympic-size swimming pool, plenty of fishing in the nearby Great Slave, extensive cross-country trails and campgrounds, and two yacht clubs.

Out and About in the NWT

If you can get to them, the Northwest Territories offer some of Canada's most spectacular and untouched areas. From the Yellowknife area, you can book chartered flights and guided trips that will take you to fantas-tic fishing holes, hiking trails and amazing wildlife areas. For other sights, you'll have to travel farther afield—even, perhaps, to the ulti-mate travel destination, the North Pole. The NWT are a huge land mass, spanning most of Central Canada's width. How far you go depends only on what you want to do, how experienced an outdoor person you are, and how much money you are prepared to spend.

Local Knowledge

Much of the land in the Northwest Territories belongs to its native peoples, who make up over half of the population. (The biggest hand-over to native groups occurred in 1993, when two million square kilometres of land and offshore area in the eastern territories were subdivided to create Nunavut, whose predominant group is the Inuit and which will have its own legislative assembly.) In general, the North's natives welcome tourist dollars, and Nunavut in particular is trying to attract visitors. Still, some land settlement zones have travel restrictions, and when you're out exploring you should be careful that you are not trespass-ing on private property. The subdivisions and various land claims is-sues can get quite complicated, but it's up to you to know where you are going. For information, call 1-800-661-0788.

Great Fishing: The Mackenzie River System

Fishing is one of the most popular tourist activities in the NWT, and it's also a good way to see the local wildlife—eagles, bears and mink among them. But the main thing is the fish. And the two huge lakes that feed into the Mackenzie River system are legendary for the number and size of the fish they produce.

Yellowknife sits on **Great Slave Lake**, a very cold and very deep lake that is a reservoir for myriad streams and rivers. In Great Slave, a huge body of water that comprises nearly 30,000 square kilometres, the most abundant sport fish are northern pike and pickerel (or walleye), and among the lakes and rivers that dot the southern territories you'll also find grayling and whitefish. The other principal town on Great Slave is Hay River, on the south side, where a small commercial fishery operates. Near it, the **Hay River Dene Reserve** offers visitor programs about native culture and area wildlife at its Dene Cultural Institute.

To the north is **Great Bear Lake**, probably one of the best sport-fishing places in the world. At more than 30,000 square kilometres, it is the largest lake lying completely within Canada, and the eighth largest lake in the world. The scenery around Great Bear is definitely Arctic—stunted spruce and flat plains characteristic of the northern taiga. The lake is frozen for eight months of the year—it sits astride the Arctic Circle—but during the brief summer it comes alive with boats and guides plying its waters for trophy-sized lake trout, pike and grayling. From the lake, you can also book a fly-out trip in search of Arctic char.

Nahanni National Park Reserve

Huge, beautiful and forbidding, Nahanni National Park Reserve occupies nearly 5,000 square kilometres of rugged rock outcroppings and mighty rivers in the southwestern corner of the Northwest Territories. The centrepiece of the park is Virginia Falls, more than 92 metres high and 200 metres wide, and Nahanni's natural splendour has earned it a World Heritage Site designation by the United Nations.

Best seen by canoe or river raft, Nahanni is an increasingly popular destination, and it has garnered a reputation as the ultimate in adventure travel. There are only two campsites, and the rest of the time you'll have to rough it along the gravelly shores of the South Nahanni or Flat River. But you had better know what you're doing before you go: there are 50-kilometre stretches in the park that are pure white water.

Nahanni is difficult to get to. There are no roads, and most people get there by air from the towns of Fort Simpson, Blackstone, Fort Liard or Watson Lake. Really, really hardy adventurers could try to get there by raft or canoe along the connecting rivers outside the park—a tough slug. The easy way is to hire a charter company out of one of the towns and let the hired help do most of the work getting to and around Nahanni. A chartered trip to Nahanni can run into the thousands of dollars. As always in the North, the easy way is the expensive way. For park information, call (867) 695-3182.

Wood Buffalo National Park

Accessible by road from Fort Smith, southeast of Hay River, Wood Buffalo is Canada's largest national park, comprising more than 44,000 square kilometres. Only a third of the park is in the NWT—the rest is in Alberta—but the only road access is from the territories. Wood Buffalo is a wilderness park, meaning that it provides only the barest amenities for visitors. The only serviced campsite is at Pine Lake, south of Fort Smith. For the rest, the best choice is hiking or canoeing. The park also runs some guided hikes or will help you hire a guide. Park staff allow only 8,000 visitors a year.

The scenery in Wood Buffalo is less than spectacular, consisting largely of low hills, boreal forest and marshlands. What people go there for is the wildlife—more than 45 species of mammals and 220 species of

Local Knowledge

The southern NWT is bug country, and mosquito season is at its worst during the dog days of July and early August. If you plan to visit Wood Buffalo National Park or other parts of the region, those in the know recommend going in May to June, or late August to early October. Even then, bring plenty of bug spray.

Northwest Territories: Major towns and outdoor attractions

birds. The prime attraction are the 3,000 or so bison, the largest free-roaming buffalo herd in the world. The park was originally home to the long-legged wood buffalo, but since the introduction of thousands of plains buffalo in the 1920s, the herd has become hybridized.

In Wood Buffalo, too, is the world's only natural nesting area for the endangered whooping crane, a huge white bird that stands nearly 1.5 metres high and whose wing span can reach over two metres. Although the birds are now one of the main benefits of the park's existence, few visitors actually get to see them: the whooping cranes' nesting areas are strictly off limits.

Aulavik National Park

If you want to get a taste of the Far (Far) North, this is one of the places you can do it. Located on Banks Island, about 800 kilometres northeast of Inuvik, Aulavik is more than 12,000 square kilometres of tundra, and home to such Arctic species as polar bears, arctic fox, lemmings and caribou. The park is better known, however, for its herd of muskoxen— between 40,000 and 60,000 of them. Aulavik is also a bird sanctuary, providing habitat for peregrine falcons, Brant geese and sandhill cranes. The area has long been used, as well, by humans. The Inuit used the

Local Knowledge

If you're camping in the Arctic, be careful where you tread and what you move—even the rocks. Many sites of archeological significance in the High Arctic and elsewhere consist of little more than piles of stones, but to the Inuit and to researchers they can speak volumes about the culture and history of the region. The common advice is that if you use rocks to anchor your tent, put them back where you found them when you move on. Be equally careful with wildlife. Bears are (of course) dangerous, and not to be approached. But don't take chances either with muskoxen, which can be very aggressive during mating season, and with foxes, which can carry rabies.

Out of the Way

This is way, way out. But if you'd like to follow in the footsteps of Peary (well, not literally), it can be done. In the popular imagination, the North Pole may be the ultimate destination on earth. Peary did it on foot in 1909, but you don't have to take the hard way. The easy way is by plane, and two airlines run tours out of the community of Resolute, on Cornwallis Island, all the way to the Pole. You have to set aside a week to 10 days to go, because flying over the pole depends on weather. Once you take off, it's an arduous journey even by plane, with frequent refuelling stops, all for the glory of seeing the barren patch of ice and snow that is the North Pole. The experience may be priceless, but the trip carries a hefty price tag: upwards of $10,000.

Thomsen River, which bisects the park, as a hunting route for centuries, and archeological sites in the area date back more than 3,000 years.

The Thomsen is still used today, but mostly by visitors. As the northernmost navigable river in Canada, it's a lure for canoeists and a good way to see the park. The only feasible way to get to Aulavik is by plane, which you can charter out of Inuvik. For park information, call (867) 690-3904.

The Least You Need to Know

➤ The Northwest Territories are huge, taking up one-third of Canada's total land mass.

➤ Travel to and within the Northwest Territories can be time-consuming and expensive, so plan your budget and your timetable carefully before you go.

➤ The capital of the NWT is Yellowknife.

➤ Among the outdoor attractions are Great Slave and Great Bear Lakes, Nahanni National Park Reserve, Wood Buffalo National Park and Aulavik National Park.

Chapter 17

Yukon Territory

In This Chapter

➤ Touring the land of the Klondike Gold Rush

➤ Exploring Yukon's outdoors

Welcome to the Yukon

Like its neighbour the Northwest Territories, much of the Yukon is made up of wild and forbidding places. Along with unspoilt tundra and raging rivers, rugged mountains—including the tallest peak in Canada —criss-cross the territory, making it inaccessible and remote. In fact, few people live there. Caribou outnumber the 28,000 or so humans by a factor of six.

And yet, the Yukon is an important part of Canadian history, if only because it was here, in 1896, that three prospectors discovered gold on the Bonanza River—and the Klondike Gold Rush began. Over the next two years, a hundred thousand men from across Canada and the United States set out for the Yukon in search of the precious metal. Only about a third made it, but along the way they opened up the North to the rest of Canada.

Today, Yukon Territory is still home to gold and other kinds of mining. But an increasing number of people following in the prospectors' footsteps are not miners, but travellers—300,000 a year. For them, the Yukon certainly holds a treasure trove, from the rich history of the Rush to the austere beauty of the wilderness and mountains.

Getting There

By air: Whitehorse is the major air destination in the territory, and Canadian Airlines runs daily flights through Vancouver from domestic centres; Air North flies to Whitehorse from Juneau and Fairbanks, Alaska. **By car:** The Alaska Highway runs from Dawson Creek, BC, to Whitehorse, a distance of about 1,450 kilometres. It's typically in better shape than a shorter and less-used route, the Stewart Cassiar Highway (Route 37), which runs for about 1,280 kilometres from Kitwanga, BC,

Local Knowledge

Robert Service, in such early 20th-century poems as *The Cremation of Sam McGee*, was responsible for much of the myth and legend that surrounds the Klondike Gold Rush (even though he arrived in the Yukon years after the rush was over), and he popularized a now-familiar description of the North, Land of the Midnight Sun.

It's true: days are longer near the Arctic Circle—but only in the summer. The physics behind the science have to do with the Earth's tilt, making the North closer to the sun in the summer and farther away in the winter. Above the Arctic Circle (at about 66 degrees latitude), the sun remains in the sky at midnight in the midsummer—and in midwinter, it never rises above the horizon.

Few northern communities exist north of the Arctic Circle (an exception is Inuvik, NWT), but they still get very long winter nights and very long summer days. It might sound odd for a region known to be so cold, but one thing you will want to pack if touring the North in summer is plenty of sun-screen and a good pair of sunglasses. The air is very clear, and there is plenty of sunshine—so protect yourself. There have even been reports of people camping in the open for a night and waking up with a sunburn.

to Whitehorse. **By boat:** You can take a car ferry from Bellingham, Washington, in the continental United States and from several Alaskan ports of call to Skagway, on Alaska's south coast near the Yukon border. From there, you can drive over White Pass to Whitehorse.

Getting Around

Touring Yukon Territory presents a similar situation to the Northwest Territories—that is, it can be difficult—but things are made a bit easier by better, more extensive highways. Many of the territory's outdoor destinations are accessible by car. The Alaska Highway crosses the southern part of the territory and into Alaska, but along the way it passes through Whitehorse and skirts Kluane National Park. It's currently undergoing major upgrades, but remains the best route through the Yukon. The Klondike Highway, meanwhile, runs from Whitehorse to Dawson City, one of the territory's most popular tourist destinations.

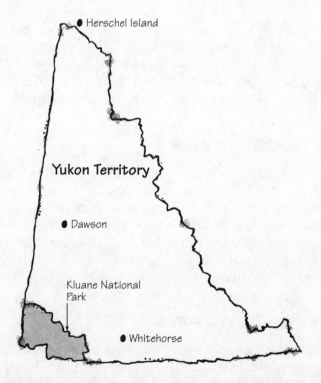

Yukon Territory: Major towns and outdoor attractions

By the Way

The Alaska Highway was an amazing feat of engineering and wartime fortitude. Started in 1942 to provide a military route to Alaska—which the United States feared was vulnerable to a Japanese attack—the highway was built through 2,400 kilometres of forbidding wilderness and vast mountain ranges (five in all) in a mere eight months. It took 11,000 US army personnel and 16,000 civilians (many of them Americans) to construct the highway, which runs all the way from Dawson Creek, in northeastern BC, to Fairbanks, Alaska.

From Dawson City, motorists can take the Dempster Highway northwest all the way to Inuvik in the Mackenzie Delta region of the Northwest Territories.

For more remote locations, you usually have to arrange air travel or go through any one of the dozens of outfitters who operate in the Yukon. Two centres for regional airlines and private travel arrangements are Whitehorse, which services the southern part of the territory, and Inuvik, NWT, the tourism centre of the Western Arctic.

Out and About in the YT

A lot of visitors go to the Yukon simply to explore its history. Along the highways and in Whitehorse and Dawson City, you'll find many of the normal amenities that cater to the tourist dollar. If you venture farther afield—and if you're the outdoor type, you certainly will—then the rules of northern camping still apply: plan carefully, leave yourself lots of time, and make sure you have the funds and the equipment to handle the Yukon's often harsh conditions.

Whitehorse and Dawson City

Nestled in a protected valley on the shores of the Yukon River, Whitehorse is home to about 20,000 permanent residents, and the capital of Yukon Territory is the usual first stop for visitors. The city, located in the far south of the Yukon, has long been a gateway to points north:

Local Knowledge

Thanks to the mountains that cut it off from the Pacific Ocean to the west, much of Yukon Territory is subject to extreme temperature shifts. Dawson, for instance, can be hot in the summer, with temperatures over 30 degrees not unheard of. Winters are another matter. The coldest temperature ever in Canada was recorded at Snag, Yukon, in February 1947, when the thermometer dipped to minus 62.8 degrees Celsius.

it got its start as a stop-over for would-be miners during the Klondike Gold Rush.

Today, Whitehorse is a small but modern city. It enjoyed a mini-boom during the 1990s, when gold prices were high on world markets. The cultural centre of the territory, its recently built **Yukon Arts Centre** houses a collection of works by Canadian and Yukon artists, as well as being the prime venue for the city's remarkably active theatre community.

Around town, you'll find plenty of attractions to remind you of the area's Klondike days. You can take a ride on the **Klondike**, a restored turn-of-the-century riverboat, or explore the **Old Log Church** (now a museum), built in 1900 to service the spiritual needs of the gold-hungry prospectors. The **MacBride Museum**, meanwhile, has galleries devoted to the natural and human history of the territory, including an exhibit focusing on the Gold Rush. Most of the attractions in Whitehorse are open only during the summer; the MacBride is open year-round. Call (867) 667-2709.

If you want to continue exploring Klondike country, take the Klondike Highway to Dawson, about 530 kilometres to the north along the Yukon River. This was the big camp for prospectors during the Gold Rush, and in 1898 Dawson had a population of 30,000—the biggest Canadian city west of Winnipeg. It's never quite been the same since, and today the town of about 1,300 relies not on gold, but on the tourist dollar.

Many of the historic buildings in Dawson have undergone substantial restoration since the 1960s as part of an attempt to make the place look and feel the way it did during the Rush. Among the more notable is the **Palace Grand Theatre**, where the local tourist association stages vaudeville-style reviews to more than 40,000 visitors every summer. In the old Arctic Brotherhood Hall, built in 1899, is **Diamond Tooth Gertie's Gambling Casino**. The old Territorial Administration Building (1901) houses the **Dawson City Museum and Historical Society**, which features detailed exhibits looking at Dawson's history. For information, call the Klondike Visitors Association, (867) 993-5575.

The Chilkoot Trail

If you were wealthy during the Gold Rush, you travelled to the North by ship. But for many of those who went, that was beyond their poor or middle-class means. For them, getting to the gold often meant passing through the Chilkoot Pass—a 1,000-metre-high break in the mountains at the Alaska-Yukon border—to get to Bennett Lake in the territorial interior, where they built boats to carry them along the Yukon River. In those days, the Chilkoot Trail was a hotbed of frontier lawlessness, and the North-West Mounted Police (later the RCMP) set up a post at the pass to deter the criminal element from taking advantage of the 30,000 or so prospectors who used the trail every year.

Today, the Chilkoot Trail is used by hikers, not prospectors. And its 53 kilometres are lined with shelters and good campgrounds, built jointly by the US National Park Service and the Yukon Government. The trail begins at Dyea, Alaska, near Skagway, and then crosses through British Columbia before ending in the Yukon southwest. It is littered with picks, wagon wheels, stoves, cans—artifacts left over from the Rush.

Despite its modernization, the trail is still a difficult hike, and you will need to be well prepared. Weather conditions can change rapidly, and a July snowfall in the Chilkoot Pass is not unheard of. But if you really want to re-create the Gold Rush, this is the way to do it. For trail information, call Parks Canada in Whitehorse, 1-800-661-0486.

Local Knowledge

Whether you're walking the Chilkoot or exploring any other outdoor area in the North, try to follow the practice of no-trace camping. That means, first of all, taking out everything—empty cans, packages, tissues—that you brought in. Respect the wild area, its plants and animals. And don't take any souvenirs. On the Chilkoot Trail, resist the temptation to pick up any of the shovels, cans or other Gold Rush artifacts you find along the way. Not only is it illegal, but it can ruin the experience for those who follow you.

Kluane National Park

In the southwest corner of the Yukon, Kluane (pronounced kloo-wan-ee) National Park, about 22,000 square kilometres in area, is dominated by the St. Elias Mountains, which are the youngest in North America. They are also among the most active, and Kluane experiences more than 1,000 earth tremors every year. The western part of the park contains the highest mountains, known as the Icefields Ranges, home to the tallest peak in Canada, Mount Logan, which rises 5,959 metres above sea level and is a challenge for even the most experienced mountaineer. Around the mountains are glaciers, and Kluane has upwards of 4,000 of them.

If you want to see such peaks up close, you had better be an experienced and hardy back-country expert, or be willing to pay big bucks for a local tour outfitter to take you there. The biggest peaks are, unfortunately, not visible by car.

But the park also offers other, more accessible glimpses of the Yukon's wonders. Besides mountains, a good chunk of Kluane is a greenbelt area, inhabited by a rich abundance of northern wildlife. The park has the largest known concentration of Dall sheep in the world, and as many as 250 grizzly bears. This part of the park lies just off the Alaska Highway, and is easily reachable by car. You can explore along well-marked trails that lead off the highway, or camp in the grounds at Kathleen Lake (on the east end of Kluane) or along the

Canada by Web

For information on Yukon excursions and attractions, check out:
http://www.yukonweb.com
http://www.yukon.com

many campgrounds that dot the side of the road. For information, call (867) 634-2251.

Herschel Island

More than 600 kilometres north of Dawson, Herschel Island was the Yukon's first territorial park, and is perched in the Beaufort Sea. To the north is the Arctic Ocean, to the south the mountainous terrain of the Yukon mainland. The only way to get to Herschel Island is by boat or by float plane, available for charter out of Dawson or Inuvik, which is only 250 kilometres away. There are only minimal facilities for camping on the island, and you will have to arrange your visit well in advance.

The interest here lies partly in the wildlife. The waters around Herschel Island are home to a rich abundance of fish and mammals, including seals and two types of whale, beluga and bowhead. More than 76 species of birds live on the island, including hawks, snowy owl and ptarmigan, and caribou and grizzly bear frequent it during the summer. In the winter, polar bears and arctic foxes ply the shore and ice floes for food.

The other attraction of Herschel Island is its human history. Archeologists have found remnants of 1,000-year-old dwellings on the island, and some suspect that habitation by people migrating from the Bering Land Bridge could date back more than 10,000 years. But the most obvious sign of human occupation on the island is much more recent. Following its "discovery" by the British explorer Sir John Franklin in 1826, Herschel Island became in the 1880s an important wintering station for American whalers. Today, the whalers are long gone, but thirteen of their buildings on Pauline Cove still exist, as do their cemeteries.

The Least You Need to Know

➤ The Klondike Gold Rush started with the discovery of gold in the Yukon in 1896.

➤ In Whitehorse and Dawson, and along the Chilkoot Trail, you can explore the history of the Gold Rush.

➤ Kluane National Park is home to Canada's tallest mountain, Mount Logan.

Tourism Agencies

Provincial Agencies

Newfoundland Tourism, Culture
and Recreation
1-800-563-NFLD

Tourism PEI
1-800-463-4PEI

Tourism Nova Scotia
1-800-565-0000

New Brunswick Tourism
1-800-561-0123

Tourism Quebec
1-800-363-7777

Ontario Travel
1-800-ONTARIO

Manitoba Tourism
1-800-665-0040

Tourism Saskatchewan
1-800-667-7191

Alberta Tourism
1-800-661-8888

Discover British Columbia
1-800-663-6000

Northwest Territories Tourism
Information
1-800-661-0788

Nunavut Tourism
1-800-491-7910

Yukon Tourism
1-800-78-YUKON

City and Regional Agencies

Tourism Halifax
(902) 421-8736

Saint John, NB
(506) 658-2990

Fredericton, NB
(506) 452-9508

Moncton, NB
(506) 853-3590

Greater Montreal Convention and
Tourism Bureau
(514) 844-5400

Quebec City Region Tourism and
Convention Bureau
(418) 692-2471 or 651-2882

Tourist Association of
Saguenay-Lac-Saint-Jean
(819) 778-2222

National Capital Information Centre
(Ottawa)
1-800-465-1867

Tourism Toronto
1-800-363-1990

Niagara Falls Visitor and
Convention Bureau
(905) 356-6061

Tourism Stratford
1-800-561-SWAN

Resorts Ontario
1-800-363-7227

Northern Ontario Tourist Outfitters
Association
(705) 472-5552

Tourism Winnipeg
1-800-665-0204

Tourism Saskatoon
1-800-567-2444

Tourism Regina
1-800-661-5099
Calgary Tourist Information
1-800-661-1678

Edmonton Tourism
1-800-463-4667

Drumheller Tourist Information
(403) 823-1331

Vancouver Tourist Information
Centre
1-800-888-8835

Vancouver Island Tourist
Association
(250) 382-3551

Okanagan Similkameen Tourism
Association
(250) 860-5999

Whistler Resort Association
(604) 932-3928

Selected Canadian Parks

Newfoundland

Terra Nova National Park
Glovertown, NF
(709) 533-2801

Gros Morne National Park
Box 130
Rocky Harbour, NF
A0K 4N0
(709) 458-2066

PEI

Prince Edward Island
National Park
2 Palmers Lane
Charlottetown, PE
C1A 5V6
(902) 672-6350

Nova Scotia

Cape Breton Highlands
National Park

Ingonish Beach
Cape Breton, NS
B0C 1L0
(902) 285-2270

Kejimkujik National Park
Box 236
Maitland Bridge, NS
B0T 1B0
(902) 682-2772

New Brunswick

Fundy National Park
Alma, NB
E0A 1B0
(506) 887-6000

Kouchibouguac National Park
Kouchibouguac, NB
E0A 2A0
(506) 876-2443

Quebec

Forillon National Park
Box 1220
Gaspé, PQ
G0C 1R0

La Mauricie National Park
Place Cascade
794, 5th Street, CP 758
Shawinigan, PQ
G9N 6V9
(819) 536-2638

Saguenay-St. Lawrence National
Marine Park
182 de l'Église Street
Tadoussac, PQ
G0T 2A0
(418) 235-4703

Ontario

Algonquin Provincial Park
Box 219
Whitney, ON
K0J 2M0
(705) 663-5572

Fathom Five National Marine Park
PO Box 189
Tobermory, ON
N0H 2R0
(519) 596-2233

Point Pelee National Park
R.R. 1
Leamington, ON
N8H 3V4
(519) 322-2365

Quetico Provincial Park
Atikokan, ON
P0T 1C0
(807) 597-2735

Manitoba

Riding Mountain National Park
Wasagaming, MB
R0J 2H0
1-800-707-8480

Spruce Woods Provincial Heritage
Park
(204) 827-2543 (May to Sept.)
(204) 834-3223 (Sept. to May)

Saskatchewan

Prince Albert National Park
Box 100
Waskesiu Lake, SK
S0J 2Y0
(306) 633-5322

Meadow Lake Provincial Park
SK Environment and Resource
Management, Box 70
Dorintosh, SK
S0M 0T0
(306) 236-7680

Cypress Hills Interprovincial Park
SK Environment and Resource
Management, Box 850
Maple Creek, SK
S0N 1N0
(306) 662-4411

Alberta

Banff National Park
Box 900
Banff, AB
(403) 762-1550

Jasper National Park
Box 10
Jasper, AB
T0E 1E0
(403) 852-6161

British Columbia

Gwaii Haanas National Park
Reserve/Haida Heritage Site
PO Box 37
Queen Charlotte, BC
V0T 1S0
(250) 559-6317

Pacific Rim National Park Reserve
Box 280
Ucluelet, BC
(250) 726-7721

Northwest Territories

Nahanni National Park Reserve
PO Box 238
Fort Simpson, NT
X0E 0N0

Wood Buffalo National Park
Box 750
Fort Smith, NT
X0E 0P0
(867) 872-2349

Aulavik National Park
Sachs Harbour, NT
X0E 0T0
(867) 690-3904

Yukon Territory

Kluane National Park Reserve
PO Box 5495
Haines Junction, YT
Y0B 1L0
(867) 634-2251

Travel Services

Railways

VIA RAIL
1-800-561-8630

Airlines

Air Canada
1-800-361-7585

Canadian Airlines
1-800-665-5554

Bus Lines

Greyhound
1-800-231-2222

Voyageur
(514) 843-4231

Car Rental

Avis
1-800-879-2847

Budget
1-800-527-0700

Hertz
1-800-263-0600

National
1-800-227-7368

Hotel Chains

Best Western International
1-800-528-1234

CP Hotels & Resorts
1-800-828-7447

Days Inn
1-800-325-2525

Delta Hotels
1-800-268-1133

Four Seasons Hotels
1-800-332-3442

Holiday Inns
1-800-465-4329

Howard Johnson
1-800-654-2000

Quality Inn
1-800-263-7137

Radisson Hotels
1-800-333-3333

Ramada
1-800-228-2828 (US)
1-800-268-8998 (Canada)

Sheraton
1-800-325-3535

Travelodge
1-800-255-3050

Westin Hotels
1-800-228-3000

Travel WEB Sites

Recommended sites are marked with an asterisk (*).

Canada: Information and Links

Government of Canada Information: www.infocan.gc.ca
Canadian Tourism Information Network: info.ic.gc.ca/Tourism
*Attractions Canada: attractions.infocan.gc.ca
Parks Canada: parkscanada.pch.gc.ca

Bed and Breakfast Online Canada: www.bbcanada.com
*Environment Canada weather forecasts: www.tor.ec.gc.ca/forecasts/index.html

Online Travel Guides

*HotWired Rough Guide: www.hotwired.com/rough/canada
Lycos World City Guide: cityguide.lycos.com/canada
The Directory for Travel: www.travel.org
*Excite Travel: www.city.net/countries/canada
TheTrip.com (for Montreal and Toronto): www.thetrip.com
World Travel Guide: www.wtgonline.com

Newfoundland

*Government of Newfoundland tourism site: www.gov.nf.ca/tourism
Newfoundland and Labrador Tourism Marketing Home Page: www.infonet.st-johns.nf.ca/providers/tourism
Newfoundland and Labrador

Traveller's Guide: www.nfld.com
Newfoundland and Labrador
Tourism Information: www.
wordplay.com
City of St. John's: www.city.
st-johns.nf.ca

Prince Edward Island

PEI Visitor's Guide: www.gov.pe.
ca/vg
PEI Virtual Tour: www.peisland.com

Nova Scotia

Nova Scotia tourism: www.gov.ns.
ca/tourism.htm
*NS Tour: ttg.sba.dal.ca/nstour
Destination Nova Scotia: www.
destination-ns.com
Virtual Nova Scotia: explore.gov.ns.
ca/virtualns
NS Online: www.nsonline.com
The Evangeline Trail Association:
www.valleyweb.com/evangelinetrail

New Brunswick

New Brunswick Department of
Economic Development and
Tourism guide:
www.cybersmith.net/nbtour
NB links: new-brunswick.net/
Saint_John/links.html

Quebec

*Tourism Quebec: www.tourisme.
gouv.qc.ca
Quebec Tourist Guide: www.
quebecweb.com/tourisme
Quebec Ministry of the
Environment and Wildlife: www.

mef.gouv.qc.ca
Montreal Official Tourism site:
www.tourism-montreal.org
*Montreal Guide: www.
pagemontreal.qc.ca

*Quebec City: www.otc.cuq.qc.ca
Quebec Winter Carnival: www.
carnaval.qc.ca
Quebec City Tourist Region:
quebec-region.cuq.qc/eng
Mont Tremblant: www.tremblant.
com
Mont Sainte-Anne: www.
mont-sainte-anne.com

Ontario

Travel Ontario: www.gov.on.ca
*Ontario provincial parks: www.
mnr.gov.on.ca/MNR/parks
Ontario travel site: www.boatfarm.
on.ca/ontario/ontario.htm
Events Ontario: www.
eventsontario.com
Ontario Hotel and Motel
Association: www.omha.com
Tourism Toronto: www.
tourism-toronto.com
*Toronto Star visitor's guide: www.
starcitysearch.com/Toronto/
Visitors_and_Getaways
City of Ottawa: www.city.ottawa.
on.ca
Ottawakiosk: www.ottawakiosk.com
Tourism Niagara: www.
tourismniagara.com
The Bruce Trail Association: www.
brucetrail.org
Algonquin Provincial Park: www.
algonquinpark.on.ca

Manitoba

*Travel Manitoba: www.gov.mb.ca/itt/travel
Tourism Winnipeg: www.tourism.winnipeg.mb.ca
Winnipeg attractions: www.mbnet.mb.ca
Whiteshell Provincial Park: www.whiteshell.mb.ca

Saskatchewan

*Tourism Saskatchewan: www.sasktourism.com
Saskatchewan Provincial Parks: http://www.gov.sk.ca/serm/WWW/PARKS
Tourism Regina: www.saskweb.com/~tregina
City of Saskatoon: www.city.saskatoon.sk.ca

Alberta

*Discover Alberta: www.discoveralberta.com
Discover Edmonton: www.discoveredmonton.com
Info Edmonton: www.infoedmonton.com
Edmonton attractions: www.cs.ualberta.com/UAlberta/Edmonton.html
Discover Calgary: www.discovercalgary.com
*Calgary Explorer: www.calexplorer.com

British Columbia

BC tourism information: www.tbc.gov.bc.ca/tourism
*Travel BC: travel.bc.ca
*Discover Vancouver: www.discovervancouver.com
Tourism Vancouver: www.tourism-vancouver.org
Vancouver tourist information: www.vancouver-online.com/online/Tourism
Whistler Resort: www.whistler.travel.bc.ca
Okanagan-Similkameen Tourist Association: www.osta.bc.ca

Northwest Territories

NWT Government: www.gov.nt.ca
*Explorer's Guide: www.nwttravel.nt.ca
City of Yellowknife: www.city.yellowknife.nt.ca
Nunavut Tourism: www.nunatour.nt.ca
*Arctic travel site: www.arctic-travel.com

Yukon Territory

Tourism Yukon: www.touryukon.com
Yukon.com: www.yukon.com
*Yukon Web: yukonweb.com

Index